Cheerfulness

Cheerfulness

A Literary and Cultural History

Timothy Hampton

ZONE BOOKS · NEW YORK

2022

© 2022 Timothy Hampton
ZONE BOOKS
633 Vanderbilt Street
Brooklyn, NY 11218

Printed in the United States of America.

Distributed by Princeton University Press,
Princeton, New Jersey, and Woodstock, United Kingdom

Library of Congress Cataloging-in-Publication Data
Names: Hampton, Timothy, author.
Title: Cheerfulness : a literary and cultural history / Timothy
    Hampton.
Description: New York : Zone Books, 2022. | Includes bibliographical
    references and index. | Summary: "This book offers the first study
    of a form of emotion that has inflected both the social life and the
    literary history of the European/American cultural tradition since
    the Renaissance." — Provided by publisher.
Identifiers: LCCN 2021007241 (print) | LCCN 2021007242 (ebook) |
    ISBN 9781942130604 (hardcover) | ISBN 9781942130628 (ebook)
Subjects: LCSH: Cheerfulness in literature. | Literature, Modern —
    History and criticism. | Affect (Psychology) in literature. |
    Self (Philosophy) in literature. | Literature and society. | LCGFT:
    Literary criticism.
Classification: LCC PN56.C46 H36 2022 (print) | LCC PN56.C46
    (ebook) | DDC 809/.93353 — dc23/eng/20210930
LC record available at https://lccn.loc.gov/2021007241
LC ebook record available at https://lccn.loc.gov/2021007242

For Jessica, Emily, and Sophia,
with love

What should a man do but be merry?

for, look you, how cheerfully my mother looks,

and my father died within these two hours.

—SHAKESPEARE, *Hamlet* (Act 3, Scene 2)

Just direct your feet

To the sunny side of the street.

—DOROTHY FIELDS

Contents

THREE: MODERN CHEERFULNESS

A Contagion, a Power

The surest sign of wisdom is a constant cheerfulness.
Its status is like things above the moon, always serene.
— MONTAIGNE, "On the Education of Children"

This book studies the multiple forms and uses of cheerfulness from the end of the Middle Ages to the twenty-first century in the Western literary and philosophical imagination. Cheerfulness is an emotional energy that can raise the spirit for a limited time. We have some control over it; we can, as the saying goes, "cheer up." This sets it apart from the passions, which are traditionally understood to seize the self, and distinguishes it from happiness or melancholy, which cannot be willed or controlled. You can "make yourself" cheerful. This feature is not, of course, unique to cheerfulness; we can "calm down," as well. But cheerfulness is also shaped by our interactions with others. As we will see in what follows, cheerfulness is a subjective emotion that is also social. It operates outside ourselves, even as, paradoxically, we seem to be able to harness it for our own well-being.

Cheerfulness does not take us "out of ourselves," as do anger and joy. It is modest. It involves a subtle readjustment of the emotions in regard to the immediate future. It is a kind of temporary lightness, a moderate uptick in mood: "A good hour may come upon a sudden; expect a little," writes Robert Burton in his 1638 book, *Anatomy of Melancholy*: "Cheer up, I say, be not dismayed." "Expect *a little*."[1]

It is possibly because of its modesty that cheerfulness has been overlooked by writers about literature and philosophy. They tend to focus on more intense emotions, such as anger, joy, and melancholy. This book aims to bring attention to cheerfulness as a force in self-understanding and a factor in writing. I want to study both the forms and uses of cheerfulness. That is, I am interested both in what people have said *about* it, and in *how it functions* as a concept, or key term, in stories and philosophical arguments. Through this double focus we will be able to trace the history of an emotion and follow its movements across many different types of writing, from theological commentary in the Reformation to modern aesthetics.

The philosopher Baruch Spinoza singles out cheerfulness as distinct from other movements of the self. Whereas some pleasures can overwhelm the body, says Spinoza, cheerfulness, which he claims resides in both mind and body, helps to *temper* their interplay. Pleasure, for example, can be excessive and can have negative consequences. The antidote to excessive pleasure is the same as the antidote to melancholy — cheerfulness. "Cheerfulness is always good," says Spinoza, "and cannot be excessive."[2] Thus, when considered within the self, cheerfulness operates as a balancing force.

Classical and early modern medicine and philosophy provided an entire inventory of the passions, which were understood to seize and shape the self in various ways. The examples most frequently discussed by philosophers were anger and melancholy. Cheer, however, fits uneasily into these categories. It is not happiness, what Aristotle called *eudaemonia*, which implies a certain moral stability. The philosopher David Hume calls cheerfulness a "quality of mind."[3] Yet it is often ephemeral. It moves. It is not optimism, which is strategic and narrative. Nor is it hope, which is philosophical and messianic. Cheerfulness is too modest to fall into step with these emotions. Barack Obama built a successful political campaign in 2008 on the single word "Hope," but no one could be elected on a platform of cheerfulness. You might express cheerfulness to put the voters at ease, but that would be performance, not policy. Cheerfulness offers no political program. It is largely corporeal and often fleeting. And yet it can transform the moral self.[4]

Much of our vocabulary for discussing ourselves stems from a kind of disjunction between our inside and our outside. In the Renaissance, this break was described through such notions as dissimulation, and *sprezzatura* — the idea, developed in Baldassare Castiglione's *Book of the Courtier*, that the most effective form of action is one that disguises all effort and strain. In this formulation, everything from the composition of verse to expertise at fencing should appear effortless. This disjunction between the striving interior and the cool, accomplished exterior of the courtier emerges as a given at the close of the Middle Ages, when our story begins.[5] It finds its modern inversion and analogue in the anxious Freudian subject, massively beset by drives she cannot understand or control, yet struggling to maintain the external semblance of balance in order to function in "normal" society.

This simple paradigm of the social self, of inside and outside, is complicated by the presence of cheer, which bridges and mediates the relationship between the interior of the self and its exterior. The English word "cheer" comes from an early word meaning "face," and cheerfulness is consistently associated with that body part. I will say more later about the etymologies and meanings that hover around the emotion. Yet even when unassociated with the implications of the English word, the movement of cheerfulness (of *gaieté* in French, of *Heiterkeit* in German) links the "inside" of the self and the "outside," shaping their relationship, making it possible for us to imagine them at all. This point is made clear by the French writer Germaine de Staël, in her widely read 1810 book *On Germany*. There, she stresses the importance of conversation for the emotional well-being of the self. She offers an account of the movement of "gaiety," the synonym generally used in French for our English word "cheerfulness": "The desire to appear amiable leads one to take on an expression of gaiety, no matter what the interior disposition of the soul might be. The facial expression influences, bit by bit, what one experiences. And what one does to please others ends up shaping what one feels oneself."[6]

De Staël offers a useful description of one way that cheerfulness works as it moves from the outside inward, shaping body and spirit. Her location of the origins of gaiety in conversation (the desire to appear "amiable") is, of course, not universal. It is rooted in her own aristocratic context and in the French tradition of valuing witty conversation. However, the movement she describes — the outside affecting the inside; the face shaping the soul — is depicted by any number of writers, from the Renaissance to the present day. In our own time, it has been recommended by everyone from Buddhist spiritual teachers to psychotherapists. We will see different versions of this movement as we go.[7] It means that cheerfulness can be a technique, a way of managing oneself and influencing others. It falls into the category of what the philosopher Michel Foucault called the "technologies of the self" — those techniques and practices through which we make ourselves into particular kinds of subjects.[8]

Cheerfulness has something in common with the affects, "those intensities that pass from body to body," as two recent scholars have described them.[9] The affects of the self have become a topic of scholarly research in the humanities and social sciences in the past several decades. Affect, in Sara Ahmed's memorable phrase, is "what sticks, or what sustains or preserves the connection between ideas, values, and objects." For political philosopher Antonio Negri, affect is a "non-place," a site where the individual can resist the late-capitalist totalization of exchange as the measure of all things.[10]

Scholarship on affect is often rooted in a celebration of difference. It tends to focus on what one scholar calls "the singularity of one's affective experiences . . . the idea of one's difference from all other subjects."[11] However, cheerfulness, as I noted earlier, also is consistently linked by poets and philosophers to the texture of community. It is social and may emerge from or toward others. It is a force, a form of energy that can influence those around us. The philosopher Hume calls it "a flame" and "a contagion." It can take over a group and change the interactions of its participants. For the gloomy French philosopher Blaise Pascal, this social dimension is also a tool of domination. In his *Pensées*, he complains that people rich in imagination are "imperious" and cheerful (or "gay") in conversation: "Their gaiety often wins over the opinion of their listeners." For Pascal, gaiety is something added to social exchanges, something in the conversation that diverts us from the argument. It doesn't shape the argument, but it makes us more likely to accept it. This recognition of cheerfulness as something "extra" — as a coloration, a supplement, or an addition — is something we will see repeated across our discussion. It may help explain why Ralph Waldo Emerson calls cheerfulness a "power."[12] And because cheerfulness has a social dimension — one that can shape others, as well as oneself — it is something that can be *used*. Cheerfulness can be appropriated, used as a tool, both for managing emotional life and for affecting others.

We can refine our description of the object of study here by pointing to the distinction between melancholia and cheerfulness. In classical accounts of physiology, which endured in the West from the Greeks well into the nineteenth century, the body is governed by the interplay of four humors, the sanguine, the phlegmatic, the choleric, and the melancholic. The emotional state that we call melancholy is the result of a humoral imbalance, coming from an excess of black bile in the system. Melancholy is conventionally set in opposition to the sanguine humor, which is associated with the blood. Cheerfulness is frequently linked to sanguinity. However it is not a humor. It is a force, almost a spur, that can stimulate sanguinity and counter melancholy. It is a technique, a "technology," to recall Foucault's term. Because you can make yourself cheerful, you can deploy cheerfulness as a weapon against melancholy, even if you are not, yourself, of a sanguine humor. And cheerfulness can be generated or stimulated through the practices of everyday life. Early modern medical writing and manuals of comportment from the Enlightenment offer advice about how to stimulate cheer. As an anonymous author from the seventeenth century in England recommends, "Generous Wine" and

"Musick Instrumental as well as Vocal" are useful techniques for generating cheer and combating melancholy.[13]

While the relationship between cheerfulness and melancholy may be a cliché, the generative power of cheerfulness is disruptive. It moves things about and unsettles them. To take a somewhat random example, we can point out that in Herman Melville's well-known sea story *Billy Budd* (published posthumously in 1924), the handsome sailor Billy is consistently described by the narrator with the adjective "cheerful." His superior, John Claggart, whose fascination with Billy leads to both of their deaths, stares miserably at him through melancholy eyes. As Claggert's hostility and fascination with Billy grow, he is described as watching "the cheerful sea-Hyperion with a settled meditative and melancholy expression." Much of the plot of the story turns on the ways in which Billy's cheerfulness—the cheerfulness of the handsome, ambitious young male—unsettles the rigidly hierarchical community of the ship on which he serves.[14] This suggests that cheerfulness functions differently according to the social identity of the character through which it is enacted and to whom it is attached. It shapes different characters in diverse ways. It has different uses. A bit later, we will look at the relationships between cheer and gender identity and cheer and race. And our discussions of Charles Dickens and Horatio Alger will consider the uncomfortable relationship between cheerfulness and male ambition hinted at in Melville's story.

The distinction between melancholy and cheer has interesting implications for the study of literature. An important strand of aesthetic thought in the European tradition focuses on the importance of melancholy as a factor in poetic composition. Poets are said to be melancholy. Albrecht Dürer's famous image *Melancolia I* is often taken as a figure for the artist. Here again, cheerfulness is overlooked. For there is a counterhistory, which I will be tracing here, that links cheerfulness to both poetry and literary interpretation. I want to see how cheerfulness raises questions about literature itself, about how reading and writing may or may not be cheerful activities.

I will show that cheerfulness has an aesthetic dimension to go along with its moral and psychological aspects. My interest extends to the history of aesthetic forms and, in particular, to the workings of artistic creation. At the present moment, as we watch the demise of traditional literary culture, that history might be useful.

My own approach, while drawing on some of the themes of affect studies, takes shape as well through an engagement with philology — that is, the study of the history of words — and with intellectual and literary history. The historical and linguistic dimensions of this project are crucial, since much work on emotion in the humanities and social sciences focuses on the present, on our life in the media-saturated world of late capitalism, on film or video. Cheerfulness, however, takes its modern shape at a much earlier moment, as I will show. It is first conceptualized in relationship to late medieval practices of piety and spirituality. While cheerfulness may be both empty and ubiquitous today, it has been an important concept in past spiritual and collective life. What we live today as "cheer" (cheerleaders, Cheerios, Cheers!) is the distant echo of that earlier moment, now largely stripped of its spiritual underpinnings. I want to listen to the resonances and echoes of that earlier history.

But first we must sketch out some parameters for the project. Much ancient moral philosophy privileged a state of stable well-being. The Greeks, from the time of the pre-Socratic Democritus, called it *euthymia*. As Democritus's biographer Diogenes Laertius puts it: "The end of action is tranquility [*euthymia*] . . . a state in which the soul continues calm and strong, undisturbed by any fear or superstition or any other emotion." The Roman Stoic Seneca translated *euthymia* as "tranquillity of mind" (*tranquillitas animi*): "A steady and favourable course . . . a peaceful state, being never uplifted nor ever cast down. This will be 'tranquillity,'" writes Seneca.[15] Later scholars have occasionally rendered this idea into English as "cheerfulness." We will certainly hear echoes of this Stoic tradition as we go, especially in such writers as Montaigne and Hume. However, as we will see, modern notions of cheerfulness imply a much more active and, indeed, social model of well-being. The modernity of these notions is part of the story told by this book.

No less important, as a kind of technical term in the classical world, is the Latin word *hilaritas*, from which we derive our words "hilarity" and "exhilarate" and which is used to describe lively conversation, general gaiety. This is a word we will see consistently translated into English as "cheerfulness" in the early modern period. Our focus will be on how that process of translation — centrally important to both the English-language Bible and other key texts — generates new layers of meaning that are in turn picked up by later writers. Together, these layers of meaning shape modern ideas of cheerfulness. But this book is not a "word study." We will also trace how the effect of cheerfulness circulates like a cloud through certain texts, even when the word "cheer" itself is absent.[16]

It is also worth distinguishing cheerfulness and *euthymia* from such notions as the Chinese *le* and *wan*, which, as Michael Nylan has demonstrated, are quite different: "Upon close examination," writes Nylan, "the semantic units routinely translated as 'happy' or 'cheerful' in English have well-defined but different social valences in classical Chinese." As Nylan goes on to point out, "The vocabulary for several American virtues relating to happiness (the virtue of 'cheerfulness,' for example) does not seem to exist in the classical writings in China, though an absence of literary evidence does not ensure that cheerfulness was absent from daily life." It is also worth pointing to the important Sanskrit Yogic tradition, which stresses characteristics of equanimity that are often translated as "cheerfulness" (linked to *sumuka* and *sumana*) as the consequence of a purification of the mind. This is, again, quite different from the modern Western notions of cheerfulness and gaiety I explore below.[17]

Yet at the same time, even in the Western tradition, because of its median position and its modesty, cheerfulness often risks turning into some less appealing version of itself, such as what the seventeenth-century moral philosopher Obadiah Walker called "mirth." Mirth, says Walker, is a vice that seems "like a virtue," but is no such thing. Cheerfulness, by contrast, *is* a virtue, at least for Walker. However, "the exact limits and boundaries [are] difficultly fixed" between the two.[18] Our task will be to study the shifting edges of the nonecstatic sensibility manifested by cheer. Just as cheerfulness can counter melancholy, it borders on more extreme forms of bliss — joy, transport, Dionysian rapture — without becoming them. It lives on the edge of these more intense emotions. As one of the characters notes in Mademoiselle de Scudéry's popular seventeenth-century prose romance, *Clelia*, there is a difference between cheerfulness and joy. Joy may suddenly arise in even the most melancholic persons, whereas cheerfulness functions differently. "Joy sometimes causes sighing, when it is extreme, whereas laughter is the perpetual effect of cheerfulness. Joy can never arise of itself alone, it must always have some extraneous cause. 'Tis not so with cheerfulness, which arises of itself. Joy is an infallible consequent of all passions when they are satisfi'd; cheerfulness subsists without aid, though it may be augmented by causes from without."[19]

Thus, cheerfulness has much in common with a kind of moderation, a form of light-hearted decorum blending body and spirit. And because of its socially moderated character, cheerfulness can be counterfeited, as we will also see. Indeed, if the excessive version of joy is a kind of unbridled ecstasy, and if the extreme of melancholic thoughtfulness is psychic paralysis, the flip side of cheerfulness is not joy, but a manufactured cheerfulness, a fake gaiety that often motivates strategies of "passing" or the strategic manipulation of social relations. This "fake cheer" will emerge through our discussion of how cheerfulness shapes literary fiction-making.

Through a series of interlocking chapters, this book tells a story of cheerfulness from the end of the Middle Ages in Europe to twenty-first-century America. It offers an account of the forms and uses of cheerfulness in the emergence of modernity. The book falls easily into three parts. Chapters 1 through 5 study the early modern period, locating cheerfulness both in medical writing and in the theological discourse of the period. Here we will study the politics of cheerfulness, depicted in Shakespeare, as well as the important reinvention of cheerfulness by the French philosopher Montaigne. Chapters 6 to 9 focus on the rise of modernity in the age of capitalism, taking us from the moral philosophy and social psychology of the Scottish Enlightenment (David Hume, Adam Smith) to the development of the classic English novel (Jane Austen, Charles Dickens) and Romantic poetry (William Wordsworth). Here we see cheerfulness interwoven with accounts of economic life, of ambition, of work, of gender identity. The last chapters study modern cheerfulness, beginning with Ralph Waldo Emerson and Friedrich Nietzsche, two writers who reimagine cheerfulness in aesthetic terms and take us into the changing function of cheerfulness in the consumer capitalism of the mid-twentieth century. We end with a consideration of the philosopher Theodor Adorno, who wrote against cheerfulness in art, and the jazz musician Louis Armstrong, who reinvented cheer against a background of African American performance.

We will see that cheerfulness migrates from one intellectual discipline to another. For the early modern period, it is deeply connected to ideas of Christian community and to theories of a healthy spiritual and physical life. In the Enlightenment, it reappears in discussions of social virtue, in ideals of philosophical conversation and friendly colloquy. In the nineteenth century, under the pressure of an emerging capitalist economy, it moves from common spaces into the individual personality, becoming a character trait, a factor in ambition or psychological healing. In the modern era, it slips its spiritual and communal moorings, to be taken up by the somber heroisms of the Boy Scouts and the slogans of the snake-oil salesman.

My approach will be not to abstract concepts from words, as if they existed apart from their specific appearances or contexts. Nor do I attempt to describe how human beings "really" are, in the ways that a psychologist or a sociologist might do. I am interested in fiction and in language. In the early sections of the book, I will look in particular at the history of key words and at the residues of historical and social experience inside those words. This is because late medieval and early modern culture is more linguistically variegated than our own, as writers shuttle between Latin, Greek, and various emerging national vernaculars. Much of the history of cheerfulness can be unpacked from the history of the word itself, which is, of course, a term in English. Yet we can responsibly approach this topic only comparatively. Whenever possible, I will expand my reach to fold in discussions of non-English terms and concepts, shadings that add texture and relief to our English vocabulary of cheer. By toggling between languages, we can sense and describe the connotative penumbra around certain words. I am interested in how words accrue layers of meaning and in how semantic nuances power philosophical arguments and fictional stories as tools for evoking and describing how certain characters act or feel. I want to build our discussion on the different terms across the European languages that seem to refer to the emotional state, whether we call it, in English, "cheerfulness" or "cheer," in German *Heiterkeit*, or in French *gaieté*. I want to explore the resonances and limits of those words and their cognates. Our inquiry will begin in the study of words — in etymologies and translations — but will quickly expand to trace the circulation of effects, images, and scenarios in imaginative writing.

But why focus on literature and language? And how do we know that when different writers are talking about cheerfulness, they are talking about exactly the same thing? Obviously, we don't, any more than we know everything that the word "democracy" connoted in fifth-century BCE Athens. Whether a philosopher in the nineteenth century would "feel" the same kind of cheerfulness as a mystic in the fourteenth century, we cannot know. But we *can* notice that the language around cheerfulness — the metaphors, the technical terms, the examples — remains remarkably consistent across time, languages, and forms of writing. Of this we will see undeniable evidence. Literature gives us history in words. It imagines the situations in which certain words are used to describe certain kinds of feelings or actions. It gives us insight into what it feels like to say those things, what they mean, what their reach is, when they are used. It initiates us into the meaning world of people who are not us, living in different spaces and times.

Moreover, because literature is fictional, it provides multiple ways for us to look at emotional and ethical valences in language. When we read *The Tempest*, we can study *both* what Shakespeare's character Prospero says about cheer and what it means that Shakespeare puts that particular word in the mouth of an Italian wizard/ prince who is trying to get his kingdom back. This access to another world's language and sensorium is one of the things that literature gives its readers. As we will see, even very abstract writers, such as the philosophers David Hume and Adam Smith, take refuge in literary examples, in fictional scenarios that can help us gauge what they mean by cheerfulness and what they think it can and can't do. Fiction drops us down into the swamp of meaning in ways that other forms of documentation do not. And, in this case, since we are often toggling between languages — looking at moments of translation, echo, citation, and so on — that swamp of meaning is particularly dense and fertile.[20] To explore this terrain, we will need a certain amount of literary fieldwork, or what is sometimes called "close reading." Though often detailed, this should not, I hope, be a slog for the reader. In any event, attention to detail is necessary, since it alone can show us not only what is said about cheerfulness, but what cheerfulness *does*.

The largely northern European and English-language tradition on which I focus here has emerged as the area of richest inquiry during my research. This is not to say, obviously, that there are not cheerful people outside of the traditions studied here. It only means that for the writers examined in the chapters to follow, cheerfulness is an explicit topic of reflection. My readings outside of the tradition that occupies me here have not revealed the same types of nuances and shifts that I trace in what follows. For example, it is simply not the case that we find the kinds of slippages and openings that we find around "cheerfulness" in the Spanish word *alegría* — a word derived from the Latin *alacritas*, which we will meet along the way. Or to take a literary example, the most influential early modern

Italian poet, Ludovico Ariosto, strikes comic poses and deploys a light-hearted attitude in his epic poem *Orlando furioso* (1532). Yet the *language* of cheer is missing. As he winds up his long poem, he proclaims a generalized climate of *allegrezza*. However, his *allegrezza* is rejoicing. It is not cheer.[21]

What follows, then, is a story of texts that take cheerfulness as both a concept and a force, as something to be explained and something to be used. It is the story of a flame, of a fleeting force that nonetheless plays a role in the emotional history of modernity. Cheer begins our history as a quality of the body, but it quickly takes on social, philosophical, and even theological implications. It thickens into a concept that accrues psychological nuances, moral implications, and aesthetic force. It helps to shape selfhood, generate stories, and structure philosophical arguments. It becomes a tool — for theology, economics, manners, poetry, social advancement, and political reconciliation. It names a form of power that has been overlooked and, perhaps, undervalued.

PART ONE

Early Modern Cheerfulness

CHAPTER ONE

Body, Heaven, Home:

Cheerful Places

Facial Stories

Samuel Johnson's 1755 *Dictionary* opens its entry on "cheer" by offering
two definitions. From the French *chère*, we are told, the word means
"entertainment." From the Spanish *cara*, he adds, it means "the countenance." "It seems to have, in English," concludes Johnson, "some
relation to both these senses." Johnson's modest acknowledgment of
the confusion and ambiguity that surrounds the term is emblematic
of its larger history. "Cheer" could indeed be linked to the Spanish
word for face, *cara*. But it certainly comes into English from the Old
French word *chiere*, which does not initially mean "entertainment,"
as Johnson says, but, also, "face." Both *cara* and *chiere* might possibly
be derived from the Greek *kara*, which means "head."

The process through which "face" comes to mean "entertainment"
is itself part of the entertaining story of cheer.[1] In this chapter and the
next, we will be looking as closely as we can at the words that seem to
shape cheerfulness, at their etymologies and translations, at borrow-
ings and meanings. Only slowly will we see the emergence of something like a modern idea of "cheerfulness," a light-hearted emotional
force through which one can shape oneself and one's relationship to
others. In medieval writers, I will show, the idea of "cheer" as face is
invested with a particular emotional charge. It moves around, and the
application of the language of cheer to different contexts or sites of

emotional experience works to expand the connotations of the word, giving it a role in late medieval mystical and religious writing. The spiritual connotations of cheer in medieval culture will return in the sixteenth century to describe communities of belief.

In medieval culture, as I mentioned in the Introduction, "cheer" is one word in English for "face." It denotes the physical human visage. But it also suggests something more, as indicated by literary uses of the term. To explore this, we might start with a quick look at Geoffrey Chaucer's *Canterbury Tales*. It makes sense to begin with Chaucer, since his book depicts, already in the 1390s, a group of people — pilgrims — telling stories in a group setting. The face is an important motif in the depiction of the action. Thus, the Man of Law begins his tale with a "sobre cheere."[2] In the "Knight's Tale" Emelye speaks to Diana "with pitious cheere." In the same tale, Palamon the knight kneels "with humble chere" before riding forth later "with banner white, and hardy cheare and face."[3] The double reference to "cheare and face" is what linguists call a "binominal," an instance of two words being used where one might suffice. Yet the double terminology is telling. The Man of Law's "sobre cheere" indicates the surface of the body. Palamon's "Sobre cheare and face" suggests that we are dealing with something slightly more than a mere synonym of *chiere* or *cara*, something located on the front of the human head and something more than that. In the prologue, the Nun counterfeits a "cheere of court," suggesting a physical presence shaped by a social situation. "Cheere" seems to imply a way of presentation, a look, an expression. It is face, but not only face. It is certainly not valued positively, as we think of modern "cheer." It only rarely appears without an adjective to modify it. It is not merely physical, but it is nevertheless rooted in the body.

These signs of the self, on the self, also describe the relationships between strangers. The "Man of Law's Tale" introduces us to the Sultan of Surrye, who would courteously welcome a merchant from abroad, "make him good chiere, and bisily espye / Tidings of sontry regnes."[4] Good cheer here involves welcome, hospitality, possibly food — it's not quite clear what "make him good chiere" actually implies. The connection may come from French, for the French had been showing their "cheer" for a good while by the time Chaucer's character shows his hospitality. In his romance about Lancelot, *Le chevalier de la charrette*, written in the 1170s, the poet Chrétien de Troyes recounts how Lancelot is welcomed into the home of a couple on his way to an ordeal that will test his courage and free his people. As he and his men ride up, the lady of the house welcomes them with a "joyful and happy face" (*chère molt joyant et liee*).

We should note the grammatical constructions used here. Later writers, as we will see, will talk of "cheerful faces"; "face" will be the noun, "cheerful" will be the adjective. Here we see joyful cheer; "cheer" is the noun, "joyful" the adjective. This means that "cheer" has no emotional essence or inherent quality. It is what is presented to another. It demands an adjective. Chrétien will speak elsewhere of a "chere dolente," or suffering face. On occasion, it can stand alone, as a body part, as when a blushing maid who has fallen in love is asked what happened to her face: "My sweet dear girl / Who dyed your face in this way?" (*Ma douce damoisele chiere, / Qui si avez teinte la chiere?*).[5] Yet even here, the physical aspect of cheer is quickly modified by a qualifier; the face is evoked only to be described as colored, "dyed," or, perhaps, "painted." For both Chaucer and Chrétien, "cheer" seems to locate us at the point where body becomes emotional—if not moral ("sobre," "pitious")—and where emotion becomes physical.

The link between hospitality and the "joyful face" or "joyful cheer" hinted at by Chrétien and Chaucer's Sultan of Surrye seems to be proverbial in medieval and early modern literature. We find it in Shakespeare's narrative poem *The Rape of Lucrece*, where Lucrece unsuspectingly welcomes the rapist Tarquin to her home: "So guiltless she securely gives good cheer / And reverend welcome to her princely guest, / Whose inward ill no outward harm expressed."[6] With characteristic nuance and complexity, Shakespeare unpacks the relationship, only hinted at in Chrétien's welcoming hostess, between hospitality, the face, and the presentation of the self. If there were any doubt that "cheer" is a form of hospitality, his Lucrece helpfully presents *both* "good cheer" and "reverend welcome," even as Tarquin's duplicity — his obviously dissimulating visage — undoes the connection between inner self and facial manifestation. Shakespeare sets forth two kinds of faceliness. For Lucrece, face and soul, body and morality, are one. For Tarquin, they are split.

The act of putting on a "good face," or a "bonne chère," then, bundles together physical presence, emotional self-presentation, and the rituals of hospitality. It involves how the self is made through its relationship to others. We can understand the logic behind this particular form of "good cheer" by placing it in the context of feudal culture, where aristocrats lived in isolated castles, surrounded by potentially hostile neighbors. The prudent response to an incursion from any stranger would be to kill him. Instead, "to put on a good face" offers a less violent response; it becomes a sign of courtesy — we might say, of civilization itself. The link between hospitality and corporeal expression accounts for what is probably the most frequent postmedieval use of the word *chiere* in French. This is the expression that Samuel Johnson has in mind, whereby "faire bonne chiere," or "to make a good face," quickly becomes a synonym for celebrating or throwing a feast. From this point on, in French, *chiere* (orthographically revised to become *chère*), like the English "cheer," begins to lose its bodily origin and become a synonym for the social habits of festival or abundance. Through this expansion of usage, "cheer" begins to take on a material connotation. It takes us to the tradition of sharing a meal as a sign of community. The "good cheer" of the generous hostess, which makes possible community and communion around the table, begins to include the food and drink.

The Face of God and Cheerful Welcome

Yet cheer is also theological. The period between Chaucer and the figures who will interest us in subsequent chapters sees the emergence of an important body of spiritual writing by lay authors; that is, by authors not linked to the orders of the Catholic Church. These authors, the most influential of whom are Julian of Norwich and Margery Kempe, help expand reflection on religion and piety beyond the confines of the priesthood. It may not be by accident that much of this writing is by women. Writers such as Julian and Kempe evoke a personal religious experience — one not mediated through a male priesthood. They depict and imagine communities that must be defined spiritually, rather than institutionally. And as we have already seen in the comportment of Chrétien's hostess and Shakespeare's Lucrece, cheerful behavior is often (though not exclusively) gendered feminine. For these authors, "cheer" is an important term because of its multiple meanings, which they use as a kind of resource for evoking spiritual experience.

Perhaps the most intense and nuanced writer in the tradition of English lay piety is the mystic Julian of Norwich. In her "showings," or accounts of her visions of God, Julian insists on the importance of God's beautiful face. God's visage is a key image for Julian, and we should not be surprised to see that she uses the term "cheer," spelled most often "chere," to denote it. She mobilizes the senses we have been tracing. For her, "chere" links face and spiritual bliss: "But I saw Him royally reign in his house and filling it completely Himself with joy and mirth," she writes in the sixth revelation, "full homely and full courteously with marvelous melody in His own fair blessedful cheer: which glorious cheer of the Godhead fills all of heaven with joy and bliss."[7] Julian here describes the presence of God as paradoxically located in a specific site, his face ("But I saw Him"), and yet spread beyond that site (it "fills all of heaven"). Her account operates through a kind of metonymy, a horizontal logical movement, to express the miracle of God's omnipresence.

The capaciousness of the word "cheer" is useful for depicting absolute presence, for the paradoxes of a theology that is both individual and cosmic. Julian plays with the overlapping we noted in Chaucer between a physical location for "chere" and an emotional charge. Here, she uses the term both to describe God's presence for the single believer (he's in his "house") and his extension through heaven. His "cheer" is visible, you can see it in a mystical vision, yet it is also extensive, a kind of feeling of bliss. As a point of contrast, we can note that Julian's near-contemporary in the European visionary tradition, Dante Alighieri, had also glimpsed the Godhead. He had described it as light, shaped as three circles (for the Trinity) with one circumference.[8] By contrast, Julian uses the term "cheer"; the twin adjectives "blessedful" (God's face) and "glorious" (the heavens) do the work of indicating how the Godhead and the blessed world are extensions of one another. This is how he can be glimpsable to the visionary and yet also all around.

This double meaning of "cheer" also has a temporal dimension for Julian. It powers her struggles to depict a world that is both histori-cal — caught in time — and eternal, always infused with God's love. Cheer, for Julian, can have an external dimension — it can be "shown," as it would be on a body, like the "pitious cheere" of Chaucer's char-acters. But it also has an internal or purely spiritual dimension. This duality seems to be part and parcel of God's presence, the "double chere" through which God contemplates the fallen world. As God looks on the fall of Adam, he expresses his pity through an "outward" cheer and his "endless love and right" through his inward cheer. The outward cheer, in turn, has two dimensions. One entails the "full fall-ing of man," that is, Adam's sin, and the other involves God's repara-tion for that fall, the unfolding of human history. When we sin, says Julian, he welcomes us back with hospitality and his glad face: "Then our courteous Lord shows himself to the soul merrily and of full glad cheer, with friendly welcoming, as if [the soul] had been in pain and prison, saying, 'My dear darling, I am glad thou art come to me in all thy woe.'"[9] Here, the emotional charge of God's presence (indicated through the binomial, "merrily and of full glad cheer") is the conse-quence of a single act of showing, of revealing his face. At the same time, the "other cheer," the inward cheer, is not divided into fall and redemption. It simply offers a vision of completeness, "all one."[10]

These complicated multiple versions of "cheer" or "cheare" are enumerated in the sixteenth revelation, where God is described as having no fewer than three different "cheers": one is the physical face he showed at the time of the Passion; the second is his pity at and compassion for our sins; the third is what we will see in heaven. Of these, Julian concludes, "Yet we may never stint of mourning, nor of weeping, nor of seeking, nor of longing, till when we see him in his blessedful cheer." In the meantime, "the blessed cheer of our Lord God works in us by grace."[11] Here again, blessedness lies in a specific place, the face of God, in such a way that we must "come here" to glimpse that face. Yet "cheer" is also understood to permeate the universe, to make creation blessed, and to sustain us until the end of time.

Julian's complex expansion of the idea of "cheer" reflects her project of depicting the intensity of the *personal* experience of God, beyond the mediation of the church, while accounting for the *collective* experience of God's goodness in a spiritual (not necessarily ecclesiastical) community. Her connection of the emotional and moral uplift of God's presence to images of wandering and return finds a more accessible analogue in the work of her contemporary, Margery Kempe. *The Book of Margery Kempe* is less a set of mystical visions than a protoautobiography, recounting the spiritual progress of the author and her engagement with different communities, both civic and ecclesiastical. For Kempe, cheer begins to take on the primarily material and communal connotations that we earlier traced to the practice of hospitality. The book is laced with depictions of social relationships informed by good cheer. Yet the word is intriguingly multifarious in its meanings. For example, early on, she recounts an accident in which she is hit by a falling beam. She is miraculously healed. She is then pulled from the rubble by "a good man, called John of Wyreham," whom she then thanks "for his cheer and his charity."[12] The proximity of the two terms suggests that emotional uplift and ethical practice go hand in hand.

The theme of cheer as hospitality is everywhere in this book, and it raises the question — central for any lay writing on religious themes — of what constitutes a spiritual community. Is it defined by the church? Or does it lie elsewhere? Kempe seems to suggest that communal spiritual experience is the consequence of both "cheer" and "charity." In chapter 49, we find her in Leicester, where the abbot and his fellows give Margery "right good wine" and "right good cheer." As she prepares to leave, "many good folk of Leicester [came] to cheer her . . . and made her right good cheer, promising her that if ever she came again, she should have better cheer amongst them than she had before."[13] Friendly hospitality, spiritual uplift, and sustenance are indistinguishable. Here, as in Julian, we can see how the diverse senses of the word "cheer" are being deployed to establish connections between experiences that might not otherwise go together. Whereas for Julian cheer had to do with the representation of the Godhead, here, the focus is social. When Kempe repeats the term "cheer" to describe the spiritual welcome of the abbot, the good food, the friendly affection of the folk of Leicester, and their promise that she will be welcomed even more warmly in the future, we can see how she is using the term to suggest the interpenetration of spirituality, fellowship, nutrition, and civic hospitality.

The association is repeated elsewhere, when Kempe travels to Norwich. There, after making a charitable donation at the cathedral, she visits an old friend, Richard Caister. He invites her directly to his house in an expression of hospitality: "And he led her with him to the place where he stayed and he made right good cheer." After remarking on Margery's "merry" countenance, despite the rigors of the journey, they linger over a meal "and had full goodly cheer" before taking their leave.[14]

We can see thus that the overlapping of emotional power and physical presence suggested in the "cheere" of Chaucer's pilgrims to Canterbury functions as a kind of linguistic resource to be expanded and exploited by later writers. The literature of fifteenth-century lay piety uses cheer as a way of explaining religious mystery (Julian) and spiritualizing social engagement (Kempe). The juxtaposition of communal fellowship and cheerful countenance seen in Kempe, in particular, sets up a close link between "cheer" and community. It raises the question of whether the "cheer" of communion and hospitality is the agent of spiritual experience or whether it's the other way around. Does the cheer that permeates the universe bring Kempe and Caister together in communion? In such a case, hospitality would be the manifestation of some higher spiritual force. Or is the good cheer of a meal together the agent of spiritual gaiety? These questions, which are here hinted at by the lay writers of the fifteenth century, will reemerge a century later, in the debates around community and spirituality accompanying the Protestant Reformation. To those debates we turn in our next chapter.

CHAPTER TWO

Among the Cheerful:

The Emotional Life of Charity

Cheerful Giving

As we move from the late medieval world into the early modern sixteenth century, the semantic richness shaping the emergence of "cheer" as both a corporeal quality and a communal virtue becomes entwined with the great socioreligious questions dominating European culture and politics. A new word appears. "Cheerfulness" is the abstract noun that turns specific instances of "cheer," with their connotations of face, hospitality, and spiritual uplift, into a general quality. According to the *Oxford English Dictionary*, the word seems to have come into English sometime in the 1530s. In Myles Coverdale's translation of sections of the Bible, which builds on the earlier work of his friend William Tyndale, we read in the first book of Maccabees (3.2) that the Maccabees fought "with cheerfulness for Israel." Here, the term picks up on the generous community exhibited by those who welcome Margery Kempe on her travels, as we saw in our previous chapter. The Maccabees, being good warriors, are willing, as well as able, to help Israel, and their spirited help is given a general name, "cheerfulness." They are quite literally "full" of the energy and power celebrated by both Kempe and Julian of Norwich. John Wycliffe's fourteenth-century Middle English Bible had used "gladness" for this passage. This rendering of the Latin Vulgate Bible's phrase "cum laetitia" — "with happiness" — as "with cheerfulness" is used again in the

King James Bible. Thereby these energetic fighters become proverbial, and "cheerfulness" begins to enter the conceptual vocabulary of
English selfhood as a term evoking good-spirited willfulness.[1]

These translation choices are important. As we will see, an entire
complex of Latin words and phrases from the Vulgate — *confidite*,
bono animo, constans esto, and so on — are all looped into a single
semantic network when they are translated into English via forms
of the word "cheer." Biblical scenes and passages that were unre-
lated in the Latin or Greek texts now echo and gloss each other. This
homogenization both corrals the diverse connotations of these other
phrases and helps to render uniform and consistent the language
of Christian community in English. It creates that community in
language. By tracing these translations, we can also see how cheerfulness itself is thickening, in the early modern world, from a term
used principally to denote the face to a larger notion that gathers and
blends diverse aspects of human experience. The good news of scripture is a source of cheer for sixteenth-century Europe. Less obvious
is how that cheerfulness may be diffused through a community.

For figures such as Julian of Norwich or Margery Kempe, the usefulness of cheer involved the connotations of the word itself, which
could represent the paradoxes of mystical experience or link spiritual
values to social gathering and hospitality. In the sixteenth century,
however, the very notion of what constituted Christian community
was thrown into crisis.

Central to the notions of charity and community put forth by
Saint Paul in his Epistles — those notions that came to the fore in the
debates around the Protestant Reformation — is the directive that
Christians must engage with each other gladly, just as, we might surmise, the Maccabees did their duty willingly, exhibiting "cheer," by
fighting "cheerfully" for Israel. Paul's letters give us two influential
formulations of this type of relationship. First, in Romans, chapter
12, Paul proclaims the famous doctrine of the Christian community
as a body with "many members," and he stresses that participation in
that community is shaped by the different "gift" offered each of us by

"grace." Let the one who gives give with simplicity, let the one who rules rule with diligence, and "He that sheweth mercy" let him do so with "cheerfulness," say Tyndale's version and the Geneva Bible's verse 8. The same phrase is repeated in the King James translation, some fifty years later. The English term conveys Saint Paul's Greek word, *ilaróteti*, which means "in a happy fashion." More important for the overwhelmingly Latin culture of the English Renaissance, it renders the Vulgate Bible's *hilariter*, which is obviously derived from the Greek. In Latin, this word evokes the Roman goddess of happiness, Hilaritas, who was often depicted on coins. To give "hilariter" in Latin is to give happily. But in English translation, it is to give "cheerfully"; that is, with a glad spirit, full of the emotion connoted by "cheer" in writers such as Chaucer and Kempe, willingly.[2]

Paul repeats the same language two books later, in an even more famous and, indeed, foundational passage. This is in the second letter to the Corinthians, where he sketches the social dynamics and ministry of the new Christian community. What is central to that community is charity, or *caritas*, says Paul, and to participate fully in it, say the Geneva and King James versions: "Every man according as he purposeth in his heart, so let him give; not grudgingly, or of necessity: for God loveth a cheerful giver." "Hilarem enim datorem diligit Deus," says the Vulgate at 9.7.[3] In a French context, Olivier Arnoullet's 1550 vernacular Bible would translate *hilarem* as *joyeusement* (joyously). However, Theodore Bèze, John Calvin, Clément Marot, and later, Sebastian Honorat, in 1566, would stress gaiety through the phrase "Dieu aime celuy qui donne gaiment." Luther's German says, "Einen fröhlichen Geber hat Gott lieb," thereby introducing *Fröhlichkeit*, the key term in Friedrich Nietzsche's 1882 book *The Gay Science*, which we will study a bit later.[4] The English-language tradition conveys this "gaiety" as cheerfulness: "God loveth a cheerful giver." The phrase "not ... of necessity" helps us grasp the nuances of the term: cheerfulness suggests the willing practice of charity, the ready commitment to help one's neighbor. Similarly, "not grudgingly" underscores the control that the cheerful giver has over her charity. Cheerfulness is not about the gift; it's about the emotion that accompanies the gift, just as "cheer," in Chaucer, seemed to suggest an emotional charge that went beyond the physical presence of the face.

These linguistic connections between cheerfulness and charity resonate across the emerging Christian humanist culture of early modern Europe. They are somewhat firmed up and given authority in the writings of Erasmus of Rotterdam, the most famous European intellectual of the sixteenth century. A moderate who favored reforming the Catholic Church from within, instead of breaking with it altogether, in the manner of Luther or Calvin, Erasmus dazzled his contemporaries with his mastery of classical and biblical texts, as well as his facility in Latin and Greek. In addition to translating the New Testament from Greek into Latin (thereby placing himself in competition with the authorized Vulgate version by Saint Jerome, on which Catholic doctrine was based), Erasmus penned lengthy commentaries and paraphrases on the Gospels and the major Pauline Epistles. These texts secured his position as, with Luther, the major biblical interpreter of the age.

In his *Paraphrases* of the Pauline letters, Erasmus elaborates on Paul's urging to practice charity "with happiness," or "cheerfully," or "gaily" (take your pick). He adds that one must not give unto others in such a way that the person receiving the gift feels obligated by it. The "happy" giver erases the difference between himself and the receiver. This detail is important, since it marks the difference between Christian practices of charity and classical or pagan ideas of gift giving, which rely upon a dynamic of debt and gratitude. For Erasmus, for the New Testament Christian, the gift is given with "cheerfulness" (repeating the Vulgate's term *hilariter*), as if it already belonged to the other: "A task done with cheerfulness is doubly gracious, since whatever is done appears to come both from within and from outside you."[5] What we give others must come from "inside" us (*ex animo*) and yet be given as if it did not belong to us at all, as if it came from someone else (*ex alieno*), as if it already belonged to our friend or neighbor even before it was given. This is how community is imagined.

Erasmus's comments echo one of his famous *adagia*, the collection of proverbial sayings that he published across his career: "He
who gives quickly gives twice."⁶ However, in the biblical paraphrase,
we find something new. The double reference to what is "inside" or
"outside" of us imports a physical dimension into charity, a relation
between my distinct body and yours. The social aspect of cheerfulness begins to take on a body. To be a cheerful giver, we must overcome our separation.

This physical nuance is carried over through mid-sixteenth-century spiritual writing, both Protestant and Catholic. For example,
Erasmus's commentaries on the New Testament were quickly translated into English by Myles Coverdale, whom we met a moment ago.
He renders Erasmus's retelling of Paul's commandment in Romans to
give willingly in this way: "But let thy thankful gyfte be encreased
and doubled with a mery looke and cherefulness, so that whatsoever
ye gyve, seme to gyve it even as it were an other mannes, and with
all youre heartes." Coverdale lends the physical presence of the giver
a visual dimension, stressing that she must have both "cherefulness"
and a "mery looke."⁷ Indeed, the phrasing here is built from an infla-
tion of good will. The gift itself is already "thankful," but cheerful giving makes it "encreased and doubled" — whatever that might
mean. Cheerfulness thus becomes a kind of supplement that simultaneously completes the gift and makes it more than it already is. By
virtue of excessive good will, charity binds body to community. And
the bond is shaped by how we *appear*, our "mery looke." It is no longer
simply an affair of the heart.⁸

Coverdale's Englishing of Erasmus is important, since it helps
calm the semantic wobbles that we have seen across and between
languages. Paul's biblical encouragements of the practice of charity
are rendered consistently by Erasmus, in his paraphrases, with the
language that the Vulgate uses to describe the happy disposition of
the giver — chiefly, again, the Latin adverb *hilariter*. However, the
Englishing of both Paul's text and Erasmus's influential glosses relies
on the notion of "cheer," or, in Coverdale's Bible, "cheerfulness." The

semantic range of *hilaritas* is vast, and like many terms denoting positive emotions, it risks turning into a parody of itself, into sarcasm,
derision (we think of the modern English word "hilarious"), or mere
"mirth." By contrast, "cheerfulness," rooted in the body and in a
network of charity, controls that semantic drift and circumscribes
the implications of Paul's phrase. By making hilarity into "cheer,"
Coverdale mitigates the risk of parody or self-subversion. He makes
cheerfulness essential to Christian community by making it nar-
rower in scope.

No less important, the introduction of "cheer" as a term of sociability and ethics has a unifying and homogenizing effect across the
different books of the New Testament. So, in Acts 23.11, Paul is visited by Jesus, who tells him in Greek to "take courage" (*tharsei*) and
in Latin to "stay constant" (*constans esto*). A moment later, in Acts
24:10, Paul gives a testimony in Latin "from good will" (*bono animo*);
this renders the Greek *euthymos*, which means "gaily," and lends it a
volitional nuance (one can also speak out of ill will). Yet all of these
phrases are cast in English as "cheerful." This integrates these diverse
Greek and Latin terms into a single semantic network. Scenes and
phrases that were linguistically unrelated in earlier Bibles are now
associated with each other in the English Bible. This creates a web of
cheerfulness to bind the Christian community together in both its
history (Maccabees, the book of Acts) and its ethics.

This nexus of concerns is then projected into the future in the
King James Version of Christ's words to his disciples about the last
days. He speaks, shortly before the Crucifixion, in the Gospel of
John. "Do you now believe? The hour is coming, indeed it has come,
when you will be scattered, every man to his home," says Christ in
chapter 16, verse 32. But in the next verse, he goes on to reassure
them, "Be of good cheer; I have overcome the world." "Confidite,"
he says in the Latin version, using a verb that contains the root for
"faith." *Con-fidere*, from which we get the English word "confidence,"
suggests something like "be assured." Thus, "have faith," or "have
confidence." The original Greek says "tharseite," which means "take

courage" (*tharros* means courage). "Be of good comforte," says Coverdale. In the King James Version, this becomes "be of good cheer."

This translational slippage turns Christ's admonition from a bit of
encouragement and an assurance that he will return (*fides* connotes
faith) into a projection of a collective emotional dynamic. No longer
"take courage" or "believe," but "keep your spirits up" — and do so
together. Here, the Greek takes on a new shading when it becomes
Latin, and the semantic complexity of the Latin is reduced when the
Vulgate is made English. Implicit are the nuances we have been tracing — a social engagement through charity, the merry look, communion in food and drink, hospitality. This capacious social and ethical
cheerfulness is what takes the place — literally — of a more rigorously
theological notion of faith, of belief in what is not seen. It projects an
image of Christian community, scattered, yet united by a brightness
of spirit, in the space between the Crucifixion and the end of time. It
socializes courage.

Paul's urging to give cheerfully helps consolidate and shape charity, in part, as Coverdale's renderings suggest, by adding a visual
component, the "mery looke" that harks back to the medieval notion
of the "face" or *chiere*. Just as we saw Shakespeare amplify the hospitality of Lucrece by noting that it includes both "cheer" and "welcome," these English versions of Paul's great pronouncements about
charity and community introduce the importance of appearance and
the "looke" that is semantically related to the "good cheer" of a happy
face. For Chaucer, cheer was bodily. For Julian of Norwich, it was
linked to the mystery of the Godhead. For Kempe, it was nutritional
and social. Now, cheer has begun to thicken. It has become one of the
hinges that turns spiritual vision into ethical social practice via the
body. Community, charity, and hospitality are linked to the status of
the cheerful face.

Policing Cheer

We can see how and why "cheerfulness" is such a useful mediating
term in early modern theology and moral philosophy. The facial or

corporeal dimension of cheer makes it individual — it includes "me" (whoever I might be), since we all have faces. Yet it involves the way I am perceived by others, so it has a social dimension. To the extent that it retains nuances of hospitality and good will, it envelops the problem of my relationship to any "other" — even a stranger or potential enemy. Thus, it helps solder community together. And its physiological and psychological nuances (linking it to notions such as "alacrity" or "gaiety") make it the counterweight to the dreaded humor of melancholy, with its antisocial and depressive connotations.

It follows from this that once cheerfulness inflects the relationship of body to social context, its manifestation can also become, by a reversal, a legible index of the inner self, a visual clue on the body through which the social or spiritual engagement of believers might be measured. If cheerfulness defines community, it henceforth becomes possible to distinguish who is in the community and who is not according to how you look, according to the perceived "cheerfulness" of your cheer. Cheerfulness can now become a sign of a particular identity — and of participation in a particular community. It can become a policing tool.

The changing link between community and face is clearest if we turn to Erasmus's contemporary, the Protestant reformer John Calvin. For Erasmus, cheerful charity was the manifestation of a link between self and other that *already* existed. It meant that you and I are already parts of a larger whole, members of the body of Christ. What is mine is *already* yours, even before I give it to you. By contrast, for Calvin, this expressive sign *of* communal identity becomes the test of one's participation *in* community. Thus, in his commentary on 2 Corinthians 9:7, he notes that when Paul "says that God loves the one who gives cheerfully, he means . . . that God rejects those who give grudgingly and with stinginess: for He does not want to dominate us like a tyrant; but just as he shows himself to be our Father, so does he require from us filial obedience — prompt and honest."[9] Cheerfulness, which Paul says comes not "of necessity," is for Calvin now a requirement. It must be "prompt and honest." It is not only the manifestation of a preexisting spiritual and moral relationship to one's fellows, as it is for Erasmus. It must be shown as the mark of one's duty to God, a sign of the inner climate of the heart, a condition of full membership in the community.

If there were any doubt as to who Calvin believes is terrifying believers "like a tyrant," as he puts it in the passage just cited, he makes the reference clear in his comments on Romans 9.1. There, he points out that the communal relationship among the cheerful is what distinguishes true Christians (Protestants) from false Christians (Catholics). He comments on Paul's exhortation that we turn away from the world and give ourselves wholly to God:

> This exhortation teaches us, that until men really apprehend how much they owe to the mercy of God, they will never with a right feeling worship him, nor be effectually stimulated to fear and obey him. It is enough for the Papists if they can extort by terror some sort of forced obedience, I know not what [*Papistis satis est si coactum nescio quod obsequium terrendo extorqueant*]. But Paul, that he might bind us to God, not by servile fear, but by the voluntary and cheerful love of righteousness [*voluntario hilarique iustitiae amore*], allures us by the sweetness of that favour, by which our salvation is effected; and at the same time he reproaches us with ingratitude, unless we, after having found a Father so kind and bountiful, do strive in our turn to dedicate ourselves wholly to him.[10]

Here, the exercise of cheerful giving is the mark of election, a free gesture. That freedom marks the difference between Protestants and Catholics. Whereas Catholics ("Papists") terrorize believers into obedience (the aside, "I know not what" is particularly creepy), the freedom of the Protestant believer resides in the fact that she freely and cheerfully turns to God, attracted by the "sweetness" of God's favor. And yet it is not just any freedom. It is a freedom that must be informed by a particular attitude. If not, God will "reproach" us. As the believer turns voluntarily to God, her cheerfulness becomes not merely the result of an appreciation of God's favor, but the visual manifestation of obedience and dedication. It turns from being the consequence or by-product of belief, as it was for Erasmus, into the very ground on which proper belief is exercised.

The manifestation of cheerfulness now becomes, in the economy of the believing self, the sign of proper spiritual practice. We must not merely pray, which is essential to the Christian's communication with God, but we must pursue our prayer without complaint, gladly, cheerfully, with a merry look. The point is made again in the commentary on the famous passage about charity in 2 Corinthians 12.8, where Calvin notes that Paul required the services of the charitable "to be rendered with lightness and cheerfulness, fearing that they might banish all grace from their service by their disdainful face — as often happens."[11] In this formulation, Calvin has expanded the role of cheerfulness to include social behavior. It is the opposite of "disdain," or pride. It stands as the necessary glue that binds social relations and fixes our relationship to God. Not to be cheerful is to undermine community.

As a gauge of the reach of Calvin's idea that the expression of cheer is a kind of measure of piety, we can note that it is a repeated theme in the work of the influential English divine Richard Hooker, who repeatedly mentions the practice of a "cheerful heart" as the sign of obedience to God. In his "Learned Sermon on the Nature of Pride," from 1553, he lists the various curses that befall the prideful before lamenting that "thou wilt not serve the Lord thy God with a cheerful and true heart, that so thou mightest be in all things happy. Hunger and thirst, and nakedness, and want of all things necessary shall be thy undividable companions."[12] For Hooker, God will not merely "reproach" us if we are not cheerful; he will punish us. Over against this, Hooker says elsewhere, "Whoso cometh unto God with a gift, must bring with him a cheerful heart, because he loveth, *hilarem datorem*, a liberal and frank affection in giving. Devotion and fervency added unto prayers the same that alacrity doth unto gifts; it putteth vigor and life in them."[13] Cheerfulness must be demonstrated, with "liberal and frank affection" ("affection" can be physical expression, as well as emotional warmth) as the measure of internal intensity.

What is remarkable here is the way that Hooker's formulation combines a language of psychic intensity with a language of physical and even linguistic energy — "devotion" is coupled with "fervency" in prayer, and "life" is linked with "vigor." This expands the function of the cheerful face to the entire body, to a particular form of acting and speaking. As cheerfulness enters the language of Protestant theology, it expands to include the actions of the believer — energy, enthusiasm, brightness. More than mere appearance, what is entailed is a kind of excess, an added quality to one's gifts and social relations. The point is made as well by Calvin in his commentary on Galatians 5.22. There, he distinguishes between the license of Christians to flout Jewish legal conventions (which, he says, involves "joy in the Holy Spirit") and the community practice that he is promoting in Galatians: "I understand joy here, not as it is understood in Romans 14.17, but a joyful way of acting, a lightness that we demonstrate toward our neighbor which is contrary to sadness."[14] In the French version of his text, he generalizes the value of cheerfulness with the expression "une façon de faire" (a way of acting, or doing). Movement itself involves cheer, and cheerfulness is a movement directed toward another.

And cheerful community is linguistic. Hooker's near-contemporary John Donne, in his 1627 panegyric for Lady Danvers, the mother of the poet George Herbert, expands on what we have just seen. What characterized the much-admired Lady Danvers, he notes, was her cheerful engagement with both the practice of worship and the reading of scripture. As soon as the doors of a house of prayer were opened, "she ever hastned her family, and her company hither, with that cheerful provocation, 'For God's sake let's go.'" And every Sabbath she led the family "with a cheerfull singing of Psalmes; This act of cheerfulnesse, was still the last Act of that family, united in itselfe, and with God. God loves a cheerfull giver; Much more a cheerfull giver of himself. Truly, he that can close his eyes in a holy cheerfulnesse, every night, shall meet no distemper'd, no inordinate, no irregular sadness."[15]

Here we see an idealized vision of the blending of piety, community, and identity in the web of cheerfulness. Calvin's notion that the cheerful giver must show his inner spirit is now made concrete through images of movement and performance, of poetry made active. Erasmus theorizes the giving of gifts. Donne presents the self itself as a gift, since God loves "much more a cheerfull giver of himself." And the performance of cheerful scripture, he points out elsewhere, is bolstered by the very form of the Bible. Thus, in a sermon preached in 1622 at Lincoln's Inn, Donne notes that God

> gives us our instruction in cheerfull forms, not in a sowre, and sullen, and angry, and unacceptable way, but cheerfully, in Psalms, which is also a limited, and a restrained form; Not in an Oration, not in Prose, but in Psalms; which is such a form as it is both curious, and requires diligence in the making, and then when it is made, can have nothing, no syllable taken from it, nor added to it: Therefore is Gods will delivered to us in Psalms, that we might have it the more cheerfully, and that we might have it the more certainly.[16]

For Donne, the cheerfulness elicited by the Psalms involves the shape of poetry, the rhythmic or metrical construction of the verse. The completeness of structure, the regularity of the line, add both cheerfulness and certainty to the argument. Cheerfulness is now a kind of writing. Rhetorical *enargeia* and devotional energy mirror each other.

Renaissance and Reformation accounts of Christian community place cheerfulness at the center of charitable practice. Paul's description of charity as inflected with cheerfulness brings together the nuances of meaning that we saw explored in earlier writers — emphasis on community, spiritual elevation, the expression of the self. Now, however, writers about the practice of Christian piety expand the notion of cheerfulness, linking it to bodily experience, to the enactment of community, to the energy and form of poetry itself. Cheerfulness as spiritual energy or force, as lightness of attitude, is inextricable from new ways of imagining the body and new appreciations of the rhetorical power of the Bible. This link between bodies and texts is richly evocative in the early modern period. It extends as well to writing about medicine and health. And as our next chapter will show, cheerfulness is the key concept shaping the interplay of medicine, literature, and ethical action.

CHAPTER THREE

Medicine, Manners, and Reading

for the Kidneys

Healthy Regimes

In early modern literature, cheerfulness becomes a force that can shape the soul and, quite literally, heal the body. It touches on a variety of activities and practices. The philosopher and historian Michel Foucault once described the sixteenth century in Europe as a time characterized by "insurrections of comportment."[1] By this he meant that social, political, and religious transformations were accompanied and, in some cases, driven by new ways of shaping the self. The Renaissance humanist attention to the texts of classical antiquity, coupled with such new technological developments as the printing press and the European discovery of gunpowder, generated a whole set of disciplines and practices that changed the way people shaped themselves: new medical techniques, new religious rituals, new forms of heresy and sexual culture, new educational ideals, new dietary options, new ceremonies for social engagement at court and in the city, the rise of table manners—all of these areas of human experience underwent transformations that reshaped the daily lives and self-conceptions of many Western European people.

In this chapter, I want to look at the role played by cheerfulness in three related areas. We have seen how ideas of religious community include images of the cheerful body. Now we will turn to the discourse of medicine to see how cheerfulness functions in physical health. Then, given the Renaissance humanist association of bodily health with good comportment, we will look briefly at writing about the educated body before turning, in a last section, to look at the work of François Rabelais, the greatest prose writer of the period, who was both a doctor and a humanist and who links discussions of cheer to the theme of reading. Thus, cheerfulness will make its full entry into the field of literature, no longer a mere body part (as in Chaucer), but a form of power.

Medical understanding in early modern Europe was shaped in large measure by the writings of the ancient Greek physician Galen. It relied on the theory that the body is governed by four humors — melancholic, sanguine, choleric, and phlegmatic — that could be regulated through processes of heating, cooling, depletion, and increase. Aristotle had written as well within this broad tradition and had studied the relationship between light-spiritedness and the humors of the body in the thirtieth book of his *Problems*. There, he devotes a passage to the variable status of black bile or the "atrabilious" humor. It is "originally mingled in the bodily nature," says Aristotle. It is a mixture of hot and cold and, like water, can take on either of these temperatures. When black bile is cold, it can produce "apoplexy or torpor or despondency or fear; but when it is over heated, it produces cheerfulness [*euthymia*] accompanied by song, and frenzy, and the breaking forth of sores, and the like."[2] Most people, says Aristotle, possess the atrabilious temperament in a slight degree and are ordinary. Those who have too much of it are prey to mood swings. Men become intoxicated by it. This heats them up and leads to *euthymia*. When their drunkenness passes, they become despondent and even suicidal. This variability among those who possess too much of the atrabilious humor is what gives certain people "remarkable gifts, not owing to disease but from natural causes."

We are obviously a good distance here from the modern cheerfulness that is our topic, where no frenzy explodes or sores erupt. Yet Aristotle is useful for the way he places bodily health in proximity to emotional exuberance. He locates the body at the center of emotion;

bursting into song and suffering sores on the skin are mentioned in the same sentence, as if there were no substantial difference between them. And yet, because ecstatic happiness is housed in the body, for later thinkers, more modest forms of delight can reside there, as well, and participate in the dynamics of healthy living.

In the early modern period that concerns us here, medical thinkers often describe cheerfulness as a counterbalance to melancholy. "Cheer" is often mentioned in the context of the sanguine humor. It takes the form of an expression of the spirit, as a kind of mediator between body and soul. For example, in his influential 1586 book, *A Treatise of Melancholy*, the English doctor Timothy Bright calls cheerfulness an "affection" linked to sanguinity, or "sanguine cherefulness," to be distinguished, for instance, from "melancholick sadness." Yet cheerfulness is not exclusively material, produced from fluids. It is principally an expression of the soul. Bright stresses the ways in which bodily experience may "declare" (that is, express, make legible) the passions of the soul, as in, for example, the experience of music, which can drive us by turns to "heavinesse," to "chearefulness," to "passion," to "rage," to "modestie," or to "wantonnesse."[3]

His list of "declarations" of the soul does not, in fact, correspond to the four humors in a one-to-one schema. The inventory of comportments is, of course, much more varied. This means that cheerfulness takes the form of an external manifestation of spirit that may — or may not — result directly from a sanguine temperament. Indeed, because it is an external manifestation, hovering, as it were, on the surface of the body, cheerfulness may become a tool to counteract melancholy. And in turn, it may be produced artificially, out of external causes such as wine, which generates a "marvelous chearing" of the self upon the first drink (no second drink is recommended).[4] Thus, "cheer" resides on the frontier between chemical and behavioral zones. And because cheer can be generated or produced by diverse factors, Bright stresses that the affliction of melancholy, his main concern, may be counterbalanced by any number of external stimuli. These involve the practice of "cheerefull music," exercise, which makes the blood a "cheerfull juyce," a "cheerfull and lightsome" habitation, and "cheerful sightes, agreeable to vertue and pietie."[5] Bright's linkage, in this last phrase, of virtue and piety to cheerful vistas suggests the overlapping of moral language with the language of the body in this corpus of writing.

The Dutch physician Levinus Lemnius, Bright's near-contemporary, is more specific and expansive in his account of what cheerfulness can do. In a 1561 discussion of "cold and dry" personalities, he links the health of the body to drink and company, through the spread of a cheer that is at once material and social:

> For when a man hath bene in pleasaunt company and at good cheere where all thinges haue bene meerilye discoursed, & the tyms ioyously passed, there appeare for the space of certayne dayes after in hys face and countenaunce, forehead, browes, lippes, eyes and beckes (for all these are be wrayers and tellers of the minde inwardly) great tokens of myrth and alacrytie and many arguments do outwardly testify the chereful dispositien of the internal Spyrits. For the body being heated wyth laughing and ioyinge, w^t kissing and dalying, wyth dauncinge, Wyne, and singing, is made fresher and better coloured, for that the Bloud is diffused into the vtter part and habite of the body.[6]

Good conversation, wine, "kissing and dalying," which are all cheerful factors, make the body flourish — and not for a moment, for some days. The cheer of conversation, of kissing, of the cheerful visage, is thus linked to the general health of the body.

The assumption that physiological stimulants can shape emotional life became part of practical medical knowledge. So a century after Lemnius and Bright, we find in William Salmon's 1696 *Family Dictionary*, a widely distributed guide "for the preservation of health," an actual recipe for a "Powder to Create Cheerfulness." Among other ingredients, it contains clove, basil, ambergris, saffron, lemon peel, ivory shavings, leaves of gold and silver, and bone shavings from the heart of a stag. This powder, we are told, will help "sweeten the breath, restore decayed strength, and dissipate

Melancholy, proceeding from an internal, or no real cause." "The Dose is from ten to twenty grains in any convenient Vehicle."[7]

The exact relationship between the interior of the self and the face was a source of great interest among early modern medical writers. Lemnius's claim that the brows and lips are "wrayers and tellers of the mind inwardly" finds its analogue in the educational writings of the ever-cheerful Erasmus of Rotterdam, whose biblical commentaries we have already encountered. European writing about the body was deeply influenced by Erasmus's several treatises on education and comportment, most famously, his *Little Book about Good Manners for Boys* of 1530.

This book gave rise to an entire current of writing about good manners and *civilité* in northern Europe over the following century. It is concerned with the relationship of the disposition of the body — most especially the face — and the state of the inner self. For Erasmus, as for Lemnius, the body is a kind of text on which we can read the condition of the mind and the soul. "The external decorum of the body proceeds from a well-ordered mind," he writes in the opening passages. In this context, he might have in mind something like the traditional phrase from the Bible, in Proverbs 15.13, where the Latin phrase "Cor gaudens exhilarat faciem" becomes "A glad heart makes a cheerful countenance" in the King James Version. Yet he also asserts the reverse — that a well-ordered body can produce decorum in the mind. Lemnius is a simple analyst of how the physiology works. Erasmus is more ambitious. He is a counselor for the improvement of the inner self. Thus, he tells us that how we hold our body shapes how our mind is disposed. And the entire first section of the book consists of a series of recommendations about controlling the body, on the assumption that a well-ordered mind and a tranquil soul will result. The face should be well arranged, calm, respectful. The forehead, above all, should be smooth, "cheerful," and "serene." Erasmus's Latin term, as in his biblical commentaries, is *hilaritas*, now paired with *serenus*. A cheerful brow is the sign of a "good conscience and an open mind."[8]

55

Erasmus and Lemnius show how writing about medicine and comportment took cheerfulness as both a legible sign of the inner self and a technique, a kind of tool for self-management. Erasmus describes cheerful activity with several words that we will see echoed in later writers, not only "hilarity" but also "alacrity" (*alacritas*, which Lemnius uses as well) — an energetic lightness in social situations. The first requirements of healthy play among boys, says Erasmus, are "alacritas" and "liberalitas." Elsewhere, he writes to his friend Thomas More about a portrait of himself by Quentin Metsys, noting that a mistakenly prescribed stomach medication had purged his bile, altering his face between the first sitting and the second, such that the completion of the painting had to be deferred until his body settled down and he could present a more "cheerful" (*alacrior*) face to the artist.[9]

Erasmus, Bright, and Lemnius all stress that self-presentation through alacrity is partly under the control of the individual. Depending on the context, it can be stimulated by wine and good conversation or enhanced by a constant turn to the good news of scripture. Through these diverse discussions of body and soul, we can see a broadening of the scope of cheerfulness from medicine to comportment. "Cheerfulness" becomes not merely a word for describing actions in the Christian community, but a term of force that connects the body to practices of self-shaping and sociability in an emerging educated society at the dawn of the modern age.

Gay Reading

For writers such as Lemnius and Erasmus, cheerfulness is no longer simply a descriptive term. It is now understood as a physical and emotional resource, a kind of force or tool that can *do* things in and through the body. As Salmon suggests, you can even access a kind of instant cheerfulness, mixed up in a powder. In order to see it in action, we turn now to the world of imaginative literature. We begin with work of the French contemporary of Erasmus, François Rabelais (1483?–1553). Rabelais is the major writer of prose fiction in sixteenth-century Europe and the first great innovator of modern literature. His stories of the giants Gargantua and Pantagruel blend the themes of the Christian moral philosophy we saw in the last chapter with accounts of the health of the body of the type just seen in Lemnius and Erasmus. Because he was a doctor (and commentator of Galen), a Christian moralist, and a fabulist of the body, he is best equipped to show us the uses of cheerfulness during the moment of the Reformation.

Rabelais often uses the French phrase "bonne chere," or "good cheer," to refer to feasting and celebration. However, it is the term "gaiety" or "gayeté" that does the most work in his discussions of emotion, community, and health. In the preface to his 1534 chronicle *Gargantua*, Rabelais sets the health of the body at the center of his work. He links it to the art of reading. He begins by comparing his book to the Silenus box. The Silenus box was a decorated container in which the ancient Greeks stored medicine. It was ugly on the outside, like the satyr Silenus, but contained healing herbs and balms on the inside. Such is his book, says Rabelais — its superficial ugliness masks salutary wisdom that lies within.

That wisdom will, quite literally, heal what ails us. Yet in order to access it, the reader must be correctly attuned. For one thing, we must be willing to gnaw on the text, as a dog gnaws on a bone to suck out the marrow. That is, even when the literal sense of the text (the bone) offers joyous material (*matieres assez joyeuses*) the reader must move beyond it to access the marrowlike message of the author. We do this by taking the text in a positive, "higher" sense: "Interpret in a higher sense what you believe, by chance, to have been spoken with a gaiety of the heart" — as he says in French, "en gayeté de cueur."[10] This sentence calls for close attention. The "cheerful heart" that we saw several authors link to the proper practice of Christian charity in our last chapter is here located in the "gay heart" of the author. Charity, it turns out, also informs literature, in the relationship of spirit, author, and community. The reader participates in the community through a kind of faith, by "believing, by chance," the good intentions of the author. This is not strict religious faith, since it comes "by chance"; we stumble across it as we read. It is faith in reading and through reading. The gaiety of the author's intention is transferred to the language of the text, which the reader, in turn, takes in the best sense.

And this gaiety shapes the health of the body. For Rabelais goes on, in the final lines of the prologue, to raise the theme again: "So, take pleasure, my loves, and *gaily* read the rest, for the ease of the body and the profit of the kidneys" (*Or esbaudissez vous, mes amours, et guayement lisez le reste, tout a l'aise du corps et au profit des reins,* my emphasis).[11] Thus, "gayeté" emerges as an equivalent of the English "cheer" that will become conventional through translations between French and English.

Cheerfulness is present, even when the word "cheer" is absent. Here, "gaiety" is the term that links the pleasure of reading with proper interpretation. It sets up a bond of faith between reader and writer. It establishes community around the book. It links the gaiety of heart found in the author with the bodily health of the reader. It will literally heal us of our kidney ailments, much as Timothy Bright and Lemnius suggest that music, flirting, and a glass of wine can rescue us from melancholy. However, the cure comes only if the book is read "gaily," in such a way that the reader takes the author's intentions in the best sense. Both reading and writing, in this sense, are forms of charity. As interpreters and scribes, we are all "cheerful givers."

There may be no greater celebration of the power of literature than this. It has a history. In his book called *On Christian Doctrine,* the early Christian philosopher Saint Augustine reminds his readers that all phenomena in the universe are signs of the presence of God. Our job is to read his presence in them. When these signs are ambiguous or confusing, when we are faced with conflicting interpretations — especially when reading the Bible — the best thing is to choose the interpretation that reaffirms our love of God and of others. Augustine wrote: "Whoever, therefore, thinks that he understands the divine Scriptures or any part of them so that it does not build the double love of God and of our neighbor does not understand it at all. Whoever finds a lesson there useful to the building of charity, even though he has not said what the author may be shown to have intended in that place, has not been deceived."[12] We love God through our love of others, and charity informs interpretation.

Rabelais mobilizes this account of interpretation for his own secular literary purposes. He points out that, even though he might have been drunk while he was writing his book, his readers should always make sure to "interpret my deeds and words in the most perfect way" — or as he puts it, with an invented Italianate phrase, "en perfectissime partie." In this way Augustine's textual focus is reforged by Rabelais into a relationship between author, text, body, and community. Reading becomes gay.[13]

As Rabelais's work unfolds, he invents his own eccentric name to denote what he here calls "gaiety." This is the idea of "Pantagruelism," or what he sets forth, in the prologue to his *Third Book of Pantagruel* (1546), as a doctrine for living that involves never taking anything "in a bad sense" (*en maulvaise partie*), but always with "good, frank, and loyal courage." A more expansive definition is provided in the preface to his *Fourth Book* (1552), where Pantagruelism is explicitly linked to bodily health. Here, Rabelais depicts himself as a doctor (which he in fact was) looking for his glasses in order to be able to see and talk to his reader. When asked about how things are going, he informs the reader that he is himself in fine health, thanks to a bit of "Pantagruelism," which keeps him spry. This he defines as "a certain gaiety of spirit, pickled in scorn for fortuitous things."[14] Here the "gaiety of heart" that inspires the writing of *Gargantua* (and is taken as such by readers) gives way to a "gaiety of spirit" or "of the mind" — a "gayeté d'esprit" — that has evolved into a philosophical doctrine. The element of chance that structured the earlier relationship of reader and writer ("what you believe, *by chance*, to have been spoken with a gaiety of the heart," as he said in *Gargantua*) is echoed, but it has now given way to a scorn for chance. The gayness that sanctions healthy reading seems to have migrated to a more general register of philosophical counsel. An image of community in the earlier book now gives way to an expression of wisdom.

The idea of indifference to "fortuitous things" evokes a kind of Christian Stoicism, which turns to faith as a bulwark against the vagaries of fortune. But gaiety also emerges here through a gesture of the individual will, which is able to set aside contingency. In the *Third Book* prologue, he calls it a "propriété individuale." The key to health is a rejection of fortuitous things. In the case of the biographical Rabelais, this involves ignoring not only the official censorship and attacks on his good name that he suffered throughout his career, but the entire political and religious upheaval that seized France in the middle years of the sixteenth century. *Gargantua* was written in the 1530s, at a moment of toleration and optimism. The *Third Book* and *Fourth Book* appeared at a time of increasing political and religious disunity in Christian Europe. They display a much darker tone than the earlier book, relying on political allegory and pointed satire. And within this dangerous setting, what can keep you healthy is a rejection of the banalities of everyday life. More charitable reading may not help you, Rabelais now seems to suggest; you have to help yourself by brushing aside the power of chance. Then gaiety can do its work as a healing force.

For Rabelais, the body is a constant point of reference. As he says a few paragraphs later in the prologue to the *Fourth Book*, "Without health there is no life, life is not liveable" (*Sans santé n'est la vie, n'est la vie vivable*).[15] For him, as perhaps for no other writer, reading and writing are corporeal practices. To heal your body, turn to gaiety. The physical nature of the process is stressed through the image of "pickling"; gaiety is "pickled" or "preserved" in contempt for contingency. The *Fourth Book* speaks of a "certaine gayeté d'esprit, conficte en mespris des choses fortuites."[16] ("Conficte" is from the Latin *comficere*, meaning "to prepare" by pickling or cooking slowly.) This "preparation" is also a tempering, a shaping of Christian optimism that is bound up with a turning away from the trials of this world.

We can see gaiety, or cheerfulness, in action later in the same book, where it is integrated into the narrative as a plot device. The *Fourth Book* tells of a sea journey on which Pantagruel and his men seek information about whether one of their group, the lusty and cowardly Panurge, should marry. Toward the end of the book, the enterprise suddenly stops as they pass the Island of the Hypocrites. The wind dies down, the sea is becalmed, and the ship loses its forward momentum. Everyone dozes off. When Pantagruel wakes from his nap, the priest Frère Jean cries out, "with great cheerfulness of spirit" (*en grande alaigresse d'esprit*), "How can one raise a wind in times of calm?" Panurge, who is generally intemperate, answers with another question, "What is the remedy for anger?" Epistemon, Pantagruel's teacher, follows up, "with gaiety of heart," by wondering, "How can you piss when you don't need to?" Another member of the group then asks how to counteract a glare in the eyes. Still another sailor wonders how to sleep in the sun when you are hungry.[17]

In the classical epics of Homer and Virgil, the plot is often motivated by bad weather as ships are blown off course. Here, by contrast, both the story and the journey have run out of breath. The scenario of a ship stranded by calm seas and a lack of wind would have been most familiar to Rabelais's readers from the accounts of travel to the New World that were beginning to circulate in mid-sixteenth-century Europe. In this case, the strange weather may also have some allegorical meaning when we remember that the island nearby, where none of the sailors will venture, is the land of hypocrites. If we were in a conventional travel narrative, prayers would be offered for a miracle, and perhaps the wind would change. In this case, something else happens. Rabelais invests the scene with a spiritual power rooted in cheerfulness.

Pantagruel tells his men that all of their questions and more will soon be answered. He then announces that it's time to eat, and the entire company sits down to a meal. When it is over, the problems have disappeared: The previously angry Panurge is now no longer upset, but "gay as a popinjay," and Epistemon needs to piss. Once the men are fed, the wind begins to rise. Spirit, body, and narrative are all healed. When asked about this development, Pantagruel says that the question of how it happened is not important. It happened, he says, by a "hidden sympathy" between their raising their glasses and the rising of the wind. They sing praise to God, and Pantagruel concludes by noting that just as wings raise the bodies of birds in flight, wine raises the spirits of people, because "their bodies are clearly cheered [*alaigris*] and whatever is earthly about them is softened."[18]

The meal enjoyed by the sailors has a sacramental dimension to it, reminding us of the Holy Communion. "Bonne chere" is present, even though the phrase is not used. But the rebooting of the narrative is also linked to bodily needs. It consists of wine and bread — the elements of the Eucharist — but also of meat (*ce bon pain, ce bon vin et frays, ces bonnes viandes*). It is spiritual, but not strictly theological, since it is also corporeal, salutary, and literary; the questions asked are questions about the control of emotions, about the care of the body, about motivation, about sleeping in the sun.

Rabelais turns the episode into a parable about community and emotion while testing out the role of cheer in the workings of a narrative plot. If cheerfulness can make things happen in bodies and communities, as Erasmus, Saint Paul, and Lemnius suggest, we here see that it can also make things happen in stories. The healing of the discomforts of the crew is set in motion by the initial "cheerful" questions raised by Frère Jean and the rest of the men. Cheerful attention to the body generates community and nourishment, which in turn heals the body through wine and the text through narrative movement.

These connections are new in our story so far. Body and community are linked to reading and to the narration of a journey. Does the healing stem from the body itself, from the wine that Lemnius and Timothy Bright remind us can heat up the stagnant humors? Does it come from the cheerful questions? From some divine mystery, as Pantagruel surmises? From the conventions of narrative itself? Rabelais explores these questions in the context of a fictional journey that stops, like a melancholy body, and then powers up again. Cheerfulness is a form of power, medical, spiritual, and literary.

Rabelais uses the language of Christian community and cheerful giving at the very moment that the health of the body seems to require a separation of the self from the hazards of this world. He brings the physiological themes of medical writers such as Timothy Bright and Levinus Lemnius together with the spiritual interests of Erasmus. His text explores the limits and possibilities of the relationship between cheer and the body. He begins to push past the purely theological cheer of the Pauline tradition toward something that might look like a psychological power in cheerfulness. However, since his characters are giants, and not recognizable "modern" literary people with "realistic" emotional lives, he is able to locate gaiety in a literary context that holds multiple intellectual traditions in a kind of suspension, where cheerfulness touches souls, bodies, communities, and even the maritime climate.

Cheerfulness is strangely motivated in Rabelais; it comes from a rejection of the contingent, a question about the wind, an act of reading. Yet the contrast among the happy group of readers in *Gargantua*, the solitary doctor who seeks to heal himself in the prologue to the *Fourth Book*, and the hungry, perplexed sailors in the scene just discussed suggests the ways in which cheerfulness and gaiety can migrate beyond the space of biblical commentary and emerge as forces in the shaping of secular culture. Rabelais uses the Augustinian notion of interpretation as a charitable activity, but he expands it to touch the individual will, the questing body, and the power of literature itself to heal us. The body of the author or curious traveler expands the reach of cheerfulness beyond the communal body of Christ's church.

When we remember that Rabelais is writing only a couple of decades after Gutenberg's invention of printing, we can understand his shuttling between a moral improvement of the self and scenes of reading and writing. Themes of charity and generosity, techniques of textual interpretation previously applied to the Bible, are now being expanded, applied to the individual will, to stories themselves. Rabelais's violent adventure tales, with their scenes of bodily excretion, outrageous appetite, and linguistic excess, ask us to think about the reader's role as both interpreter and ethical actor in the world. Gaiety emerges as a conceptual node that ties together literature, health, and ethical action. Rabelais achieves this unity by implicating us, as readers, in his text as members of his reading community. The gaiety of his strange characters is our gaiety, as well, as we read his book, "for the ease of the body and the profit of the kidneys." His near-contemporary, Shakespeare, to whom we turn next, will also be interested in health, community, and reading. But his vision of cheerfulness will unfold in a world of communities in crisis.

CHAPTER FOUR

Shakespeare, or

the Politics of Cheer

"Set It Down"

Cheerfulness is not only spiritual and medical. It gives emotional content to new political cultures that emerge in the late Renaissance. We might, in this context, think of Baldassare Castiglione's *Book of the Courtier*, which appeared in Italian in 1528. It sparked a vogue across Europe for books on courtliness and civility. This was a new kind of writing, distinct from the Christian moralism seen in writers such as Erasmus of Rotterdam, whom we looked at in previous chapters. Castiglione's book and those like it offered a guide for success in the new court societies that were beginning to develop across Europe, from the Tudor court of Henry VIII (Thomas Hoby's English version, *The Courtyer of Count Baldessar Castilio*, appeared in 1561) to the Versailles of Louis XIV.

Book 3 of the *Courtier* focuses on the lady at court. Along with good conversation and musical skills, it notes that beauty is an especially useful attribute. It is a natural gift, *a bellezza vaga ed allegra*. The adjectives are suggestive: *vaga* implies both charm, or lightness, and a general lack of location or focus (see our "vagabond"); *allegra* takes us back to *alacritas*: happiness, energy, perhaps. But this beauty is also something that can be enhanced or developed through practice and cultivation. Hoby calls this attribute a "sightlye and cheerful beawtie," noting that it can be increased through "gestures, wordes and apparaile."¹ Hoby's phrase "sightlye and cheerful" draws on the idea of the "cheer" as "face," but also on the energetic lightness that we saw in our last chapter.

While Hoby's phrase may seem like a detail, it points to a new type of social experience. We have been studying the role of cheerfulness in spiritual communities. There, it is a kind of force that can loop together individual emotion, bodily health, and collective virtue, as emblematized in Rabelais's community of sailors, who change the weather with their gay questions and cheerful fellowship. When we come to Hoby and Castiglione, we are reminded that the manifestation of cheerfulness is also a way of influencing people. It shapes you, but it shapes others, as well. And you can enhance its power, as Hoby suggests, with gestures, words, and clothing. Hoby locates us in a context that is quite different from the languages of self-care or Christian community that we have described in the previous chapters. It emerges as a force in the interpersonal politics of court societies. At times, cheerfulness is a tool for cultivation through gestures and words, as Castiglione would have it. At other times, it may be a mask.²

The theater is the literary form that explores the illusions and surfaces of court society, so we should not be surprised to find that William Shakespeare is interested in the workings of cheer in courtly gatherings. Shakespeare shows us a world of performers, people caught up in games of dissimulation and illusion. He explores the uses and limits of cheerfulness. He shows us communities in crisis. And as we will see in this chapter, the language of cheer offers a way for Shakespeare to represent the effect of collective crisis on individual characters. At the same time, he carefully evokes reflections on cheerfulness at moments of transition or crisis in the plots of his dramas. This means that he turns the evocation of cheerfulness into a literary device, a technique of fiction-making that links individual emotion to literary genre and form.

The transition from a theologically themed cheerfulness of community to a politics of representation is central to *Richard III* (1593),

the dark conclusion to Shakespeare's first quartet of historical dramas.[3] An important theme in the play is the fragility of community,
be it Christian or national. The famous opening lines of the play —
"Now is the winter of our discontent / Made glorious summer by
this son of York" — mobilizes an image that we will study in more
detail later whereby the warming sun brings "cheer." Yet the image
is double-edged, since it both suggests that York has brought sun
to a chilled English polity — he's cheered things up — and that his
ascendancy has opened the way for Richard's own winterly resentment to appear as something it is not. Already we are in a world of
dissimulations. Resentment masquerades as cheerfulness. Richard,
who is physically handicapped, is certainly lacking in the "sightlye"
advantages of Hoby's beautiful court lady, but he can and will use
language to shape the climate in which he can seize power.

Richard's cheerfulness is cheerfulness stripped of charity. If charity — love of God through love of one's neighbor — is the quality of
Christian community, Shakespeare's play sets up Richard as a figure
of anticharity. The first act of the play unfolds in a systematic manner
through a series of scenes in which charity and community are set
in conflict. This is made explicit in the second scene. When Richard
calls for the dead king Henry's corpse to be set down by his bearers,
Lady Anne says, "What black magician conjures up this fiend, / To
stop devoted charitable deeds?" (1.2.32–33).[4] He turns her language
back against her fifteen lines later, enjoining her not to reject *caritas* by cursing him, "Sweet saint, for charity be not so curst." And a
moment later, as he begins his seduction of her, he repeats the same
language, "Lady, you know no rules of charity, / Which renders good
for bad, blessings for curses" (1.2.66). Richard exploits her expression
of charity as a collective Christian virtue, nudging the meaning of
"charity" into the realm of sexual favor. Then, a moment later, when
she threatens to destroy her own beauty rather than entertain his
suit, he turns to the conventional natural metaphor that opens the
play, "As all the world is cheered by the sun, / So I by that; it is my day,
my life" (1.2.127). Thus, from the outset, Richard takes us a good way

from Saint Paul's counsel to be a cheerful giver. He uses the language of cheer and charity to manipulate those who are in his way.

The perversion of charity as a glue of community is then expanded again, a scene later, where Margaret, the widow of the dead king Henry, upbraids Richard and his minions. Richard's unctuous side-kick Buckingham tells her to be quiet: "Have done, for shame if not for charity" (1.3.273). She ripostes,

> Uncharitably with me have you dealt,
> and shamefully by you my hopes are butchered.
> My charity is outrage, life my shame;
> And in my shame still live my sorrow's rage.

As Richard turns the language of charity against itself, appropriating it for his own advantage, Margaret altogether recasts the language of community. What binds me to you is not my love *for* you, but my rage *against* you. This anticharity binds people together through their hatred of a common enemy, not through their love of God. It is the origin of tribal politics. The characterization is continued when the doomed Clarence evokes a nostalgic ideal of community against which he measures the current situation as he informs his execu-tioners in the Tower, sent by his brother Richard to murder him: "Our princely father York / Blessed his three sons with his victorious arm / And charged us from his soul to love each other" (1.4.214–16).

As a counterweight to the theme of broken community, the play introduces the theme of cheer. When used for legitimate purposes, cheer is a force of life. Thus, early on in the action, we learn that Richard's brother, the king, Edward IV, is ill. Cheer binds him to life, as the queen's son, Lord Grey, urges her to entertain the king and "cheer his grace with quick and merry words" (1.3.5). Thirty lines later, Buckingham reports that hope is warranted because "his grace speaks cheerfully" (1.3.34). Authentic cheer and cheering may thus be seen as qualities that can hold the king's natural body alive. Whether it can heal the body politic is less obvious. Thus, the insistence on cheer is a kind of literary blinking light, alerting us through the language of emotion that what is at issue is the destiny of national community.

As the story moves toward its climax, cheer migrates from character to character, powering the action, but constantly in play. Richard seems to claim it in one of the play's most extraordinary moments, when he suddenly accuses Edward's wife of witchcraft by asserting that his withered arm is her doing. This occurs at the exact structural center of the play, in the third act of five, in the fourth scene of seven. Richard's dramatic claim is prepared by a dialogue between Hastings and Stanley about Richard's countenance, which all agree is transparent and easy to read. Says Hastings, "His grace looks cheerfully and smooth today. / There's some conceit or other likes him well / When he doth bid good morrow with such a spirit" (3.4.53–55). The "smooth" nature of Richard would seem to be an echo of Erasmus's claim that a "serene" face is the mark of the cheerful man. Hastings's misreading sets the scene for the dramatic gesture in which Richard declares himself bewitched. Richard's serenity could thus either be dissimulated serenity or a serenity at the fact that he alone knows what he has planned. Either way, it is misread, and the implication is that all cheerful expressions are unstable in meaning.

Yet the cheer that falsely testifies to Richard's personality also signals the turning of fortune in the play, for the same language reappears at the crisis point in the story. On the eve of his climactic battle with the Earl of Richmond, as Richard prepares to bed down, he checks on the situation of his men: "Saw'st thou the melancholy Lord Northumberland?" he asks Ratcliffe. Northumberland and Surrey, he learns, have gone off through the army, "cheering up the soldiers." The joke here would seem to be that the job of cheering the soldiers falls — and not by Richard's command — to Northumberland, the figure of melancholy. Even at the level of emotion, things are topsy-turvy in England. Shakespeare goes on to expand the theme. "So I am satisfied," Richard continues. Then, taking a bowl of wine, he reflects on his situation: "I have not that alacrity of spirit / Nor cheer of mind that I was wont to have. / Set it down," he instructs his loyal henchman Ratcliffe. "Is ink and paper ready?" (5.3.69–76). At the moment of reflection, when the self-conscious Richard turns from soliloquizing about dissimulation to contemplating his destiny, he reflects not on his conscience, but on the loss of cheer. And he wants that loss noted for posterity, for us.

Here we see the destiny of national community depicted as a transformation of the self. The juxtaposition of Northumberland's urging of the soldiers with Richard's self-analysis splits the notion of cheer from the ideals of community favored by Erasmus and Calvin. We can begin to grasp what cheerfulness was in the play, because it is now gone. Cheerfulness was what came before. We saw Richard use it against his neighbors. His energy and good cheer were a kind of weapon, turned against charity and community. His self-conscious description of his state of mind envisions what later chroniclers and biographers would say of him — that he was a cheerful type. He is writing his own emotional biography. From this moment of the loss of cheer and "alacrity," we can deduce that Richard's actions throughout the play have, in fact, been inflected with a "cheer" that offered some alternative version of selfhood to the struggles of his victims to reconstitute community. This is the cheer of a self that is cut loose from God. The delamination of cheer from community is underscored by the reference to Northumberland "cheering" the troops. Publicly, cheer has degenerated into a kind of rhetoric. It emerges as the trick of the powerful to control their subjects. The "cheer" that incites the members of Richard's army counterbalances and outweighs the charitable cheer that should bind the country.

Perhaps what is most striking about Richard's acknowledgment of the loss of his cheer is what it tells us about literature. It signals a change in the register of the play. Whereas in Rabelais gaiety bound the characters together, Shakespeare calls forth the conventional language of community to underscore the solitude of the tragic protagonist. It is almost as if Shakespeare were telegraphing to his audience that we are moving out of the realm of historical narrative, where cheer is up for grabs as a tool of power, and into the space of tragedy, where characters must confront their destinies without masks. The reversal in the plot coincides with the loss of cheer in the main character. Put differently, the loss of cheer offers the emotional parallel to Richard's upcoming defeat in battle. This is not an instance of the much-discussed "private self" that scholars have often seen as an innovation in the early modern period. Rather, it is a literary technique that can represent how public crisis feels to the individual. It prepares the way, at the level of character, for what is about to take place in the plot. It is a loss or failure of the self that resonates both backward and forward, telling us that up to now Richard has been a cheerful fellow, but hinting that cheer and tragedy may somehow be incompatible. It ties character to literary genre.

"Meeting Were Bare Without It"

Fortune has indeed turned. A second after Richard's moment of tragic self-consciousness, we see cheer migrate to his military opponent, the Earl of Richmond, the good guy in the play. Holinshed's *Chronicles*, one of Shakespeare's source texts, had noted that generally, Richmond's "countenance and aspect was cheerful and courageous."[5] Shakespeare stresses this by providing him with cheer at the very instant that Richard loses it. In the same scene where Richard acknowledges his "lost" cheer, the ghost of the murdered Prince Edward appears to him and to Richmond as they sleep. To Richmond, he urges, "Be cheerful" (5.4.100); to Richard, he says, "Despair and die" (5.4.105). And Richmond takes this to heart, recalling upon waking that "my soul is very jocund / In the remembrance of so fair a dream" (5.4.211). A moment later, he concludes his oration to his soldiers by urging, "Sound drums and trumpets bold and cheerfully! / God and Saint George! Richmond and victory!" (5.4.248–49). While the loss of cheer is the mark of tragedy for Richard, the spread of cheer becomes the energizing element to a new collective destiny under the cheerful Richmond's command. The failed charity of the earlier generation gives way to a military victory over the evil usurper. This shift in momentum is indicated by the shift in the location of cheerfulness. Cheerfulness doesn't bind community, as it does in Rabelais. It moves between warring factions.[6]

Richard is not alone among Shakespeare's villains in his failure to generate "cheer" at the moment he is tested. In act 3, scene 4 of *Macbeth* (again, at the exact center of the play), Lady Macbeth chastises her husband for his inability to mix with the guests at the banquet celebrating his accession. She points out that food alone is not what makes a banquet, that people dining in someone else's house want hospitality and high spirits. Food must be accompanied by ceremony and welcome, the rituals of sociability:

> You do not give the cheer: the feast is sold,
>
> That is not often vouch'd, while 'tis a-making,
>
> 'Tis given with welcome; to feed were best at home;
>
> From thence, the sauce to meat is ceremony;
>
> Meeting were bare without it.[7]

It is cheer, now linked again to "welcome," which distinguishes the mere collecting of bodies in the same space from the establishment of an actual community. And as in the case of Richard, it is what, at a crucial moment in his story, the villain Macbeth cannot mobilize. Four lines later, he tries to rouse the company by toasting the absent Banquo, "our country's honour" (3.4.39), whom he has just murdered. Instead of binding the company together, his toast conjures up the ghost of his dead friend. Macbeth is overcome with terror. Not all killers, it would seem, can spin cheerfulness with the same ease as Richard III. "Meeting were bare without it," indeed.

The social climber and seducer Richard defines himself—indeed, describes himself—in terms of his now lost cheer: "Set it down." He is the ambitious man who has appropriated sociability in order to "pass," to invent a royal personality for his most unroyal self. He is the actor par excellence. Macbeth is a theatrical character, too, but he is not a mere actor. He never descends to Richard's level of pure dissimulation, and from his failure to generate cheer come both his isolation and, in part, his dramatic power.

As Shakespeare's works unfold, ironic representations of "cheer" in the ambit of villains — and the subsequent loss of cheer — proliferate. This motif structures some of the most interesting moments of self-presentation in *Hamlet*. The play is extremely suspicious of "cheer" or cheerful activity. Claudius's early expression that Hamlet needs to stay put in Elsinore is articulated through a language of the face: "We beseech you, bend you to remain / Here in the cheer and comfort of our eye, / Our chiefest courtier, cousin, and our son."[8] Claudius's formulation suggests the extent to which cheer has become, for Shakespeare, a term of power, a resource to be manipulated. Here, cheer defines the "eye," yet the eye is at one and the same time the tool of company and the tool of surveillance. It is that thing that Claudius wants to keep trained on Hamlet while pretending to bond with him.

Claudius's ambiguous manipulation of cheer is contrasted with yet another scene of loss. In the midst of the play within the play, the Player Queen almost seems to be channeling Lady Macbeth when she laments the melancholy of the doomed Player King: "But woe is me, you are so sick of late, / So far from cheer and from your former state that I distrust you."[9] The loss of cheer is tantamount to a breakdown of the self, to an isolation that here takes the form of dissolution of the bond between mates. It recalls *Macbeth*'s image of broken, cheerless community. And as in *Richard III*, the recognition of lost cheer both points back to an earlier image of self-assurance and adumbrates tragedy.

What is striking is the epistemological certainty and moral clarity of the Player Queen's lament. In contrast to Claudius's earlier ambiguous manipulation of the language of cheer, the Player Queen says unequivocally what she knows. Faces are notoriously difficult to read in *Hamlet*, but the Player Queen is a certain and steady reader. Moreover, she knows what she's talking about. There is bad business afoot. And it is characteristic of *Hamlet*'s exceptional complexity that this moment of certain and accurate interpretation of another's face can only occur inside the play within the play. Only inside a self-conscious fiction can faces can be read in ways that they cannot in Elsinore more generally.

We can see here that cheerfulness in Shakespeare is both a key term for depicting emotion and a literary device. It shows us the effect of public crisis on the emotional world of the individual, and it functions as a marker of literary genre. To underscore the point, we can contrast these tragic moments with an account of cheerfulness in comedy. Thus, in *As You Like It*, the young hero Orlando reminds his servant Adam to "cheer thyself a little" (2.7.6), despite the fact that they are lost in the woods and have neither shelter nor food. The encouragement seems to work, for not ten lines later, following a joke, Orlando senses that Adam is doing better: "Well said, thou look'st cheerly, and I'll be with thee quickly" (2.7.13–4).[10] This is one difference between comedy and tragedy. In comedy, cheer lies within the reach of characters in times of trouble. In tragedy, it is lost.

Even more interesting is the role of cheerfulness in *Romeo and Juliet*, a play that, more than any other in Shakespeare's canon, wavers between comedy and tragedy. We are given two moments of cheerfulness in the play: The first comes in act 2, scene 3, where the sanguine counselor Friar Laurence makes his first appearance, praising the beauty of the new day and the sun's capacity "to cheer, and night's dank dew to dry."[11] Yet he also hints at what Richard III knows, that cheerfulness may be deceptive. He juxtaposes the cheering of the day to his work as a herbalist. One plant has the power to poison, yet its smell is appealing—"with that part cheers each part" (2.3.21). It can lure us to our doom. The metaphor of the plant looks like an allegory of cheerfulness gone wrong. Beware of cheer, he seems to say. It is a force that disguises the true character of things. And, sure enough, the friar's lightness of spirit is recalled at the outset of act 5, when Romeo, now living in exile in Mantua and involved in a scheme to redeem his love for Juliet, wakes to recount a dream he has had. "My dreams," he says, "presage some joyful news at hand." He echoes Friar Laurence's talk of cheerfulness. But he alters the good friar's language, for it is not the new day that cheers him, it is his dream, which spills over into the day — just as the poisonous part of the plant can "cheer" the rest: "And all this day an unaccustom'd spirit / Lifts me above the ground with cheerful thoughts." He goes on to tell us that he dreamed himself dead, but was revived by Juliet (5.1.5–6). Yet he is a dupe to believe his dream as the force of cheer, rather than the new day. And so a mere two lines later, Balthasar enters to reveal that he has seen Juliet "dead." This sparks Romeo to return to Verona and set in motion the misunderstanding that leads to his premature death and to tragedy for the entire city. With uncanny precision, here, as in *Richard III* and *Macbeth*, cheer is evoked to correspond to the onset of disaster. Its disappearance or mistaken use provides the psychological character marker for shifts in the direction of the plot.

"Strange and Admirable"

"What cheer, my love?" asks Theseus of his fiancée Hippolyta at the outset of *A Midsummer Night's Dream* (1595).[12] The question is a good one. Hippolyta is an Amazon queen, from a tribe of independent warrior women. She has been "woo'd with [the] sword" by Duke Theseus and brought to Athens for marriage. And she has just watched a scene in which the Athenian maiden Hermia, in love with Lysander, has been humiliated in public by both the duke and her father and commanded to marry Demetrius, whom she doesn't love. If Hermia refuses, she will be condemned either to death or a nunnery. Theseus's question about Hippolyta's "cheer" is the line that directly follows his command to Hermia: "To death, or to a vow of single life" (1.1.122). No wonder Hippolyta's "cheer," suggesting both face and spirit, seems at a low ebb. She must be wondering what she's gotten herself into.

Theseus's question suggests that cheerfulness has a limit. In this case, it is bounded by community and gender. The manipulations of cheerfulness seen in the courtly political contexts of *Hamlet* and *Richard III* may not be universal. Hippolyta is the witness on whom cheerfulness is being tested out. She is the spectator of the complicated love intrigues that make up *A Midsummer Night's Dream*. Yet she is also from a different emotional and ethical world, a world of war and female heroism. She occupies the position that Sara Ahmed has called the "affect alien,"[13] the person from a different dispensation, ignorant of the rituals of sociability that pertain in a community. Her presence brings to the fore the educational theme that runs through Shakespeare's play and that is sometimes hidden from sight by its amorous complications By bringing Hippolyta to Athens, Theseus wants to civilize her to the ways of the Athenians. Her education, like ours, takes place through the processes of watching. Yet she disrupts the smooth political surface of the play. First, she watches the humiliation of Hermia. Then, later, as the play winds down, she is prominent among the spectators of the performance of the story of Pyramus and Thisbe, a story of "very tragical mirth" put on by the workingmen of Athens. She is impatient with their crude performance ("This is the silliest stuff I ever heard" [5.1.208]), as if her concerns were elsewhere — which, judging by Theseus's concerned comment cited earlier, they may well be. The cheerful one, during the performance, is Theseus, who is emotionally generous toward the clumsy workingman-actors. He takes on the role of the gay or cheerful reader whom we saw earlier in Rabelais — the reader who takes all things in the best sense. When Hippolyta complains about the bad acting of the mechanicals, Theseus counters that "the worse are no worse, if imagination amend them" (5.1.209). She answers acerbically, "It must be your imagination then, and not theirs" (5.1.210).

The exchange between Theseus and Hippolyta affirms the "civilizing" power of the cheerful interpretation we saw earlier in Rabelais — the sense that the imagination can counter melancholy and critique by simply taking things in a positive way, "in the best sense." But it also points to the limits of that capacity.

Hippolyta the Amazon seems to want none of it. She has seen the domination of Theseus's goodwill over Athenian women. That Theseus's rejoinders about charitable spectatorship should be made to Hippolyta, whose earlier witnessing was stressed, makes clear the link between his generous reading of the workingmen's play and the "law" that condemns Hermia to death. Theseus can watch the workingmen's play charitably for the same reason he can condemn Hermia to death—because he is in power. His reading of the "Athenian law" in act 1 is of a piece with his reading of the performance in act 5. He is at once reader, legal interpreter, and cheerleader. And so it is not by chance that Hippolyta, alone among the nobles of the court, believes the group of young lovers when they say that they were enchanted in the forest during a midsummer's night. She grasps the fact that something unusual is afoot, something that cannot be resolved by cheerful acts of the will: " 'Tis strange, my Theseus, that these lovers speak of" (5.1.1), she says to begin act 5 of the play. Theseus responds with a long and famous speech on lovers, lunatics, and poets, pointing out that they are all prey to the imagination. He dismisses all the enchantments of the forest as a kind of madness or illusion. Hippolyta is not so sure: "But all the story of the night told over, / And all their minds transfigur'd so together, / More witnesseth than fancy's images," she responds. And the dialogue breaks off, unresolved, with her closing comment: "Strange and admirable" (5.1.21–25).

As the outsider, the witness figure who tests the limits of cheerfulness, it is no accident that Hippolyta is a woman and a foreigner. Ever since the householder's wife in Chrétien de Troyes's *Lancelot*, whom we saw welcome the knight with "good cheer," women have been the vehicles of cheer. The hermeneutic dimension of cheerfulness, the gaiety that takes things in the best sense, is both the characteristic of a "civilized" social sphere and the duty of females who are subjugated to the laws of men in power. Hippolyta is both wary of a system that puts women in convents and open to an order of experience that lies outside the bounds of Athenian law. She is the figure who absorbs and registers the "strangeness" of the magic that dominates the world of the forest: "More witnesseth than fancy's images." Thus, even as Shakespeare, in his tragedies, uncovers the rhetorical resources of cheerfulness as a form of power, he here questions the limits of the tradition of "cheerful" or "gay" reading. A cheerful hermeneutic works, it would seem, only when the community of readers already shares a certain set of ethical principles.

The problem of how to interpret is brought together with the political dimension of cheer in the romance adventure of Shakespeare's last single-authored play, *The Tempest*. There, we learn of a community that has been destroyed by political intrigue. This fracturing is reflected in the violence of the sea storm (which might remind us, by contrast, of Rabelais's sea journey in unnaturally calm weather, studied earlier). There is need for both political and spiritual repair. As Northrop Frye noted some years ago, *The Tempest* feels like it is the conclusion and resolution to an earlier story of the type that Shakespeare gave us in his political tragedies—a story of betrayal and skulduggery set on the mainland of Italy.[14] We should not be surprised, then, to find that the play opens with a series of urgings of the type we have now seen several times—people being told to lift their spirits in a time of trial, when community is at risk. "What cheer?" the Boatswain asks the Master in the second line of the play, and when he is told that danger is near, he turns to the crew with "Heigh, my hearts! Cheerly, cheerly, my hearts!"[15] He repeats the exhortation a moment later after having told the aristocrats to stay off of the deck.

"Cheer" here means something like heart or spirit. However, these evocations will be echoed, in a register that will bring us back to the great themes of community studied above, at the play's end, as if cheer were bookending the action. Cheerfulness is linked to reading, to how we read signs, to how we understand the phenomena around us. This point is made clear in the final moment of *The Tempest*. Here, after the wizard Prospero has astonished his estranged brother Alonso with the wonders of the island and shown him the spectacle of the son he thought dead playing chess with Prospero's daughter, Miranda, he leaves him to contemplate what he has seen:

> Do not infest your mind with beating on
> The strangeness of this business; at pick'd leisure
> Which shall be shortly single, I'll resolve you,

Which to you shall seem probable, of every
These happen'd accidents; till when, be cheerful,
And think of each thing well. (5.1.245-50)

In other words, as Rabelais would say, until I explain it all, take these events in their best sense — "en perfectissime partie."

Here is the answer to Hippolyta's claim that the events of the forest were "strange." "The strangeness of this business" will be explained. In the meantime, read the events we have all just witnessed with good cheer. That cheerful reading turns a story that would be tragic for Alonso into something more productive. Unlike Hippolyta, he will be integrated back into community. Cheerful interpretation holds Alonso's attention while Prospero cleans up the rest of the action elsewhere on the island. It prefigures our own imagined cheerful interpretation of Shakespeare's play, which is now moving from romance magic back to political reconciliation. The loss of cheer for Richard III, the onset of tragedy, is answered by the recovery of cheer in the romance world of *The Tempest*.

Prospero's recommendation to his estranged brother, "be cheerful / and think of each thing well," supplements the question, "What cheer?" and the calls of "cheerly, cheerly" that open the play. These evocations of cheer are linked to the destiny of community. The initial calls of panic seek to hold off the threat to community and survival, yet they cannot heal a community that has lost its spirit. Prospero, by contrast, knows that cheerful reading has a political dimension. True political reconciliation can never take place by simply unmasking old grievances and punishing evildoers. Such punishment simply leads to more vengeance in a later generation — as the history of tragedy and politics, from Marlowe to Racine, from Lincoln to Trump, reminds us. Instead, if politics is to be healed, events must be read — reread — in the best sense. The resolution of a political schism is not only about shifting power back where it belongs. It is also about reading the past in the best sense. This does not mean, obviously, that Alonso — or anyone — should avoid reading the past in all of its complexity and violence. Prospero is not advocating the sugarcoating of events, only a cheerful recuperation of the grounds of community.

The cheerful hermeneutic links the act of reading to the disposition of the body and community. It brings the story back from the realm of tragedy to comedic resolution, just as, conversely, Richard III's "Set it down" takes us from historical chronicle to tragedy or as Romeo's loss of cheer takes us from comedy to tragedy. What for Rabelais was a motif of Christian charity in the relationship of reader and text becomes, in Shakespeare, a marker of generic change, like a shifting of literary gears. The healing sought by Prospero can come only through a combination of charitable reading and the cultivation of a cheerful spirit. These are the qualities that Prospero will stress in the epilogue to the play, when he turns to the audience to ask them to "pardon" him for his mistakes. In literary terms, they provide the generic alternative to the lost cheer and personal estrangement of tragedy. Whether they can satisfy the Amazon Hippolyta remains an open question.

In the late Renaissance in Europe, the quality of cheerfulness undergoes a shift. Whereas mid-sixteenth-century writers, struggling with the implications of the Reformation, circled around the concepts of charity, hospitality, and community that had been set forth in the New Testament, with Shakespeare we see the limits of those concepts. In the political world of court society, in struggles over the control of authority and the meaning of history, cheerfulness becomes a form of dissimulation or trickery, like the "sightlye and cheerful" beauty of the courtier. Moreover, Shakespeare points to the mobility of cheerfulness by deploying it as a literary device. It appears and disappears at crucial moments, when his plots modulate between generic registers. He teaches us something about how character and plot intertwine to create an effect of personality in fiction. Cheer, or its absence, does work in describing the interiority of his characters as they take their places in the unfolding of stories. Cheerfulness becomes the sign of a psychological dispensation at the moment that history and narrative take a turn. For Richard and Macbeth, the loss of cheer marks the failure of the self. For Theseus and Prospero, the turn to cheerfulness aims at redemption or reconciliation.

This relationship between cheerfulness and individual character will become the preoccupation of Shakesepeare's contemporary, the philosopher Montaigne, to whom we turn next. For the moment, Shakespeare's tragedies have unmasked the earlier idealism of cheerful readers and actors as a kind of naivete, raw material for the con man, a shiny distraction on the eve of disaster. Prospero suggests that there is a counterweight to revenge and violence, if we just read cheerfully. But then, Prospero lives on an enchanted island.

CHAPTER FIVE

Montaigne, or

the Cheerful Self

Exhausted Reading

The French philosopher Michel de Montaigne was Shakespeare's slightly older contemporary. His *Essays*, written in the two decades after his retirement from a public career in 1571, take as their professed center of focus the changing thoughts and tastes of the essayist himself. As Montaigne writes down his moods, describes his health problems, and registers his opinions about current events, he paints a picture of a literary self that is strikingly modern. He gives us one of the first images in European literature of a private, secular individual. He is clearly attuned to both the religious questions addressed by Erasmus and Rabelais and the power politics we saw in Shakespeare, but he presents himself as neither a spiritual seeker nor a political actor. Montaigne shows the possibilities of a cheerful "self" while also pointing out its limitations. Thus, he clears the space for the emergence of an emotional regime that we will see developed fully a bit later, in the Enlightenment values of conversation and self-cultivation.

The *Essays* traveled quickly and well. They were translated into English and Italian shortly after publication and were widely read across Europe. By moving between Montaigne's French and John Florio's influential 1603 English version (read by Shakespeare, Francis Bacon, Robert Burton, and many others), we can build on what we have learned about early modern cheerfulness so far while beginning to address topics of importance to our later discussion of English and American texts. In part, Montaigne's influence is tied to his great literary invention, the "personal essay," which moves between local anecdote and general philosophical commentary. The relative shapelessness of the form makes it ideal for addressing the intersecting moral, medical, and political themes that have helped us locate cheerfulness so far. Moreover, we know that Hume, Emerson, and Nietzsche, whom we will look at a bit later, were all deep readers of Montaigne. In this chapter, we will see Montaigne repurpose the inherited language of what he calls "gaiety" for a project of self-definition that flouts both convention and tradition.

The *Essays* end with a prayer and a recommendation. The final essay, "Of Experience," closes with a passage from Horace's *Odes* in which the poet, in old age, prays to Apollo for a life filled with poetry and not devoid of honor. The aging Montaigne comments on how we might spend what is left of our lives. "Now old age needs to be treated a little more tenderly," reads the penultimate sentence. And he concludes: "Let us commend it to that god [Asclepius] who is the protector of health and wisdom, but gay and social wisdom." Florio's Elizabethan translation of the last sentences asks for wisdom that is "blithe and sociall." The original French says, "gaye et sociale." Such are Montaigne's last words.[1]

It is striking that the beautiful final sentence contains a qualifier, "*but* gay and social." We can surmise why wisdom should be "social," since it is well known that Montaigne loves conversation. But why should it be "blithe" or "gay"? Several pages earlier, after having listed many of his own preoccupations and habits, Montaigne turns to a summing up of his own life. "As for me," he begins, in the final section of the essay, "I love life and cultivate it just as God has been pleased to grant it to us" (p. 857). And this gift of life includes a duty to care for the world. "I accept with all my heart and with gratitude what nature has done for me, I am pleased with myself and proud of myself that I do. We wrong that great and all-powerful

Giver by refusing his gift, nullifying it, and disfiguring it" (p. 855). In French, the gift of life is taken "de bon coeur, et recognoissant"; for Florio it is done "cheerefully and thankefully, and with a good heart." All of these formulations suggest Montaigne's acceptance of all of creation, both the metaphysical realm of the spirit and the physical world of sex and appetite. An acknowledgement of the beauty of the world imposes an ethical and even political duty upon the individual to bring all aspects of life together: "To what purpose do we dismember by divorce a structure made up of such close and brotherly correspondence?" he asks a moment later. "Let the mind arouse and quicken the heaviness of the body, and the body check and make fast the lightness of the mind" (p. 855). Thus, the *Essays* end with a reflection on the coherence of the self—body and soul together—that is framed by two encomia of cheerfulness.

What form would such cheerfulness take? Earlier, in our discussion of Erasmus and Calvin, we saw that cheerfulness carries a spiritual and social resonance for many early modern thinkers. It works to bind the human subject to her community. It both directs the self (we are enjoined to be cheerful) and represents it (if you are a cheerful giver, that means something). It is both what makes community happen and the evidence that community exists. For Rabelais, who explores the intersection of medical cheerfulness and religious gaiety, the cheerful giver is also a cheerful reader and writer. The charity of the Christian is also an interpretive generosity. Gaiety is a literary affair. It can heal community.

Montaigne offers an alternative to the "cheerful" or "gay" reading we saw advocated by Rabelais's narrator and Shakespeare's Prospero. This comes in the tenth chapter of the second book of his *Essays*, the essay entitled "Of Books." There, he tells us that he has a mind that loves to jump about. This makes sustained study a problem. If he picks up a book and finds it difficult, instead of struggling with it, he simply sets it aside: "If I encounter difficulties in reading, I do not gnaw my nails over them; I leave them there after making one or two attacks on them" (p. 297). Such is the description of reading in the initial version of the *Essays*, published in 1580. Eight years later, Montaigne publishes a second edition of the same essay, adding some more text: "What I do not see at the first attack, I see less by persisting," he inserts. "I do nothing without gaiety; continuation... dazes, depresses, and wearies my judgment." At the end of his life, he expands the text still further, with the tag, "My sight becomes confused and dispersed" (p. 297).[2]

The first thing we might note about this account of reading is how, as Montaigne expands his text for each new edition, it becomes increasingly gloomy and skeptical. This isn't gay reading; it's exhausted reading. The more Montaigne writes about reading difficult books, the more negative the effect on his state of mind. His initial impatience, in the 1580 version, turns into an exhaustion and even saddening of judgment in 1588. Then, in the last version, it becomes a veritable physical disability as he ends up not even able to see what he's looking at.

This is of course the exact inverse of what Rabelais says about reading. In the famous preface to *Gargantua*, written forty years earlier, Rabelais describes his reader as a dog gnawing a bone, troubling it and picking at it, looking for deeper meaning inside the text. Rabelais's reader is persistent, evincing a gaiety that leads to health; he reads for his kidneys. Montaigne's reader is fickle. Even more striking, what for Rabelais is a charitable act, binding reader and writer, becomes for Montaigne a scene of depression. The more he tries to read, the more his vision is overcome and his judgment is depressed and exhausted — it becomes "triste" and "las." Reading doesn't heal the body; the body gets in the way of reading.

No less interesting in this moment is the curious blending of the struggles of the judgment and the struggles of the body. Which affects which? Does vision become exhausted because one can't understand, or can one not understand because the eyes get tired? My exhaustion doesn't come from the fact that I see less each time I read; rather, I am certain that I'm not seeing things because I am worn out trying. And from my physical condition, I can posit that there is something out there that I'm not seeing in the text.

At this point, we can note the work done by Montaigne's proclamation at the center of this discussion: "I do nothing without gaiety." Gaiety is included in the description of reading, but it is repurposed from what we saw in Rabelais and Shakespeare. The counterbalance to an exhausted sense of judgment is the bright claim that what seems to be interpretive failure is in fact an attribute of the self. The assertion compensates for Montaigne's weakness. What looks like exhaustion turns out to be gaiety. And that quality of the self extends far beyond the scene described here. Not, "I read with gaiety," but "I do nothing without gaiety"; "je ne fais rien sans gayeté" — or, as Florio's translation would have it, "without blithenesse."

Thus, gaiety emerges as the characteristic flavoring or modality that shapes not *what* Montaigne does, but *how* he does it. He cannot be a gay reader, but he can be gay. Gaiety is the aspect of any action that saves it from being meaningless, even — or perhaps especially — when it is ineffective. A slightly broader version of the same idea appears later, in the ninth essay of the third book, the essay on vanity, where Montaigne discusses his vexed relationship to the chateau he has inherited. There, he laments his inability to keep his father's house in good condition while noting, at the very moment in the text where he turns to discuss the paternal castle, that he generally prefers being elsewhere: "It is pitiful to be in a place where everything you see involves and concerns you. And I seem to enjoy more gaily the pleasures of someone else's house, and to approach them with a purer relish" (pp. 725–26).[3] Then he adds, in an insertion for a later edition, that the Cynic philosopher Diogenes remarked that the best wine is wine that comes from somewhere else, that is unfamiliar. Just as the act of reading implies a freedom from obligation to study, the gayest experience of domesticity is in someone else's house.

Thus, the key advantage of gaiety for Montaigne would seem to be that it frees him from obligation. The theological and ethical shading that marked gaiety in our earlier discussions has now faded. And this revision extends to politics. As he notes later on in "Of Vanity," the best political service is what comes through free choice, rather than through conventional obligation. I love the private life, he says, not because I don't like the public life, but because I have freely chosen it, "it is by my own choice" (p. 756) (*c'est par mon chois que je l'ayme*, p. 966b). I chose it because of my "complexion," and my free judgment. "I serve my prince the more gaily because I do so by the free choice of my judgment and my reason" (p. 756) (*j'en sers plus gayement mon prince par ce que c'est par libre eslection de mon jugement et de ma raison*, p. 966b). Forget Shakespeare's association of cheerfulness with royal power. This is a different approach. In all of these formulations by Montaigne, gaiety redeems or compensates for judgment. When judgment, hindered by the body, fails in the act of reading, it is redeemed by the assertion of gaiety. Gaiety seems to be the modality of the self that signifies its freedom from external constraint.

Cannibal Gaiety

This account of cheerfulness, of course, elides the kind of manipulation we saw in Shakespeare's *Richard III*, where cheer was a mask. In the political realm — and we remember that Montaigne wrote in the midst of a massive social and religious war — Montaigne's gaiety has the potential to look like arrogance or even subversion of princely authority. Yet he makes it clear that when judgment is freely exercised, gaiety follows, and political obedience is strengthened. His phrase "I serve my prince the more gaily by the free choice of my judgment" suggests a voluntary political association, but a strong one.

The scent of political restiveness hovering around Montaigne's hostility to convention and duty is why he is careful to build a fence around the implications of individual gaiety. The translator Florio seems to be conscious of the potentially disruptive willfulness in Montaigne's version of cheerfulness, for when Montaigne says he serves his prince "gayement," Florio helpfully adds in two terms, "joyfully and genuinely," which temper the claim and reaffirm that conventional pleasure is also royal service. And again, a few pages later, in "Of Husbanding the Will," the tenth essay in the third book, we learn, as Montaigne discusses his time as mayor of Bordeaux, that he hates social and political commitments, which involve the self in passionate obligations. The best thing is to use one's own judgment, for this produces more flexibility: "He who employs in [politics] only his judgment and skill proceeds more gaily. He feints, he bends, he postpones entirely at his ease according to the need of the occasions; he misses the target without torment or affliction . . . he always walks bridle in hand" (p. 770).[4] The image of the bridle — the metaphor for self-control since the ancients — here suggests that Montaigne is keeping within convention, policing himself. He brings his own bridle to the paddock.

Thus, Montaigne is using the idea of gaiety to promote personal agency. He frees the self from external constraint — the constraint of convention, scholarly boredom, drudgery, or domestic duty — while carefully erecting limits to appropriate forms of action. Gaiety operates as part of the self's relationship to itself. In this way, Montaigne can hold his own reins.

The freedom from obligation that Montaigne associates with gaiety is linked to the body. In his early essay "On the Education of Children," he stresses the ease and pleasure that should accompany the study of philosophy. In contrast to the current grim practice of scholastic philosophy, he notes, there is nothing gayer than the philosophical life: "There is nothing more gay, more lusty, more sprightly, and I might almost say more frolicsome" (p. 118) (*il n'est rien de plus gaye*, p. 160a), or as Florio has it, interestingly, "there is nothing more beauteous" (p. 123). And he recalls an exchange between "Demetrius the grammarian" and a group of philosophers in which Demetrius is told that only pedants struggle and wrinkle their brow — "rider le front" (p. 160a) — whereas the sweetness of philosophy produces "a peaceful and gay countenance" (p. 118) (*contenance . . . paisible et . . . gaye*, p. 160a). Healthy philosophy, he concludes, should render the body healthy, as well.

Yet if gaiety is a kind of emotional mechanism that balances freedom and self-control, the self-control is clearly linked to the disciplining of the body. This is explored in the fifth essay of the third book, the essay on sex and language called "On Some Verses of Virgil." There, Montaigne stresses the close link between body and soul. As he approaches death, he says, he tries to isolate his spirit, giving it wise advice, reminding it of the examples of Seneca and Catullus, yet to no avail. If the body is unhappy, he says, so is the spirit. And he goes on to assert the originary dominance of the body. Whereas philosophers often attribute the transports of the soul to divine visitations, or to wine, or to poetry, what they should do is pay attention to the body, for when one is young and in good health, it is health itself, a "boiling health" (*une santé bouillante, vigoureuse*, p. 821c), that generates the "fire of gaiety" (*ce feu de gayeté*) and drives us into moments of enthusiasm when we seem to transcend our own selves.

This is a remarkable moment in the *Essays*. At one level, it seems to evoke Aristotle's idea, mentioned in our Chapter 3, of *euthymia* as a kind of frenzy. But it also touches on Montaigne's aversion to the divine transport celebrated by fanatics on both sides in the French wars of religion. Here, the idea of ecstasy is cast not as divine transport, but as the body's own life force. The body explodes into cheer not because God has possessed it, but on its own power. Enthusiasm and ecstasy come not from some mystical inspiration (be it Protestant or Catholic), but from simple good health, from the fire of gaiety proper to youth.

The advantage of such a model is that whereas mystical visions cannot be managed, "the fire of gaiety" can be tempered. It can be controlled by our relationships with those around us. Montaigne quotes a line from Horace that says that while we can, we should all banish old age, then adds, "I love a gay and civil wisdom" (p. 641) (*J'ayme une sagesse gaye et civile*, p. 822b). This is the phrase that is echoed on the very last page of the *Essays* with which I began, where he wishes for "a gay and social wisdom." Gaiety frees us from stifling convention, but sociability and civility moderate gaiety. The self is free of custom, but not free of social obligations. Cheerfulness has migrated to the space between individual will and social convention.

It should be obvious here that Montaigne's cheerfulness or gaiety takes us in a different direction from the spiritual or religious senses of cheerfulness set forth by Erasmus, Calvin, and Rabelais. Montaigne makes this clear through his discussion of a series of exemplary figures who manifest gaiety. Chief among these are the Tupi natives of Brazil, mentioned in the famous essay "Of Cannibals." When the cannibals are captured by their enemies and are about to be roasted and eaten, we are told, they do not despair. To the contrary, they "wear a gay expression" (p.157) (*portent une contenance gaye*, p. 211a), or as Florio has it, "ever carry a cheerefull countenance" (p. 169). In a similar vein, we hear of the Eastern nations where a woman follows her spouse to death with "a gay countenance, as if going . . . to sleep with her husband" (p. 535) (*d'une countenance gaye*, p. 685); with "a cheerfull countenance" (Florio, p. 635). For these heroic figures, cheer is the manifestation of their independence from their tormentors and from conventional attitudes toward death. It is that thing that defines their difference.

These two examples are particularly complex, since they both fulfill and transcend the indifference to death often associated with the great Stoic exemplars whom Montaigne mentions elsewhere in the *Essays*. On the verge of being executed and eaten, the Brazilian torments his captors by pointing out that he has been nourished by their own ancestors, captured in earlier wars. Thus, when they eat him, they are in fact eating their own flesh. In this context, the gaiety of the cannibal is intended to signify at once his indifference to death and his delight in standing up to his tormentors. His death is both the consequence of his gaiety and its realization. He is stoical to the extent that he faces death unafraid, but more than stoical to the extent that his expression represents a particular ethics of hostility toward his enemies.

Gaiety might thus be seen as the result of stoicism placed in a scenario of cultural or political difference. The classical Stoic, a figure such as, say, Seneca, goes to his death unmoved and unafraid, bolstered by his constancy. In a situation of rivalry, the cannibal exhibits not merely constancy, but energetic gaiety in the face of death. His gaiety is a kind of supplement to classical Stoicism. It communicates tranquility of the soul, but also goes beyond it. For him, gaiety is a kind of excess that both suggests individual transendence of suffering and the triumph of one cannibal clan over another. Similarly, the Indian woman who gaily follows her husband's body onto the funeral pyre does so to represent an extreme version of love and duty. She is not resigned; she is more than resigned—beyond resigned. For these martyrs, gaiety becomes an extra thing, the element in an action that makes it the testimony of an ethical self.

No less important are those whose gaiety is not merely the product of a moment of extremity, but seems linked to their very makeup. These are the classical heroes whom Montaigne singles out for their self-possession, several of whom Florio makes "cheerful," despite their lack of gaiety in the French: Alexander the Great, who is noted in Montaigne for "la debonnaireté de sa complexion" (p. 733) is seen, in Florio's version, to draw praise for "the integritie and cheerfulness of his complexion" (p. 677). And Caesar, who has a "visage plein" (p. 707) in Montaigne, gets a "cheerful and seemely countenance" (p. 653) in English. This cheerful overkill is developed in the essay on the education of children cited earlier, where Montaigne goes on at some length about the importance of philosophy as a form of healthfulness. Here is Florio's rendering: "It ought to sharpen and modell all outward demeanor to the modell of it; and by consequence arm him that doth possess it, with a gracious stoutness and livelie audacitie, with an active and pleasing gesture and with a settled and cheerful countenance" (p. 123). Montaigne simply wants a "contenance" that is "contente et débonnaire" (p. 160), happy and debonaire.

The Gay Countenance

It is important that Montaigne should choose the French word *contenance* (which passes easily into the English "countenance"), rather than the more conventional French term for face, *visage*, as the term to be modified by *gaye*. The terms *visage* and *contenance* are often used interchangeably in critical accounts of Montaigne's somatics, yet the phrase "un visage gay" appears only once in the *Essays*.[5] The two words imply the face differently. *Visage*, with its derivation from the Latin *videre*, "to see" (whence our word *video*) is what is seen, the passive object of observation. *Contenance*, derives from the Latin *continere*, "to hold together." It implies an active self-presentation, a composition of the face as it is presented to others, such as when the cannibals defy their captors "both in speech and countenance" (p. 169) (*de parole et de contenance*, p. 211a). Montaigne seems to understand the terms differently, since in "Of Giving the Lie," he speaks of his pleasure of learning about "the habits, the face, the expression ... of my ancestors" (p. 503) (*les meurs, le visage, la contenance ... de mes ancestres*, p. 647a, my emphasis).[6]

Thus, the "gaiety" that Montaigne evokes and that Florio renders as "cheerfulness" or "blitheness" implies a freedom from obligation, an ability to move without being forced to. "Cheerfulness," which for the English versions of Erasmus and Calvin implies the proper relationship *to* obligation, is recast in Montaigne as freedom *from* obligation. Montaigne's gaiety frees the subject without disrupting social structures. It is consistently linked to a form of disposition of the body, most often the countenance. It implies a moral subject who can "hold together" (*con-tenere*), unconstrained by duty or obligation, but limited by "civility."

Here, in this blending of a private disposition and a publicly composed body, we might locate the "free" Montaignian subject and the "gay wisdom" he seeks in the last sentence of his book. It breaks with earlier forms that we have seen. In the bargain, it reverses a particular grammatical construction that we saw earlier in medieval accounts of cheer. Whereas for Chaucer, "cheer" is the essence of the face, the surface of self-presentation that must be modified by an adjective ("drooping," "pitious," and so on); now it is "countenance" that takes the role of the noun, to be modified by "cheerful." Cheerfulness has become a modality of being as the grammatical function of the term has shifted. It is now rooted in the self, but available to all.[7]

Montaigne sets the self free into a gaiety of movement and a movement of gaiety. He explores what happens when the individual takes gaiety upon himself or herself, seizing it as a quality of self-presentation. For him, gaiety is a way of acting, a power that enables the rejection of convention and the assertion of the individual. As we have seen, it is worked out through the improvisational form of the essay itself, in which the author reserves the right to change his mind, reverse course, put down a book if he so chooses. Neither a tool of political manipulation (Richard III) nor a hermeneutic technique for healing community (Prospero, Rabelais), gaiety becomes a characteristic of the self, a way of approaching the everyday activities of reading, conversation, exercise. In some instances — the "gay" Brazilian cannibal, the Indian woman who cheerfully follows her husband onto the funeral pyre — it signifies an absolute courage. Yet because it implies the willful exercise of the self, it brings with it a modicum of self-governance. By acting gaily, the self learns, as Montaigne puts it, to carry its own bridle.

Gay Conversation

Montaigne's account of gaiety locates it in individual action, but stresses that it must be "social" and even "civil." This points us toward the forms of association that will come to dominate French culture in the century following Montaigne — the world of courtliness and salon culture characterized by conversation and wit. Indeed, as the poet Jean de La Fontaine would write some eighty years after Montaigne, modern fashion requires new things, "novelty and gaiety." "I do not call gaiety what makes us laugh," he says, "but a certain charm, an agreeable air which one can give to all kinds of subjects, even the most serious ones."[8] He is channeling Montaigne: "I do nothing without gaiety."

Montaigne's vision of a willful, self-regulating, gay self is deeply aristocratic. It has its roots in a culture of classical heroism, even as it clears the space for new types of self-definition and social interaction. And as European high culture begins to move out of the age of religious conflict and into a period characterized by salon culture, learned academies, and an increasingly cultured bourgeoisie, the "social" and "civil" images of human interaction evoked by Montaigne are revisited repeatedly by writers and artists. We can see one direction in which Montaigne's version of an individually powered, yet socially framed cheerfulness might take us by leaping ahead a bit in time.

In 1761, the Italian journalist Giuseppe Cerutti, who lived and worked in France during the years before the Revolution, published a text in answer to a question posed by one of the French academies. The question was whether intellectual enlightenment or royal decree had been more effective in mitigating the "fury" that led to dueling.[9] It was a question about whether culture or law is more important in shaping behavior. Cerutti's text takes the form of a letter to an unidentified friend. In it he focuses on the importance of gaiety, which he calls "the distinctive characteristic of your nation" (*le caractère marqué de votre nation*).[10] Other nations are weighed down by melancholy, he says, but the French lighten everything up.

Cerutti locates French gaiety in three different factors. First is the climate of France, which he contrasts with Spain (too hot) and Germany (too cold). The second factor is government. You can have gaiety only in a monarchy, says Cerutti. In a tyranny, everyone is oppressed, and in a democracy, such as England, the average man spends his time worrying about the common good. The Spaniard sees no one as equal to him. The Englishman sees all men as equal. Neither can be gay. By contrast, the Frenchman compares himself with everyone else all the time — and believes himself superior. "He takes ceaseless pleasure in believing himself the vanquisher of all of his equals" (*Il a sans cesse le plaisir de se croire le vainqueur de ses égaux*). French gaiety is thus based on a form of self-delusion, but it is also based on social interaction, which is Cerutti's third reason for French gaiety: "To please someone else," he says, "you must humanize yourself and soften your dealings with him" (*pour plaire à quelqu'un, il faut s'humaniser, s'adoucir avec lui*).

Thus we return to the idea of community, but now as a *national* community. Cheerfulness defines not the Christian, but the French subject. As we noted in our Introduction, Cerutti's near-contemporary Madame de Staël presented a similar formulation in her book on Germany written twenty years after his pamphlet. We can quote her again here, since the implications of her formulation should be much clearer now, coming on the heels of our other discussions: "The desire to appear amiable leads one to take on an expression of gaiety, no matter what the interior disposition of the soul might be. The facial expression influences, bit by bit, what one experiences. And what one does to please others ends up shaping what one feels oneself."[11]

De Staël offers the secular analogue of Saint Paul's "cheerful giver." She suggests that gaiety is generated not out of charity, but out of sociability. She provides a doctrine that Montaigne's disruptive vision of gaiety seemed to gesture toward. This secular economy of gaiety removes it from the Christian social world of obligation and community depicted by Rabelais, but reasserts it as a technique of self-transformation — through conversation, rather than faith.

However, the question remains of how this new conversational gaiety — which is deeply aristocratic in Montaigne — can regulate itself and avoid degenerating into the kind of tool of power and dissimulation that we saw in Shakespeare's tragedies. Montaigne's individualistic model of cheerfulness will be taken up and reimagined, through the concept of "social virtue" advanced by the thinkers of the so-called Scottish Enlightenment. They will clarify for us the relationship between cheerfulness and bourgeois modernity.

PART TWO

Cheerful Economies

and Bourgeois Culture

CHAPTER SIX

Social Virtue,

Enlightenment Emotion:

Hume and Smith

Radiating Hilarity

For some people — enlightened aristocrats, wealthy burghers, curious philosophers — the middle years of the eighteenth century in Europe seem to have brought a good deal of pleasure. Interesting scientific experiments were in the news. Serious political change was an exciting, if still distant idea. Hygiene had improved. Conversation was cultivated. There was great music in the capitals. What new modes of comportment and feeling characterize this pleasing cultural moment? Can we find cheerfulness here, as we move past the great religious struggles of early modernity? In this chapter I will look at how cheerfulness moves and where it comes to reside when it is no longer understood primarily to unite Christian believers or heal the melancholy body. Enlightenment cheer is conversational cheer; it provides both the vehicle and the emotional energy for an emerging secular modernity.

Teresa Brennan has noted that eighteenth-century accounts of the passions often dwell on the importance of sight, which would seem to make us "discrete," distinct from each other, whereas the transmission of affect "breaches individual boundaries." The eighteenth century would seem to be caught between these competing models of emotional energetics. Brennan argues that the "energetic dimension" of the transmission of affect (what connects us) hovers like a kind of ghost around modern discussions of affective life. Yet as I will show, Enlightenment cheerfulness remains deeply invested in the idea of a social world. Sight may make us "discrete," as Brennan argues, but communities involve more than visual experience.[1] In this chapter, I will study how a new bourgeois culture of conversation and sociability reconfigures cheerfulness. Montaigne's idea that cheerfulness could serve as the attribute of an individual subject, presenting an energetic "gay countenance" and flouting convention, resonates across the salons and academies that emerge in the seventeenth and eighteenth centuries. It is retheorized in Enlightenment ideals of conversation.

The physiological connotations of cheerfulness as a kind of tool to counterbalance melancholy (encouraged, as we saw earlier, by one glass of wine and good lighting) were already beginning to shift. In his posthumously published *Ethics* (1677), Baruch Spinoza argued that like all things, human beings are shaped by striving, or what he calls in Latin *conatus*: "Each thing, as far as it can by its power, strives to persevere in its being," and "any thing whatever, whether it is more perfect or less, will always be able to persevere in existing by the same force by which it begins to exist; so they are all equal in this regard."[2] Human life is divided between actions that increase our perfection and those that diminish it, and each action is shaped by what Spinoza calls an "affect" (in Latin, *affectus*). The affects structure, as it were, our movement toward or away from perfection.

The key here is the idea of passage. Spinoza conceives of human life as a process, as a set of movements. Thus, he says, "Joy is a man's passage from a lesser to a greater perfection. . . . I say a passage. For joy is not perfection itself. If a man were born with the perfection to which he passes, he would possess it without an affect of joy" (p. 104). Affects are thus powerings, motivations that push us back and forth between extremes.

For Spinoza, cheerfulness is a subset of joy. Whereas joy involves a movement *between* body and mind ("that passion by which the mind passes to a greater perfection"), cheerfulness (or, in his Latin, *hilaritas*) resides in both. This lends it a crucial role, for one of the challenges to the philosophical self for Spinoza involves the excessive power of certain affects on the body. The self constantly needs to manage the affects, since some can unbalance mind or body. Thus, pleasure, which *seems* to be good, can sometimes be evil, since it overwhelms part of the body. It becomes "stubbornly fixed in the body, and so prevents the body from being capable of being affected in a great many other ways. Hence, it can be evil" (p. 139). By contrast, cheerfulness, residing in both, helps to *temper* the relationship of mind and body. The antidote to excessive pleasure is cheerfulness. "Cheerfulness is a joy which, insofar as it is related to the body, consists in this, that all parts of the body are equally affected" (p. 139). In this way "the body's power of acting is increased or aided, so that all of its parts maintain the same proportion of motion" (p. 138). In this regard, concludes Spinoza (in a phrase we quoted in our Introduction), "cheerfulness is always good, and cannot be excessive" (p. 138). In Latin he says, "Hilaritas semper est bona, nec excessum habere potest" (p. 406).

In the economy of self-management, cheerfulness thus seems to be primarily a tempering force. It both participates in the interplay of inclinations that threaten to overwhelm the self and plays a crucial role in physical well-being.[3] This means that even though it lies within the ambit of joy, as a kind of subset, it is also beginning to be understood outside of the heroic self-control of the sage philosopher or brave general. No longer tied to specific actions such as, say, acts of charity or reading, cheerfulness now seems to roam about. It's a bit like a fog bank, enveloping the individual. For the emerging bourgeois culture of the Enlightenment, suspicious of excessive passion, cheerfulness plays into a strategy of self-control.

This radiating aspect of cheerfulness, located in the body, is especially of interest to thinkers who explore it outside of the metaphysical underpinnings essential to Spinoza's thought. For the philosophers David Hume and Adam Smith, to whom I now want to turn, the decentered character of cheerfulness gives it the contours of a social virtue. It contributes to what cultural historian Michael

McKeon has called the "social psychology" of the Enlightenment.[4] It is generated or produced in relationships. Both Hume and his contemporary Smith use cheerfulness to help develop their ideas of virtue. They remove the practice of virtue from its traditional locations in the soul and in the actions of a heroic (or ignoble) individual and consider it in terms of its effect on groups, on what we might call civil society. They reinvent cheerfulness for the era of bourgeois capitalism.

Civility and Cheerfulness

Hume's project, in both his early *Treatise of Human Nature* (1739) and the later reworking of the *Treatise*, titled *Enquiries Concerning Human Understanding and Concerning the Principles of Morals* (1748), is to lay out a model of virtue that would be both good and pleasurable. Whereas Spinoza is concerned with the ways in which the self can manage desire, Hume's focus is on linking virtuous behavior to pleasant sensations so that virtue will be reconceived as no longer the enemy of pleasure. Cheerfulness can help in this reconceptualization.

While useful and agreeable things are generally useful either for the person possessing them or for others, true virtue must do good in society and also please the individual. In the conclusion to the *Enquiries*, Hume claims that "Personal Merit consists in the possession of mental qualities, *useful* or *agreeable* to the *person himself* or to others."[5] Moral action must imply "some sentiment common to all mankind," and it must "extend to all of mankind" (p. 272). Other passions may move the self ("many strong sentiments of desire and aversion, affection and hatred," p. 272), yet unless they satisfy these conditions, they cannot be understood as truly moral.

Hume's work ranges across the passions in an attempt to isolate movements of the self that would help to ground a moral philosophy at once agreeable and social. To do this, he must separate out the self-pleasing or the merely useful from socially oriented goodness. Thus, the early *Treatise of Human Nature* paints a picture of the "qualities of the mind" that help in the conduct of life, but that are not necessarily good for others. These include temperance, frugality, economy, and resolution. Wisdom and good sense are also useful. On the other hand, wit and eloquence are *agreeable* to others, but don't necessarily please the self. By contrast to both of these, "*good humor*" is loved because it is *both* good for others and "*immediately agreeable* to the person himself" (p. 661, his italics).

Hume's example of this is a company in conversation, which is where cheerfulness comes in. He notes that "a chearful good-humour'd companion diffuses a joy over the whole company, from a sympathy about his gaiety. These qualities, therefore, being agreeable, they naturally beget love and esteem, and answer to all the characters of virtue."[6] Cheerfulness takes on its full power and significance *between* people, as it *moves* from one to another. It is linked to the concept of "sympathy," a kind of magnetic power that draws humans together in community and fellow feeling.

Sympathy is crucial for Hume, as it is for many of his contemporaries. In his description of cheer as a virtue, he uses the notion of sympathy to move past a tradition that locates virtue in individual cultivation and self-presentation — say, Montaigne's gay cannibal or Shakespeare's brave Earl of Richmond. In lieu of the themes of charity and alacrity that linked Christians for Erasmus or Calvin, here it is sympathy that mediates between community and individual action, making it possible for certain qualities of the self to be at once social and virtuous.[7]

This aspect of Hume's thinking is developed in the last section of the *Treatise*, the section on morals. There he takes issue with those innate characteristics of certain human beings that would set some of them apart, in splendid isolation. These are what he calls the features of "natural excellence"; that is, those qualities ingrained in the self from birth. "No distinction is more usual in all systems of ethics," says Hume, "than that betwixt *natural abilities* and *moral virtues*; where the former are plac'd on the same footing with bodily endowments, and are suppos'd to have no merit or moral worth annex'd to them" (p. 656, his italics). Hume takes issue with those who would suggest that certain natural endowments, such as a gift for empathy, seem to have no more moral value than does the ability to run fast, since they come to us from beyond our striving. For, he goes on, this distinction between natural endowments and moral virtues is false in practical life. Both of these categories are "mental qualities," and "both of them equally produce pleasure; and have of course an equal tendency to procure the love and esteem of mankind" (p. 656). In other words, because actions should be understood in terms of their *social* implications — rather than some adherence to an abstract ideal of good or evil — what is natural to us may well be the same as what is learned or adapted. Natural abilities and moral virtues are "on the same footing, both as to their causes and effects" (p. 657).

In this way, Hume codifies what we have noticed in earlier thinkers, that cheer and gaiety are social qualities that have an effect that *looks* very much virtue, without actually fitting into any scheme of virtues and vices. For him, this virtuous effect stems from the fact that cheerfulness can please both the possessor and those around her. Cheerfulness is not a virtue, but it acts like one in the way it affects people.[8]

Hume's account of the power of cheerfulness to shape social situations is expanded in the reworked version of his text, the *Enquiries*. His focus continues to be on a model of virtue that would be social, yet pleasing to the individual. Again, his example is the scene of conversation, though his figural language intensifies his appreciation for cheer over his earlier formulation. Anyone who has ever passed an evening with "serious melancholy people," he points out, can surely acknowledge that when a good-humored or gay person enters the room "cheerfulness carries great merit with it, and naturally conciliates the good will of mankind" (p. 250).

> Others enter into the same humour, and catch the sentiment, by a contagion or natural sympathy; and as we cannot forbear loving whatever pleases, a kindly emotion arises towards the person who communicates so much satisfaction. He is a more animating spectacle; his presence diffuses over us more serene complacency and enjoyment; our imagination, entering into his

feelings and disposition, is affected in a more agreeable manner than if a melancholy, dejected, sullen, anxious temper were presented to us. (p. 251)

Indeed, "the flame spreads through the whole circle and the most sullen and morose are often caught by it." The role of cheerfulness is the sign, in fact, that there is "another set of mental qualities" beyond those usually noticed. These are the qualities that do not project beyond themselves some kind of advancement (as, say, frugality might make one richer). Rather, they require no "utility or tendency to farther good." They are simply qualities that "diffuse a satisfaction on the beholders, and procure friendship and regard" (p. 250). They are agreeable to the individual, yet they spread to others. Hume's language is extreme here to suggest how everything has changed: "a *more* animating spectacle . . . *more* serene complacency . . . a *more* agreeable manner."

Here we can see the mediating function of cheerfulness, the way it moves between individuals to shape them. For Spinoza, *hilaritas* tempered the body simply by its diffusion throughout the self. It stood in contrast to those affects that seize one part of the body and lead us, through excess, into morally questionable behavior. For Hume, cheerfulness tempers the social body. It links self and group through sensation. This is not the Christian community of Calvin, with its "cheerful giver," but now cheer moves beyond the individual, binding the group through a general sense of well-being, generating, to recall Hume's terms, "friendship and regard." Hume's choice of words in this last phrase is particularly telling, since "regard" involves a respectful appreciation for the other, even as it suggests some type of gaze—the "seeing" that frames the "animating spectacle" of the cheerful person. Cheer does its work through a kind of theater of conversation and sympathy. It involves a form of "spectacle," yet is also encompassing; it infects the company. It's a "flame."[9]

The larger implications of this model for the relationship between selves and communities are hinted at in Hume's 1741 essay "The Epicurean." There, like Montaigne or Erasmus, he stresses the tension between the surface of the body and the heart. Offering a good face to the world, he says, "can do more than regulate the outside, and, with infinite pains and attention, compose the language and countenance to a philosophical dignity, in order to deceive the ignorant vulgar."[10] It changes the self, but through an economy of emotion. "Confine me not within myself," he goes on, before urging that pleasure can be linked to virtue only in social relations. When virtue is social, it becomes "the gay, the frolic Virtue" (p. 80). Cheer, which follows, is mutually reinforcing: "You partake of my delights, and discover [that is, reveal] in your cheerful looks the pleasure which you receive from my happiness and satisfaction. The like do I receive from yours. . . . In our cheerful discourses, better than in the formal reasoning of the schools, is true wisdom to be found" (p. 80). Cheerfulness is a kind of contagion that is also an economy. It involves exchange, "better than in the formal reasoning of the schools." Traditional philosophy is cast aside. This is the onset of modernity, the triumph of bourgeois sociability over aristocratic self-cultivation. We can make our own philosophy, our own virtue, our own cheer!

The sense of cheer as a kind of contagion or flame is central to Hume's conception of virtue as both pleasant and useful. It might be seen as the lubricant of relations in an ideal community. And in the conclusion to the *Enquiries*, he returns to the topic of social virtue. Whereas self-love is "peculiar" (p. 274), that is, limited, virtue must be universal. Moreover, the moral sentiments, because of their social nature, are able to temper those passions that would destroy society. "These principles . . . are social and universal; they form, in a manner, the *party* of humankind against vice or disorder, its common enemy" (p. 275). Social virtue is at the center of civilization itself.

Because his goal is to make universal arguments about human behavior, Hume's writing tends to be abstract. It deploys categories and terms that seem to float in space, without the historical examples or anecdotes used by earlier writers, such as Montaigne. And yet in the closing section of the *Enquiries*, Hume feels the compulsion to move from theoretical exposition to character. He turns suddenly to

everyday, practical life. He claims that the kind of virtue he is trying to describe may be seen right before us in the everyday world.
He gives an example. He mentions a man who has given his daughter's hand to another man, a certain Cleanthes. And not surprisingly,
given his interest in the social sphere, he describes Cleanthes not
as he knows him, but as he is *seen* by a group of friends. Each man
describes him in turn. We get a word picture, a composite portrait.
That is, Hume shifts gears in his own writing to show in language the
kind of friendly community he repeatedly praises. The first friend
tells us that Cleanthes is known to be fair and kind — that is, ethical.
The second notes that he is successful and honorable in business. The
third says he possesses the social qualities that Hume favors, having
been seen in "the gayest company," where he was "the very life and
soul of conversation" (p. 269). Yet all of these qualities are trumped
by the fourth feature of his personality, mentioned by someone who
knows him more "familiarly" than the others. This is his cheer: "That
cheerfulness, which you might remark in him, is not a sudden flash
struck out by company: it runs through the whole tenor of his life,
and preserves a perpetual serenity on his countenance, and tranquility in his soul." Yet he is not without depth of courage: "He has met
with severe trials, misfortunes as well as dangers; and by his great-
ness of mind, was still superior to all of them" (pp. 269–70).

The sign of this superiority is his cheerfulness, which blends the
traditional Stoic idea of the tranquility of the soul with a modern
social presence. This is the Stoic philosopher as businessman and
witty conversationalist. Hume concludes that here we have the image
of "accomplished merit." This is the figure of a man, says Hume, who
exceeds all of the ideals described by the famous moral philosophers
Gracián or Castiglione. "A philosopher might select this character
as a model of perfect virtue" (p. 270).[11] A philosopher — in this case,
Hume — already has.

A number of aspects of this remarkable conclusion are worth
commentary. The first is that with Hume, we see the bourgeois sensibility take form from inside the traditionally aristocratic language

of moral philosophy. We see an attempt to blend the rhetoric of traditional moral philosophy, which emphasized the "great soul" (Socrates, Cato), with a bourgeois world of social conversation. In place of heroic virtues — fortitude, constancy — we get cheerfulness. Hume's cheerfulness is social, but not mere wit, "a sudden flash struck out by company." It is both the bodily manifestation of virtue (it can be "remarked") and the deepest indicator of its presence in the human being: it cuts through the "whole tenor" of the virtuous life. It is general, infusing the entire self. It is a psychological characteristic that is rooted in social relations and visible on the body, yet still a deep moral force.

It is also worth noting the approach Hume has used to persuade us of the practical viability of his version of virtue. His generally abstract writing style suddenly gives way to what is in effect a shift to a different literary genre. This genre is the "portrait," an idealized description of a particular personality. Portrait writing was popular in the seventeenth and eighteenth centuries. Hume presents Cleanthes through a series of "views." The social dimension of virtue is acted out, quite literally, as each of Cleanthes's friends describes him. The culmination of the process is the acknowledgment of his cheerfulness, which comes from the figure who knows him best. Thus, the presentation of philosophical goodness comes through a rhetoric of perspective — we see Cleanthes from a variety of angles — that is also a narrative of unveiling. We wind up at his deepest self, which, it turns out, is also shaped by the force that marks his most superficial relations.

The final passage suggests the extent to which any philosophical account of cheerfulness in language is inevitably a literary exercise. Cheer structures character as much as character embodies cheer. This is made clear by Hume's insertion of his own authorial persona into the end of the scene. Having described the revelation of Cleanthes's cheerfulness, he addresses the imaginary community he has just called into being: "The image, gentlemen, which you have here delineated of Cleanthes, cried I, is that of accomplished merit. Each of you has given a stroke of the pencil to his figure" (p. 270). Here is community—a community of philosophers constituted by the text itself, by the collective project of depicting cheerfulness in a kind of drawing. And we end with evocations of two modern moral philosophers, the Italian humanist Castiglione and the Spanish moralist Gracián, both of whom Hume now replaces as the literary authority on virtue. Yet at the same time, his turn to the community of "gentlemen" who have both witnessed and painted Cleanthes's virtue underscores that those infected with the "contagion" of cheerfulness are also literary constructs. Hume invents a community that can bear witness to the contagious effects of cheer while authorizing it as a mark of moral virtue. He then tips his hand by pointing to the literary artifice that makes the entire system run. In this way, he reinvents cheerfulness, locating it in the world of conversation. It is a virtuoso rhetorical performance, as powerful, in its way, as Richard III's self-consideration on the eve of the Battle of Bosworth Field or Rabelais's account of gay reading.

The Working Cheerful

Once cheerfulness becomes a concept and a practice of selfhood freed from the dramas of Christian community and self-display seen in Renaissance and Reformation writers, it begins to take on an economic cast. Cheer produces cheer. It spins around the room, making merry those who are gloomy. In face-to-face situations, it also circulates and is exchanged for other emotions and affects.

If cheerfulness is economic, we might also wonder if economics might be cheerful. And, indeed, it falls to the first great theorist of capital, Adam Smith, to link the two. In *Wealth of Nations* (1776) Smith sets up a contrast between economies that are "progressive" and those that are static or even in decline. Progressive economies tend to be those that employ freemen, not slaves, and that generate wealth through increased acquisition and freely circulating labor, without having yet reached an apogee of productivity or wealth. In these "progressive" (that is, progressing) societies, says Smith, "the great body of the people seem to be the happiest and the most comfortable." Smith goes on to contrast these systems in terms of the quality of life within them: life in the "stationary" economy is "hard"; in the "declining" economy, it is "miserable." By contrast, he concludes, "the progressive state is in reality the cheerful and the hearty state to all the different orders of the society. The stationary is dull; the declining, melancholy."[12]

Here we get the traditional opposition of the cheerful and the melancholic. Yet Smith applies these terms to societies and economic systems. And it is interesting that he describes unproductive economies, first as "hard" and "miserable," then as "dull" and "melancholy." The first term in each of these pairs of words describes the *material* conditions of life in different economies. The second provides an *emotional* explanation. Between these two accounts, he evokes the "cheerful and hearty" progressive economy. "Cheer" would seem to participate in both realms of experience; it is both material and emotional. He then goes on to suggest the advantages for the worker — both materially and emotionally — of the rising wages that a progressive economy generates: "A plentiful subsistence increases the bodily strength of the labourer, and the comfortable hope of bettering his condition, and of ending his days perhaps in ease and plenty, animates him to exert that strength to the utmost. Where wages are high, accordingly, we shall always find the workmen more active, diligent, and expeditious, than where they are low" (p. 69). A "cheerful" economy thus disperses its cheer to the individual, and everybody wins.

Yet a moment later, Smith cautions against the excesses of this same cheerful state. One of the problems with increasing wages and providing the worker with hope of improvement, he notes, is that workers will become focused only on betterment and overwork themselves through "mutual emulation and the desire of greater gain" (p. 70). "Ramuzzini, an eminent Italian physician," he adds helpfully, "has written a particular book concerning such disease."[13] Indeed, he observes, we don't normally consider soldiers to be particularly good workers, yet when they have been given work that is "liberally paid by the piece," their officers have been forced to limit what they can earn, lest they harm their health through overwork and thereby, it is implied, place at risk the security of the state. And he concludes by noting that those who work less intensively preserve their health and, as such, ultimately work longer and are more productive.

Smith's curious aside on the risks of overwork and excessive "desire of greater gain" among the laboring classes brings forth two features of his reflections on cheerfulness that distinguish them from what we have seen in earlier writers. They establish his modernity, with regard even to Hume. The first is that cheer is seen to reside in the system of production itself. It no longer inheres in the individual soul, as it did in Montaigne, and scarcely even in friendly conversation, as it did in Hume. In fact, with Smith, cheerfulness seems to have become unmoored from the earlier tradition of moral philosophy and religious thought. It is now seen as something that is dynamically generated, as ever, "between" human beings, but now in their interactions with labor and money. The "betweenness" of cheer now becomes a characteristic that can link psychology to economic exchange. The cheerful economy makes people cheerful, giving them hope and leading to ever more productivity and consumption — which are the marks of the cheerful economy.

Yet at the same time — and this is the second point — because cheer is generated through economic interactions and labor (rather than, say, through the stimulus of wine or the practice of charity), it threatens to take on a life of its own. No longer a virtue, it is now something bigger than the individual, something that takes her over and shapes her. Too much cheer leads to excessive desire for betterment, which leads to exhaustion and, potentially, to an economy that is powered by burned-out workers. Cheer, then, must be moderated and contained, lest it overheat itself and convert a "progressive" economy into a "miserable" one.

The Wealth of Nations is not Smith's only major publication. His first book, *The Theory of Moral Sentiments*, had appeared almost two decades earlier, in 1759. We can set the account of cheerful economics just studied next to his moral writings. In *The Theory of Moral Senti-ments*, Smith builds on aspects of Hume's writing discussed a moment ago. However, Smith differs dramatically from Hume in that the powering force of sympathy in Hume is involuntary. For Smith, it involves choice on the part of the observer. In the conclusion of the *Enquiries*, Hume notes that one thing that keeps the individual on a moral path is the sense that he is being watched by the entire world. The "love of fame," which is also the desire for a good name, is what instills in us "the constant habit of surveying ourselves" (p. 276), a habit that in turn leads us to ask how we may appear to others. This figure of the self as a kind of spectacle for itself becomes generalized in Smith's *Theory of Moral Sentiments*, where he introduces the notion of the "objective observer," or the "Spectator" (a figure widely pres-ent in eighteenth-century English culture) who can judge our actions and see them as either moral or immoral.

Smith always locates his accounts of moral action in a particu-lar "theater" that determines propriety. When the context and the action are seen together, the moral implications of particular actions become clear. So, he notes early on, we feel sympathy with our fel-lows to the extent that we are able to observe their responses to dif-ferent situations. At minimum, we judge that "his behavior is genteel and agreeable who can maintain his cheerfulness amidst a number of frivolous disasters."[14] However, the "most lively sympathy" is gener-ated when we see someone who has suffered unjustly — often physi-cally — but who has borne this misfortune with "the firmest counte-nance" and who seems to feel no humiliation (p. 166).

Here, as in Hume, cheerfulness is the marker of true virtue. In a bourgeois culture where virtue is no longer demonstrated through heroic actions, cheerfulness becomes the external marker of inner strength. Moreover, it is the feature of particular actions that gives them some general meaning, raising them to the level of the uni-versal, for as the cheerful sufferer bears her suffering gladly, we, as "spectators," acknowledge the appropriateness of her response to a terrible situation. These two reactions — sympathy for our fellow human and surprise at her cheer — together constitute "what is properly called admiration" (p. 60). Thus, Smith's introduction of the spectator or observer into the dynamics of moral action solves the rhetorical problem posed by Hume's more abstract musings. Here we can see philosophy in action.

Smith's emphasis on personal merit in diverse situations takes on its most interesting coloration when he turns to discuss how virtue can be "universal." If we are admiring of instances of specific virtue, what would a universal virtue look like? This comes in chapter 3 of the sixth section of *The Theory of Moral Sentiments*, "Of the Character of Virtue." Here, Smith notes that "the wise and virtuous man is at all times willing that his own private interest should be sacrificed to the public interest of his own particular order or society" (p. 277). And in turn, those orders should be sacrificed to the interest of the entire universe, "of that great society of all sensible and intelligent beings, of which God himself is the immediate administrator and director" (p. 277). So private interest gives way to public interest, which gives way to God's will.

Smith expands Hume's sense that virtue should be primarily social and radiating beyond the scope of the individual actor to embrace the diverse situations in which it can be understood. Yet the sheer multiplicity of such situations requires that the image of the spectator become generalized in the gaze of God. In this formulation, actions become social when they are submitted to the authority and approval of a higher power who can see them. What, then, accounts for the generation of socially based virtue? Smith offers an example. When soldiers trust their generals, he says, they are willing to sacrifice themselves to the greater good, for then they march into battle, "to the forlorn station, from which they never expect to return," with "more gaiety and alacrity" than they would display going into a less terrifying situation. "They cheerfully sacrifice their own little systems to the prosperity of a greater system." Indeed, it is the hierarchy itself that leads them to this cheer. They submit not only "with humble resignation" to duty, but "with alacrity and joy" (p. 278).[15]

We are all spectators of each other, but God is the master spectator, and our interest is to be submitted to God's will, cheerfully: "Every other thought necessarily appears mean in the comparison" (p. 279). In this way, Smith is able to suggest how and why virtue expands beyond the limited ambit of the individual actor. When we act, we are to act with an awareness of the presence of God ("certainly of all the objects of human contemplation by far the most sublime," p. 279) and with the sense that God controls "the immense machine of the universe." Taking our place within that machine, we pursue our duty cheerfully. And conversely, our cheerfulness is the mark of our pursuit.

It is striking that Smith turns to the figure of the soldier at two key moments in his discussion of cheerfulness: when he analyses the disruptive power of cheerfulness in *The Wealth of Nations* and when he talks of community and duty in *The Theory of Moral Sentiments*. The small community of the military provides an example through which the group dynamics of cheerfulness can be studied. Hume gives us philosophers in conversation. Smith gives us soldiers. And, whereas the civil society of Hume necessarily includes the philosopher — as we saw in the final sketch of Cleanthes — by focusing on military organization, Smith can play the objective observer, standing, God-like, outside of networks of cheer.

Hume and Smith help articulate the ways in which cheerfulness functions in emerging bourgeois, postheroic cultural contexts. Both writers want to think generally about virtue and pleasure. To give their arguments cogency, they root their discussion of the social dimension of virtue in accounts of imagined small communities. For both of them, cheerfulness transcends the individual — even as, in some cases, it is essential to moral identity. Yet as we move from Hume to Smith, the paradoxes of cheerfulness in the new social and economic order become clear. Within bourgeois society, cheerfulness is a potentially disruptive force. It is the sign of dynamic economies, yet in practice can exhaust and overrun the best-intentioned workforce. It must be controlled or managed. The metaphor of the military community, in which soldiers take their cheer *both* from their communal experience and from their submission to authority, offers the solution to the conceptual paradox of imagining a cheer that is at once dynamic and controlled.

Figures such as Spinoza, Hume, and Smith contribute to the intellectual currents of skepticism and rational critique that sweep away the religious groundings for cheerfulness we saw in the world of both Shakespeare and Rabelais. As we move into the eighteenth century, an emerging bourgeois social sphere relocates intellectual activity beyond the confines of courtliness, placing it in cafés and learned academies. As part of this process, cheerfulness migrates from the metaphysical center of Christian collective to civil society. For Spinoza, cheerfulness emerges as a mediating term that can balance the relationship of body and soul, a kind of utopian affect. For Hume, cheer is linked to small-group sociability, and the conclusion to the *Enquiries Concerning Human Understanding* gives us the portrait of a fictional "cheerful" man, seen from the multiple viewpoints of those whom he draws around him in community. It is Smith, however, who seems to grasp the larger stakes of the newly civil cheerfulness. Smith understands that cheerfulness involves power. That power may be disruptive to the social order, as in the case of the workers evoked in *The Wealth of Nations*. Consequently, images of control and monitoring are brought forth, such as the depiction of the soldiers marching cheerfully to war under the eye of both Adam Smith and God.

Smith and Hume thus both expand and circumscribe the regime of cheerfulness. Their Enlightenment universalism seeks to imagine concepts of social virtue that would apply to all people. Yet the emotional vocabulary of their writing is restrictive. They reimagine the causal relationship between affect and community. No longer the "cheerful giver" of the New Testament, whose cheer was the expression of a relationship to a community grounded in the word of God, it is now *emotion itself*—the "flame" of cheerfulness—that makes the community. And if communities are bounded by affective pleasure, those excluded from that pleasure remain outside of community. For the philosophical world of Smith and Hume, the excluded are people of color, the poor (however much one may "admire" their good spirits in adversity), the disabled, and women. In other words, cheerfulness binds groups together, but they are groups of similar types — soldiers, philosophers, men of "good standing." The cheerful communities theorized here point us ahead to the "gaiety" that will come, over the ensuing century and a half, to characterize any number of small modern collectivities — college fraternities, private men's clubs, elite universities. For these communities, to be cheerful or gay is also to perform group identity. Cheer becomes the marker of those who are clearly and firmly in their own element, among their peers. However much these communities may offer abstract, Enlightenment-based, ideals that promote inclusion, their emotional vocabulary remains exclusive. Smith's account of the worker whose cheerful energy leads to exhaustion offers the darker vision of this group dynamic, suggesting the need for hierarchy and control.[16]

To understand how such cheerful communities confront their limits, we should look to fiction. The tension between cheerful small groups and those who witness cheerfulness from the margins will help shape the world of the classic English novel, to which we now turn.

CHAPTER SEVEN

Jane Austen, or

Cheer in Time

Elastic Cheerfulness

What does it mean to come of age cheerfully in the era of bourgeois culture? In the previous chapter, we traced the tendency of Enlightenment thinkers such as Hume and Smith to reimagine cheerfulness in secular and social terms. It is mobile and productive. It shapes and powers action in small communities, enveloping and transforming individuals. It provides the emotional vocabulary for the productive capacity of capitalism itself. Given the claims of these thinkers to speak about humans in universal terms (even as they describe groups of European males), and given their emphasis on forms of social interaction that inform the rise of bourgeois values (property, polite conversation, public virtue, commercial exchanges, and so on), it is worth asking what happens when these forms of cheerful behavior are set loose in the world.

For this, we must turn to the great literary genre of the bourgeois era, the nineteenth-century "realist" novel, which we will study in this chapter and the next. In this chapter, I will look at the novels of Jane Austen. In her depiction of the marriage game among the provincial gentry of early nineteenth-century England, Austen explores the emotional landscapes, social conventions, and economic pressures that shape the emergence of high bourgeois culture. For her, cheerfulness gives emotional content and shape to the experience of time.

When Jane Austen's last two novels, *Northanger Abbey* and *Persua-sion*, were published in 1818, they were accompanied by a biographical notice by the author's brother, Henry. Austen had died the preceding year, and her brother provides important information about his sis-ter. Recounting the circumstances of her death, he notes that during her last months, she endured "all the varying pain, irksomeness, and tedium, attendant on decaying nature, with more than resignation, with a truly elastic cheerfulness."¹ Her love of God and of her fellow creatures remained strong, and she retained her faculties to the last.

Austen's brother depicts her death as exemplary, in a fashion. Her cheerfulness is seen as an element in the human spirit's struggle against "decaying nature." The (male) Stoic in classical deathbed scenes may die passionless, exuding constancy. Jane Austen goes beyond this model. She dies cheerfully, exuding love, with "more than resignation." Cheerfulness is the extra quality that makes her unique.

Henry Austen's curious description of his sister's attitude as "truly elastic" can help us begin to think about the pliancy and resilience of the characters in her novels. If cheerfulness implies a relationship to the future, suggesting a raising of spirits to transcend the moment, Austen's cheer in the face of death is truly extraordinary. We might think of elastic cheer as an emotional quality that evades the pressure of the future.

Austen's heroines are buffeted by the forces of emotion as they seek to find their ways in a world of social constraints, inconstant male suitors, and meddling relatives. They must show accomplish-ment in skills (conversation, music, art), beauty in manner and per-son, and constancy of mind, even as they are held to account and compared with, on the one hand, an older generation that we hope they never come to resemble and, on the other hand, a set of "fallen" counterexamples whom we hope they will never join.² Within this constellation of forces, the practice of cheer is set out as an ideal of the well-adjusted personality. Whereas for Hume and Smith cheer-fulness is spatial, inhabiting companies, for Austen, it is primarily *temporal.* At one level, this temporality involves habit, repetition through time. Cheer is often taken in Austen as a kind of mark of the stability of things. Thus, in *Sense and Sensibility*, we meet Mrs. Dashwood, who demonstrates "her usual cheerfulness" when her daughters leave (p. 109), even as Mrs. Jennings greets them with "her usual noisy cheerfulness."[3] In *Pride and Prejudice*, Elizabeth Bennet returns home to confront a difficult situation "with the wish of appearing cheerful as usual."[4] Mr. Weston is "cheerful as usual" in *Emma*,[5] and Isabella is "cheerful and amiable as ever" in *Northanger Abbey*.[6] For Austen's miniature economies of social advancement and marriage to function, it would seem, cheerfulness must pertain, at least as an ideal.

And yet within this general theme of "usual" cheer, there are variations. In the late novel *Persuasion*, the older and wiser unmarried Anne Elliot is surprised when she encounters her old school friend Mrs. Smith, who lives in "cheerless" conditions after having been widowed and lost her money. Mrs. Smith's ability to be "cheerful beyond her expectation" — yet another depiction of cheer as something "extra" or supplementary — is described as "that elasticity of mind, that disposition to be comforted."[7] Such a description recalls Austen's own "elastic" disposition in the face of death. It also offers a mirror into Anne's own situation, following the heartbreak of her earlier truncated engagement to Wentworth.

At one level, of course, the promotion of cheer might be seen as a moral exigency for an English landed class hemmed in by provincial boredom, inbreeding, and miserable weather. But where can one find Austenian cheer? Probably not in books. *Persuasion*'s Captain Benwick is the great reader in Austen's novels, "though principally in poetry" (p. 601), and Anne Elliot is compelled to lecture him on the importance of reading more prose. When he finally allies himself with Louisa Musgrove, it is hoped that she will learn to love Byron and Scott, and he will "gain cheerfulness" (p. 648). Poetry and cheerfulness will be exchanged for each other to make a perfectly stable couple. Literary taste becomes a code for describing sensibility and fixing the structure of the bourgeois pair. Spinoza tells us that we can't have too much cheer; too much poetry, however, may not be a good thing.

The social basis of cheer is of paramount importance. In the final paragraphs of the first half of *Northanger Abbey*, Catherine Morland tells John Thorpe that "company is always cheerful" (p. 438), to which he replies, "Give me but a little cheerful company, let me only have the company of the people I love ... and let the devil take the rest." Obviously, the rub here is whether "the company of the people I love" is necessarily "cheerful company" and — most crucially for Austen's marriageable heroines — whether one can, in fact, figure out whom one loves. This is not inconsequential for our purposes, since, as we will see when we turn to Dickens a bit later, cheerful ambition destabilizes bourgeois respectability. In the short run, it will be useful to think about whether cheer binds the Austenian community despite gender differences or whether it is in fact the thing that divides that community along gender lines.

Austen's later novels are somewhat less interested in the dynamics of cheer than are her early ones. So it is to her first published work, *Sense and Sensibility* (1811), that we can turn for insights into how cheer works in the new literary world of the bourgeois novel. *Sense and Sensibility* expands and parodies the pious sentimental literature of the eighteenth century — a literature that draws in many ways on the moral languages we saw in Smith and Hume. And the very first paragraphs install cheer at the center of Austen's vision. Mr. Henry Dashwood, the father of the heroines, Elinor and Marianne, is introduced at the moment he is disadvantaged by the death of his uncle, who fails to leave him control of the estate of Norland. Mr. Dashwood is disappointed, "but his temper was cheerful and sanguine, and he might reasonably hope to live many years" (p. 5). Dashwood here seems to reverse the trend we saw in Shakespeare's tragedies whereby cheer abandons the unfortunate victim of fate at the onset of disaster. Aristocratic cheerfulness, we saw, was figured in terms of the rise and fall of kings. Bourgeois cheerfulness aims at a kind of stability. A good temper can keep you going, despite the vagaries of fortune. Yet only for a brief time, it would seem, since Mr. Dashwood dies a year later, leaving his daughters and wife dispossessed. For her part, Mrs. Dashwood is introduced as a person of extremes: "In seasons of cheerfulness, no temper could be more cheerful than hers, or possess, in a greater degree, that sanguine expectation of happiness which is happiness itself. But in sorrow she must be equally carried away by her fancy, and as far beyond consolation as in pleasure she was beyond alloy" (p. 6).

What strikes us about both of these descriptions is the relationship between the sanguine or cheerful personality and time. It is unclear whether Mr. Dashwood is cheerful because hopeful of a long life or hopeful of a long life because cheerful. In Mrs. Dashwood's case, we learn that happiness is, in fact, the expectation of happiness. It is a kind of trajectory. For both of the Dashwoods, cheerfulness is something that involves the future. It is no longer inflected with the tragic accents of Shakespeare's Richard III. Nor yet is it linked to the social mobility of the cheerful characters in Dickens, whom we will meet in our next chapter. Yet there is a difference between them. For Mr. Dashwood, the future is shaped by the self-discipline of frugality. By contrast, for Mrs. Dashwood, the first of the great Austenian mother figures, cheer is linked to *imagination*, to a fantasy of happiness. The expectation of happiness, a moral state, manifests itself as cheerfulness, an emotional quality. And because eventual happiness is assumed, "expected," cheerfulness in the present is also a form of happiness. In this regard, we can say that cheerfulness, which is predicated on the future, infuses the female character with content in the present. "I expect, therefore I am," might be her motto. This is neither Christian hope nor the long-term optimism of the stock investor. It is an interpersonal economy, involving the emotional investment of the self in a social ideal.

Certainly, cheerfulness always implies some kind of relationship to time. To be cheerful, one must entertain a certain confidence in a brighter future, even for the moment. If you are suffering, cheer can get you through the next painful hour. Austen expands this temporality of cheerfulness into a full-scale set of values. She uses the presence of cheer to think about how time and female identity intertwine. Elinor echoes and unmasks her mother's naive relationship to time a few pages later when she thinks that for Mrs. Dashwood, "to wish was to hope, and to hope was to expect" (p. 15). We can note the distinction between the narrator's account of Mrs. Dashwood's cheer ("the sanguine expectation of happiness") and Elinor's. For Mrs. Dashwood, in the narrator's formulation, to expect cheer is to know cheer. The journey and the arrival are the same. The more critically nuanced Elinor, however, glosses the narrator's description. She can see that such a model of emotion can be buttressed only by a kind of fiction-making, a slippage through which desire ("to wish") takes on a temporal dimension ("to hope"), which modulates into illusion ("to expect"). Thus, cheer is closely linked to a kind of fictional cloud within which the married Austen females must live. Mrs. Dashwood is playing a role that both infinitely defers an actual arrival at emotional stability (happiness as the expectation of happiness) and masks the reality of what is happening around her in the present. And indeed, much of Mrs. Dashwood's behavior stems from a mistaken expectation generated by her own cheer. She is not ridiculous, as will be some later Austen mother figures (we think of Mrs. Bennet in *Pride and Prejudice*), but she is a parody. She parodies the excessively gay reader of the type we saw in Shakespeare and Rabelais, the one who always takes things in the best sense. This is what happens when a contagious post-Humean cheerfulness spreads through bourgeois society. It becomes a social norm. Thou shalt be cheerful, at least if thou art woman. Elinor is not so sure.[8]

Cheer and Will

The relationship between will and cheer is a theme of much of the advice literature for young women during Austen's time. In one of the most widely circulated texts from the late eighteenth century, *The Polite Lady; or, A Course of Female Education in a Series of Letters, from a Mother to a Daughter*, the mother advises her daughter against the excesses of anger. Instead, she offers a different approach:

> For this purpose, let me advise you, my dear, to maintain a constant cheerfulness and alacrity in every part of your behaviour. This is the outward garb and expression of good-nature . . . and though thereby might be an appearance of this virtue without the reality, yet, by preserving the appearance of it habitually, you may come, at last, to acquire the virtue itself. For 'tis almost impossible for any one to personate a character through her whole life, without imbibing, in some degree, the true spirit of the character she represents. Thus, by a kind of innocent deceit, you may not only cheat the world into an opinion of your good-nature; but, what is more, you may even cheat yourself into the actual possession of this amiable quality.[9]

The author of *The Polite Lady* articulates in moral terms an effect of cheerfulness on the self that we have seen described several times now, from Erasmus to Madame de Staël. In this version, we are all in disguise, passing, putting on a facade of cheer. You can "cheat" yourself into taking on qualities if you pretend to have them. She goes on to stress the importance of conversation with other "friends and well-wishers" who will reinforce this "innocent deceit."

For the Dashwoods, cheerfulness might be linked to the belief in stories—in the stories that are generated by one's own desire. This link is reinforced at the first crisis point in the novel, which comes in chapter 15. Mrs. Dashwood and her newly impoverished daughters leave Norland and set themselves up at Barton Hall, living off the generosity of their cousin, Sir John Middleton—who is himself possessed of a "good humored countenance" (p. 22) and a jolly vulgarity that suggests the labile frontier between bourgeois cheerfulness and crude mirth. A chance meeting between Marianne, the youngest daughter, and the handsome, dashing young John Willoughby leads to what appears to be a courtship. Mrs. Dashwood, in particular, is convinced that a marriage proposal is in the offing. However, things take an unexpected turn when she and Elinor leave Marianne conveniently alone with Willoughby as they go off to visit their friend Mrs. Jennings.

They return home to find a crisis, with Marianne "apparently in violent affliction." Here Mrs. Dashwood's illusion of future bliss and her model of cheerful expectation are broken, for what ensues, we are told, is "what no foresight had taught her to expect" (p. 54).

Mrs. Dashwood confronts Willoughby as Marianne runs from the room in tears: "Is she ill?" "'I hope not,' he replied, trying to look cheerful; and with a forced smile, presently added: 'It is I who may rather expect to be ill — for I am now suffering under a heavy disappointment'" (p. 54). And he reveals that he must leave the region indefinitely, thereby smashing any expectation that he might propose to Marianne.

What is key here for the emotional landscape of the book is Willoughby's attempt to "look cheerful." If cheer, as we have noticed several times in earlier sections of this book, is defined by a melding of the presentation of the body with an action of the will — we can "make" ourselves cheerful — the failure of that gesture, or rather, in this case, the inefficacy of the attempt to carry off that gesture, inflicts a wound on both the emotional fabric of the novel and its representation of time. Austen's vagabond narrative voice is maddeningly elusive here. In a book that is so much about how people observe and judge each other, it is unclear who is making this all-important evaluation of Willoughby's discomfort. Who says he is "trying to look cheerful"? What would that even look like? In any event, the attempt at cheer here seems to fail — or, at least, Willoughby's expression, whatever it is, is interpreted for us by the narrator as a failed cheer. And that failure constitutes a kind of emotional violence that the Dashwoods cannot quite grasp. "So suddenly to be gone!" exclaims Mrs. Dashwood. "It seems but the work of a moment. And last night he was with us so happy, so cheerful, so affectionate" (p. 56). Willoughby's natural cheer has given way to a phony cheer, an attempt to put on a performance through a "forced smile" — whatever that would be.[10]

This emotional violence is also a crisis of knowing. The break in the consistency of Willoughby's character renders his actions resistant to any kind of cheerful interpretation. Unable to "read" him,

Mrs. Dashwood and Elinor are forced to invent a story for why he would suddenly seem to have become someone completely unlike the Willoughby they have known: "This is what I believe to have happened," posits Mrs. Dashwood a moment later, as she suggests that Willoughby's aunt, Mrs. Smith, has sent him away. This narrative redeems Willoughby's character, making him the pawn of his evil aunt. When she asks Elinor what she thinks of this theory, Elinor, like Shakespeare's Cordelia in *King Lear*, simply answers, "Nothing." Mrs. Dashwood counters with a criticism of her daughter's reading methods: "Then you would have told me, that it might or might not have happened. Oh! Elinor, how incomprehensible are your feelings! You had rather take evil upon credit than good" (p. 57). The incomprehensibility of Willoughby's actions seems to have elicited equally incomprehensible responses from Elinor.

We have here a full-scale crisis of community, unfolding around a set of questions about fiction. It is a crisis that tests the mother-daughter bond as it tests the cheerful disposition of the Dashwoods' group of friends. Mrs. Dashwood and Elinor take refuge in the language of fiction-making and literary hermeneutics. They strive to write a story that might explain Willoughby's "departing from his character" (p. 57). Over against her mother's generosity, Elinor practices the hermeneutics of suspicion. She notes that Willoughby "did not speak like himself" (p. 58) upon their meeting. And she admits that she should not suspect someone simply because his behavior offers "a deviation from what I may think right and consistent" (p. 59). Yet while rightness and consistency have not been totally destroyed, Elinor refuses to lend credence to any story that would excuse Willoughby completely. "It is an engagement in some respects not prosperously begun," (p. 59), concludes her mother, persisting in her fantasy that an agreement was reached between Willoughby and her daughter. On this interpretive impasse, with both characters trying to parse Willoughby's forced smile, the colloquy ends.

This is the first moment in Austen's writerly career at which the making up of stories is set center stage. We seem to have arrived at a place where the entire emotional and ethical weave of the cheerful economy is beginning to unravel. Willoughby's failure of cheer, his inability to "look cheerful," brings with it both a crisis of character and a crisis of time. Because he is a man, Willoughby can assume what Mrs. Dashwood calls a "carelessness of the future" (p. 58). His relationship to time differs from hers. He imposes on the Dashwood women a need to reinterpret events, to construct a new narrative that is now devoid of "expectation." In the process, community is broken and mother pitted against daughter. The slash across Willoughby's identity — signaled by his forced smile — imposes a revaluation of the narrative of cheer that had, until now, defined the feminine ideal of Austen's first published novel.[11]

The rest of *Sense and Sensibility* is an attempt to repair the wound inflicted by Willoughby on the emotional economy of the Dashwoods' world. In the default model of female subjectivity, the universe is a place of plenitude. The expectation of happiness generates cheerfulness. Yet this narrative relationship to the future is torn when counterfeit cheer appears in the forced smile of Willoughby — that same Willoughby whose very name parodies the relationship between will and cheerfulness. His failure both stresses the violence of the moment and the deeply gendered nature of the wound inflicted on Marianne.

Cheerful Grammar

The question that remains is how Austen brings us back from this break in the surface of character and company. She returns to these themes in the other signal moment in the novel at which issues of reading, interpretation, and imagination are stressed. This is the moment that repairs and offsets the moment we have just witnessed. Marianne and Elinor have gone to London, during which time Marianne has seen Willoughby again, an occurrence that brings on a crisis of health, taking her to death's door and back. Now she is beginning to recover as the daughters return to Barton Cottage and the country. In the meantime, Willoughby has confessed his indiscretions and weaknesses to

Elinor, who has more or less forgiven him. Their long-suffering friend Colonel Brandon has revealed to Mrs. Dashwood his love for Marianne, and Marianne is on the mend. A fullness overtakes Elinor, who is possessed by "an agitation of spirits which kept off every indication of fatigue" (p. 236). She dedicates herself to her sister, as does her mother, who returns to her habitual state of mind and expresses it without reservation: "Marianne continued to mend every day, and the brilliant cheerfulness of Mrs. Dashwood's looks and spirits proved her to be, as she repeatedly declared herself, one of the happiest women in the world" (p. 237). Austen's own language suggests the dynamic at work here, as the referent of the "her" in the phrase "proved her to be" may either describe the mother or articulate her unspoken fantasy about her daughter. Either way, Elinor remains skeptical of her mother's joy, attributing it to her "active fancy, which fashioned everything delightful to her, as it chose" (p. 238). And at the very least, what we are offered is the drama of Mrs. Dashwood's return to cheer. Cheerfulness is back, but not necessarily for Marianne.

Thus, Mrs. Dashwood remains a figure of fiction-making, someone who is unable to leave the regime of "fashioning" things as she chooses. This fantastical aspect of her character is stressed a moment later when Colonel Brandon comes to visit Marianne. Here, the stress is on reading. Brandon has declared his love, but Elinor knows that he is also fascinated by Marianne's strange resemblance to his lost fiancée, Eliza Williams. His "varying complexion" on seeing Marianne is read by Elinor as a moment of recollection; Marianne's recovery from death reminds him of Eliza's descent into fatal weakness. By contrast, Mrs. Dashwood sees "nothing . . . but what arose from the most simple and self-evident sensations" (p. 241). What is at play here is not merely the differing perspectives of the foolish mother and the critical daughter. Austen is asking us to think about how people read each other and, more important, about how the emotional compass of cheerfulness may be recalibrated and discerned on the body. Once the sin of Willoughby's "false cheer" has entered the world, all faces are open to skeptical interpretation. Reading itself is at issue.

Austen is deliberate in describing the emotional steps through which Marianne returns to health. As the Dashwoods journey home to Barton, Elinor watches Marianne carefully for signs of her inner disposition. We are told that the solicitude of her mother and sister were rewarded with "her bodily ease and her calmness of spirits" (p. 242). Elinor's "anguish of heart" at Marianne's weakness now begins to shift as she sees "an apparent composure of mind" that she attributes to "serious reflection." This, we are told "must eventually lead her to contentment and cheerfulness" (p. 242). Yet whether "apparent" in the sentence above means "seeming" or "obvious" is far from obvious to us.

What is striking about this process is the way in which it reverses the "outside-in" model of emotional movement that we have seen associated with cheerfulness in many earlier writers, including the author of *The Polite Lady*. The moral education through religious assurance seen in such writers as Calvin, as well as the contagious cheer that runs around the room in Hume's happy company of philosophers, now gives way to a deep interior work — or at least Elinor reads it as such, for we never know what process Marianne is actually going through on her way back to health. We are told that "serious reflection . . . must eventually lead her to contentment and cheerfulness," though we do not know who is making this claim. What we do know is that Marianne eventually reenters society and language. She says little as the family returns to Barton, with its memories of Willoughby, but "every sentence aimed at cheerfulness." When a sigh escapes her, "it never passed away without the atonement of a smile" (p. 242). This focus on sentences and smiles reworks the representation of time seen in Mrs. Dashwood's cheerful "expectation" at the outset of the novel. Willoughby's forced smile and false cheerfulness are echoed in Marianne's response to her own sighs. Her smile becomes the supplement or corrective, not the expression of inner bliss. It is the smile of self-consciousness, of an ironic awareness that cheer is not, in fact, yet at hand. Its referent is not emotional contentment, but the sigh just emitted.

In this way, emotional healing is stretched along a temporal string of words. Indeed, if anything, it is grammar itself that seems finally to be reinstating lost cheerfulness and rebuilding the world. This is how Austen projects, in language, an effect of psychological interiority, of work on the self. Over against the normative idea of a performative "innocent deceit" set forth by the author of *The Polite Lady*, here we get a progressive emotional transformation that we can follow, more or less, by the progress of Marianne's sighs and smiles. It is given shape by cheerfulness, which has now become a target, projected once again into the future, though now as goal, not as expectation, through the very unfolding of each phrase: "Every sentence aimed at cheerfulness." If Marianne can just *reach* cheerfulness in every utterance, her journey back from death will have been completed. Indeed, she speaks a moment later of her sister Margaret's return, of "the dear family party, which would then be restored, of their mutual pursuits and cheerful society as the only happiness worth a wish" (p. 242). Now no longer a general, customary feature of the social order, cheerfulness has been relocated as a force in the development of the bourgeois individual. It becomes what we might call a personality trait — diffidently hinted at in Marianne's embarrassed smile, yet always on the horizon.

The point here is that while Austen's novels are famously about the marriage market and about getting young women settled with the men they deserve and love, there is another narrative at work. This is the narrative of cheer, which guides these characters in different ways. We might even posit that they take their "character" (in all senses of that word) from their relationship to cheerfulness. Mrs. Dashwood's mindless cheerfulness is in fact nothing but fiction-making. Willoughby's cheer is revealed to be the thing of a moment, and the unmasking of it is the unmasking of an entire set of conventions upon which the social world relies. By contrast, Marianne can be brought back from death only by "aiming" for cheerfulness, by taking it as a target. The difference between her and her mother is that for Marianne, the expectation of cheer is not itself cheer. This targeting — which only the narrator seems certain about — is what sets Marianne apart from the older generation and the normative cheer that pertains in the social circle of the novel. Cheer comes easily to some, but for others, the wounded, it takes work, a "resolute firmness" (p. 242) to confront and overcome adversity.

For her part, Elinor seems to have little interest in the cheerful. Instead, she is the witness to the cheer of others. In this, she stands as the figure whose very presence points to the limitations of the Humean or Smithian company of cheery philosophers. Her very act of witnessing suggests the limits of female agency in a world of male actors who, like Willoughby, find themselves "trying to appear cheerful" as they determine the destinies of young women who can only escape to disgrace or watch in dismay.

Sense and Sensibility sets forth cheerfulness as a power that shapes the world of bourgeois English social relations at the turn of the nineteenth century. Cheer is both a social value and, for Austen, a literary tool. It is the emotional given of society; it is the glue that holds that society in place through friendly engagements and conversational ritual. Women are buoyed by it as it both shapes their personalities and defines their relationship to time and destiny. As a literary device, it gives narrative form to character. Yet as we have seen, it is not impervious to shock. Here, as in Shakespeare, the tragic figure loses cheer. When moral or even social impropriety enters the scene, cheer becomes a parody of itself, as we saw in Willoughby's attempt to mount a cheerful facade in the presence of his potential accusers. These moments of crisis are depicted by Austen in literary terms, as crises of narrative, of reading, and of writing. Yet in contrast to Shakespeare's aristocratic world of political destinies, cheer in Austen can be regained through a work on the self. Through Marianne's effort of moral will, backed by the encouragement of the narrator, who assures us, and Elinor, of things no one can actually see, the regime of cheer can be reinstated. This new cheer — "atoned for" by a smile — will, however, be of a less certain order than the default version of feminine conformity sketched in the early pages.

This dialectic of cheer and willful self-control reappears across Austen's work. It is thematized again in her third novel, *Mansfield Park*. There, we meet the figure of Fanny Price, who, like Elinor Dashwood, is a witness, a watcher of the actions of others. As the poor relation of the Bertram family, she has the opportunity to accept the hand of the appealing, but morally unstable Henry Crawford. In chapter 4 of the novel, her cousin and confidant, Edmund, advises her to take the offer. When Fanny objects that she and Henry are completely dissimilar ("We have not one taste in common"), he objects that their difference in temperaments is exactly the point. She is "easily dejected" and sees difficulties where there are none. By contrast, Henry is cheerful, "pleasant," and "gay." "His cheerfulness will counteract this" (p. 805).[12] And Edmund goes on to note that the tension between Fanny's melancholy and Henry's cheer is, in fact, an advantage. One wouldn't want it any other way. It is in fact a "favourable circumstance" to have different tempers, since husband and wife can temper each other: "Some opposition here is, I am thoroughly convinced, friendly to matrimonial happiness" (p. 805).

Here we see Edmund as a cheerful reader, taking problems for advantages, gaily asserting the best. It is the privilege of the male reader. In the process, he writes cheerfulness into matrimony, not as a feature of female identity, but as a goal of personal development. The skeptical witness Fanny will become an agent of her own destiny by accepting the gaiety of Henry, who will pull her along. Yet Fanny refuses to take the bait, for she is suspicious — not of Henry's temper, but of his moral sense: "I cannot approve his character," she says (p. 805).

This tension between character and temperament offers a gloss of what we saw played out in narrative terms in *Sense and Sensibility*. It stresses the paradoxical nature of cheer in Austen's work more generally. Her fictional universe is defined by cheer, which is either injected into characters as their personality or, for the female characters, posited as a goal, somewhere they need to end up. For the noncheerful, the skeptical witnesses such as Elinor and Fanny, that cheerful regime is faulty. And in the end, those characters who are strongest and most perceptive are those who live without cheer. Between cheery mothers and suspicious older daughters stand characters such as Marianne Dashwood, a victim of thoughtless social cheer who nevertheless struggles to regain cheerfulness. In her struggle, we can locate the modern subject, shaped by "personality traits" and "temperament," anxiously aiming for normalcy. Whether the "elastic" cheer evinced by Austen in her final days included and transcended this struggle, too, we cannot know.

CHAPTER EIGHT

Cheerful Ambition

in the Age of Capital:

Dickens to Alger

Self-Help

When Jane Austen's young protagonist John Willoughby reneges on his expected offer of marriage to Marianne Dashwood in *Sense and Sensibility*, he upsets the entire emotional economy of the novel. More broadly, he exposes the limits of a patrician world in which cheerfulness is taken as a given, as the emotional index of a stable social system. The small groups of friends that populate Austen's world are *understood* to be cheerful, cheerfully disposed, cheerful with each other, cheerful about the future. Women, especially, are expected to exemplify cheer. Yet as the nineteenth century unfolds, a new type of cheerfulness emerges. This is the cheerfulness of the ambitious lower-class male, of the figure who wields cheerfulness not to grease the wheels of a stable social structure, but to push his way up the social hierarchy. We see these figures, for example, in the novels of Balzac and Stendhal, where dynamic young men such as Lucien Chardon (in *Lost Illusions*) and Julien Sorel (in *The Red and the Black*) struggle to impose their will on society. These often low-born characters, heirs to an earlier literary tradition of picaresque heroes, reflect a new era of social mobility. Their values are at odds with the well-born characters of Austen, who jockey for position in the marriage market or the game of inheritance. In this chapter, we will see that cheerfulness is crucially present in the depiction of hard work and social advancement. It is a virtual job requirement for the low-born, ambitious personality. But, at the same time, it is a quality that can only rarely be mentioned. So it emerges in the margins, like reflected light, in offhand comments or ironic observations. Literature thus provides oblique or mediated reflections on the uneasy relationship between cheerful selfhood and the values of bourgeois society.

In the English tradition, we find the new literary and social type of the ambitious, low-born hero most prominently in the work of Charles Dickens. Dickens's heroes desire to rise from misery to wealth, yet much of the unique flavor of Dickens's books comes from the fact that his main protagonists exhibit little of the ruthlessness or amorality we find in, say, Balzac, Stendhal, or Dostoevsky. There is intense ambition in Dickens, but it is often deflected away from his main protagonists onto secondary characters. Similarly, the nasty problem of earning money is often marginalized, mentioned in passing, or taken as a given. Success seems to descend on Dickens's heroes, romancelike, in the form of long-lost relatives or mysterious gifts from strangers. When his heroes do work — as does David Copperfield, laboring in a warehouse, then as a copyist, and then as a writer — the details of building a fortune are rarely discussed. In no small measure, this is because money itself is largely a taboo subject for bourgeois culture. Dickens is no exception. Thus, he makes a useful test case for thinking about the relationship between cheerfulness and ambition.

While we often use the term "Dickensian" to refer to situations of poverty, set in polluted cityscapes, there is another current of Dickens's work that has an investment in cheerfulness. He is, after all, the author of the Christmas stories and the chronicler of remedial English sociability in hard times. Indeed, *Martin Chuzzlewitt* even features a pair of characters called the "Cheerly Brothers." Cheerfulness seems in some respects to permeate Dickens's universe. Yet where, specifically, may it be located? And how does it work?

As Austen's depiction of the weak and duplicitous John Willoughby in *Sense and Sensibility* suggested, male cheer is, if anything,

a dangerous quality. Dickens's protagonists are generally not explicitly or aggressively (or mendaciously) cheerful. These qualities are
reserved for minor characters, such as Mr. Micawber in *David Copperfield*, whose cheer is excessive and blind, or Uriah Heep, whose
performance of cheer is fake. We might thus take as our point of
departure the hypothesis that cheerfulness is "around" in Dickens's
novels, part of the atmosphere, permeating the air, but not explicitly
attached to heroic protagonists such as Pip or David Copperfield.
How, then, does the form of Dickens's novels carry out the corral-
ling of cheerfulness and the linking of cheer to the ambitious male
protagonist? And what does Dickens tell us about the uses and transformations of cheerfulness as we move into the modern world of
industrial capitalism?[1]

We can see the shift from Austen's world to Dickens's by turning
to one of the most popular manuals of Victorian moral philosophy,
Samuel Smiles's book, *Self-Help*, which was first published in 1859 and
had an acknowledged influence on Dickens. Smiles's book features
a number of "portraits" of eminent and successful Englishmen who
are presented as models of good comportment for the reader. And
just as cheerfulness helps shape the female experience of time in Austen — expectation of marriage, hope for the future — it here frames
male ambition by coloring the relationship of work and time. Success, argues Smiles, requires hard work and patience: "Great results
cannot be achieved at once . . . often we have to wait long, content
meanwhile to look patiently forward in hope. . . . To work patiently,
however, men must work cheerfully. Cheerfulness is an excellent
working quality, imparting great elasticity to the character." He
adds, a bit later, this general counsel: "One of the most valuable,
and one of the most infectious examples which can be set before
the young, is that of cheerful working. Cheerfulness gives elasticity
to the spirit. Specters fly before it; difficulties cause no despair, for
they are encountered with hope, and the mind acquires that happy
disposition to improve opportunities which rarely fails of success."[2]
The "cheerful elasticity" that, as we saw in the last chapter, Jane

Austen evinced on her deathbed is here recommended as a quality not of Stoic virtue, but of hopeful ambition. Cheerfulness is linked not to civil society, as we saw in Hume and Austen, but to work. Time was full for Austen's heroines, who were cheerful in expectation of cheerfulness. Here, time is structured in terms of a goal of eventual success. Cheerfulness is linked to patience, which is both a moral quality (it is long-suffering) and a practical quality (it takes the form of waiting). Cheerfulness is the emotion that makes patience accept-able and work tolerable.

The intersection of ambition and cheerfulness is explored in *David Copperfield* (1850), Dicken's loosely autobiographical story of ascent from destitution to prosperity, from abandonment to commu-nity. From the very outset, in the famous opening sentence, Dickens raises the question of who will actually be the center of attention, and thus, for us, who will embody and enable cheerfulness: "Whether I shall turn out to be the hero of my own life, or whether that station will be held by anybody else, these pages must show."[3] Our task will be to locate the play of cheerfulness, whether in Copperfield, in his relationships with others, or in those around him.

The plot of the novel is structured around Copperfield's move-ments between different small communities: the home of his aunt, the house of the Wickfields, who take him in as a boarder, his school, the boathouse in Yarmouth that is home to Mr. Peggotty, the home of his boss and future father-in-law, and so on. These comings and goings are often moments of great affective charge because everyone is more or less happy to welcome Copperfield. His mobility makes him an agent of cheer.

We can see the energy generated by these moments of meeting in what is perhaps the merriest scene in the novel. This comes in chapter 21, when Davy is sent off by his aunt to take a few weeks to consider his future career. He visits the Yarmouth boathouse that is home to his beloved nurse Clara Peggotty's brother Daniel, Mrs. Gummidge, Ham, and Little Emily. Copperfield makes it clear that his arrival, in the company of his friend Steerforth, upends the rhythm of the little house. The habitually glum Mrs. Gummidge becomes "unusually excited" (p. 307), Mr. Peggotty is delighted, and Emily is "delighted with Mr. Peggotty's delight." Ham gives himself over to his biggest and happiest grin. The party heats up, however, when stories begin to circulate. Mr. Peggotty tells of the courtship of Ham and Emily, and Copperfield is "filled with pleasure . . . an indescribably sensitive pleasure" (p. 311). When Steerforth takes the floor, all are drawn in, "a charmed circle" (p. 311), as Steerforth tells of "a merry adventure" recounted with "gaiety": "We all laughed . . . in irresistible sympathy with what was so pleasant and light-hearted" (p. 312). "We parted merrily," recounts Copperfield. "I never saw people so happy," he concludes. "How delightful to see it" (p. 313).

Here we see the kind of small-group cheer discussed by our Enlightenment thinkers, David Hume and Adam Smith, complete with a mention of the "sympathy" linking the group. The contagion of merriness binds the small community together in "a charmed circle." Yet what is important is that this moment of utopian community is made possible only by the intrusion into the world of the working class by Copperfield and his high-born friend Steerforth. Dickens's utopian moment suggests that it is through the *contact* between social groups that cheer is generated. This is quite different from what we saw in Jane Austen.

Dickens locates this small-community cheer in a "primitive," or socially "low" context, almost as if it were the vestige of some earlier economic or social organization, the village world of the fisherman. Davy and Steerforth function as conduits and observers, like the "objective observer" of eighteenth-century moral philosophy; through them, lower-class cheer comes to our attention. Yet all is not well, for while Copperfield's arrival generates good cheer, Steerforth's stories push that cheer toward "indescribably sensitive pleasure." This intensification suggests the fragility of the moment of communion. And immediately upon leaving, Steerforth shares with Copperfield his contempt for Ham and his attraction to Emily — hinting at his own forthcoming seduction of her. He turns the idea of a sympathy between social groups into a travesty as he refuses to stay in his own class and preys on the innocent. One visitor brings cheerfulness, the other eventual misery.

It is over and against this type of spontaneous moment — as rare as it is dangerous — that we might see the working out of the dynamics of cheer in the rest of the novel. Even as such characters as Micawber and Heep play out versions of excessive or fake cheer, the book features a series of scenes in which characters from different social groups are, as it were, led into cheerfulness. This initiation or conversion — if that is the correct word for it — comes in response to a moment of trial or crisis. It is *against* travail that cheer fully emerges in the novel, just as, for Samuel Smiles, it is in the face of adversity that cheerfulness defines the success of the working man.

These scenes begin early on, when young Davy is sent away from his happy home to spend two weeks in Yarmouth, in the old ship that serves as a house to Peggotty and her brother. There he meets Emily, and there he glimpses Mrs. Gummidge, whose very name seems difficult for Davy to process: "'That's Missus Gummidge,' said Mr. Peggotty. 'Gummidge, Mr. Peggotty?'" (p. 34). Much of the action in the Peggotty household is punctuated by Mrs. Gummidge's melancholy memories of "the old one," her lost husband. She emerges quickly as the explicit negation of cheerfulness. Mr. Peggotty takes a turn at the tavern, leaving the group to work "cheerfully" (p. 40) as Davy, ever the agent of cheer, reads to them. Mrs. Gummidge never looks up, and upon Mr. Peggotty's return, she only shakes her head. "Cheer up, old mawther," cries Mr. Peggoty, which only inspires tears in the widow (p. 40). "I really couldn't help thinking," says Davy, "as I sat taking in all this, that the misfortune extended to some other members of that family besides Mrs. Gummidge. But Mr. Peggotty made no such retort, only answering with another entreaty to Mrs. Gummidge to cheer up" (pp. 40–41).

This brief exchange and Davy's comment establish the close bonds of the community and the essentially sympathetic nature of cheerfulness in Dickens. Mr. Peggotty's urging comes as an urging on behalf of the entire little community, which Mrs. Gummidge seems to infect with her self-pity. Yet at the same time, because of her misery, the rest of the community is bound together around her, united in their need for a cheering. She both lends particularity to the little group and resists integration into its emotional world. There appear to be some wounds that cannot be healed.

Or perhaps they can, for at the virtual midpoint of the novel, Mrs. Gummidge suddenly loses her melancholy. This comes when it is revealed that Little Emily, David's childhood friend and the betrothed of the stolid and virtuous Ham, has been compromised and run off with the dastardly Steerforth. Mr. Peggotty announces that he will now leave, that his "dooty" is to seek his niece wherever he can. As he prepares to depart, reports Copperfield, the entire company pitches in to prepare for his departure. "What a change in Mrs. Gummidge in a little time!" says Copperfield (p. 450). "She was another woman . . . she was so forgetful of herself, and so regardful of the sorrow about her, that I held her in a sort of veneration." Indeed, Mrs. Gummidge throws herself into the work, preserving "an equable cheerfulness in the midst of her sympathy, which was not the least astonishing part of the change that had come over her" (p. 451). Copperfield concludes that he "could not meditate enough upon the lesson that I read in Mrs. Gummidge, and the new experience she unfolded to me." Here we see some version of Samuel Smiles's idea of "cheerful work." Yet even more important is that cheerfulness appears through the moment of crisis in community. It emerges not as a *practice* of everyday life, but *in response* to catastrophe. It is the reaction to an action, brought on by external stimulus.

Cheerfulness under Pressure

The sense that cheerfulness must arise in response to disaster is what sets Dickens's Victorian meliorism against the expected and hoped-for cheer of Austen's heroines. And it is reflected at another level of the narrative, in the story of Copperfield's own emotional life and professional development. Early on in the novel, Copperfield runs away from the miserable job to which he has been relegated by his wicked stepfather and makes his way to Dover, where he is taken in by his aunt, Betsey Trotwood. At the bottom of his fortunes ("I had nothing left to dispose of," p. 187), he is eventually placed in the home of the local solicitor, Mr. Wickfield, while he attends school. There he meets Wickfield's daughter, Agnes, whom he will eventually marry.

Copperfield's first glimpse of Agnes is remarkable for the way in which she is associated with her father's house. It is a welcoming house, full of "nooks and corners" (p. 220), featuring a beautiful staircase. And there, Copperfield first glimpses Mr. Wickfield's "little housekeeper, his daughter Agnes" (p. 221). The description of Agnes's appearance is striking: "I cannot call to mind where or when, in my childhood, I had seen a stained glass window in a church. Nor do I recollect its subject. But I know that when I saw her turn round, in the grave light of the old staircase, and wait for us, above, I thought of that window; and I associated something of its tranquil brightness with Agnes Wickfield ever afterwards" (p. 221).

Agnes, then, is saintly, like a figure in a church window. No less important is that she is herself a kind of copy, a version of an image that Copperfield has glimpsed only a moment earlier, down on the ground floor. There, he came face to face with a portrait of Agnes's mother, now long since dead, whose "very placid and sweet expression of face" looks down on Copperfield as he waits (p. 217). When Agnes appears, "It seemed to my imagination as if the portrait had grown womanly, and the original remained a child. Although her face was quite bright and happy, there was a tranquility about it, and about her — a quiet good, calm spirit — that I never have forgotten; that I never shall forget" (pp. 220–21). In a curious twist of time, Agnes is now depicted as the "original" of her mother's portrait, which depicts her as she will someday be. The melding of the two characters is such that Copperfield's phrase "there was a tranquility about it" could apply to either the mother's face or the child's. This descriptive language is repeated a moment later, where the "tranquility" of the face modulates into the "tranquil brightness" of the stained-glass window in whose light Agnes first appears.

What is important for us is the way in which all of these description focus on Agnes's "tranquility." Dickens uses this word over and over again to describe her. He stresses that hers is a tranquility placed at the service of others. As the evening wears on, Mr. Wickfield, "for the most part gay and cheerful with us" (p. 222), falls into moments of reverie—at which point Agnes, like the Elizabethan doctor Timothy Bright, whom we met in Chapter 3, raises his spirits with a bit of wine.

Yet just as the crisis of Emily's seduction jolts Mrs. Gummidge out of her melancholy, Agnes deals with a moment of reckoning at which her affect shifts. She is converted from "tranquility" to "cheerfulness." Two-thirds of the way through the novel, Copperfield falls in love. He loses his heart to the beautiful, but shallow Dora. He proposes to Dora one afternoon in chapter 41, when he visits her family in the company of his trusted friend Tommy Traddles, who has his own beloved, Sophy, to pursue. The difference between a "Sophy" (as the embodiment of wisdom) and the gold-plated, but superficial "Dora" should warn us that this won't turn out happily. But Copperfield plunges ahead, and upon receiving a positive response to his proposition of marriage, writes to his aunt, who, we are told, "was happy to see me so happy" (p. 593). As for Agnes, upon learning of the match, she writes back with a letter that is "hopeful, earnest, and cheerful." Copperfield adds, "She was always cheerful from that time" (p. 593).

Whereas Agnes has been consistently described as "tranquil" throughout the first two-thirds of the book, she is now, of a sudden, "cheerful" and will remain so through the ensuing chapters. The threat from another woman for Copperfield's affections transforms Dickens's description of Agnes, and the shift from "tranquil" to "cheerful" occurs with almost mathematical precision. Indeed, when Agnes and Dora meet for a party a moment later, we learn that the company is gay because "the gentle cheerfulness of Agnes went into all their hearts" (p. 601). After the party, as Copperfield and Agnes walk home, tranquility has again given way to cheer: "That cheerfulness that belongs to you, Agnes (and to no one else that I have ever seen), is so restored, I have observed to-day, that I have begun to hope you are happier at home." " 'I am happier in myself,' she said, 'I am quite cheerful and light hearted'" (p. 603).[4] Thus, we have, quite literally, a change in the emotional lexicon of the novel.

These shifts touch on the depiction of Copperfield's own emotional world. The strong female characters (Aunt Betsey, Agnes) emerge as mirrors or reflections of Copperfield's own situation. They reflect cheerful ambition back onto him. He seems void of affect without their presence. Copperfield's cheer is acted out, but never given its own descriptions. When he falls in love with Dora (his boss's daughter, no less) and is forced to leave her to return to his fledgling career, he descends, in chapter 26, into a kind of depression. He is constantly "low." He is rescued by his landlady, Mrs. Crupp, who comes to him seeking a remedy for her own "disorder" (Copperfield dispenses brandy) and comments on his low spirits with some clear advice: "Cheer up, sir" (p. 391). She discloses what is obvious, that "there's a lady in the case" and that if the lady doesn't smile on Copperfield, others will. "You are a young gentleman to be smiled on, Mr. Copperfull, and you must learn your walue, sir," she adds in her eccentric language. She goes on to note that her young male borders sometimes dress badly and sometimes well, "according as the young gentleman has his original character formed," but that when there is a "lady in the case," suffering ensues. Indeed, Copperfield's predecessor in the same rooms took his own life. "My adwice to you is, to cheer up, sir, to keep a good heart, and to know your own walue" (p. 392). She recommends that he take up the game of skittles to distract himself.

This is a useful moment in the novel because it gives us one of the few accounts we receive from an objective observer of Copperfield's emotional makeup. Here, he, like Shakespeare's Richard III (though for different reasons), seems to have lost his cheer. Mrs. Crupp's description of his situation reveals to us that one of the characteristics of this ambitious young hero is in fact his cheerfulness, his high spirits — what he calls, in speaking of his friend and double Tommy Traddles (and echoing Samuel Smiles), "his cheerful confidence and sprightly patience" (pp. 397–98). This language lies beyond the range of Copperfield's own self-description. He can act cheerfully and generate cheer in others, but he cannot say that he is cheerful. Just as ambition can be thematized only in the evil and unctuous figure of Uriah Heep, cheerfulness lies beyond the self-analysis of the narrator.

In the end, it is Agnes, following her conversion to cheerfulness, who must give language to the emotional life of Copperfield. She fills in a blank spot in male subjectivity, embodying the cheer that the narrator cannot pronounce when he describes his younger self. In the competitive world of industrial England, Copperfield rises from the lowest rung of society to become a successful barrister and then a writer. "And grown so *famous*! My glorious Copperfield!" (p. 813), cries Traddles when they meet again at the end of the book. Yet the struggle for fame and wealth, which necessarily involves no small amount of psychic anguish and competitive drive, is rarely alluded to. As Alexander Welsh has noted, "So lightly does the narrator of his own life touch upon his career that as readers we are a little taken aback and have to remind ourselves that this is a novel about a novelist."[5] The dark forces of professional competition and struggle are never shown to the reader. It is only through such "mirroring" figures as Agnes — cheerful to the end — that the emotional tenor of the novelistic world reveals itself.

The novel's silence regarding Copperfield's cheer makes all the more important the role of his double and friend Tommy Traddles. Traddles gives voice to what is implicit or acted out in the life of the main character. And so he lets us in on the secret to a good marriage. At the novel's end, Copperfield meets Traddles, now happily wed to Sophy (the wedding invitation never reached our hero) and hosting Sophy's sisters in their rooms in London. "The society of girls is a very delightful thing, Copperfield. It's not professional, but it's very delightful" (p. 814). "It's not professional," indeed. Copperfield has pursued professional success, eschewing the emotional pleasure that Traddles obviously enjoys with Sophy and her sisters. And a few pages later, Traddles reveals the secret to his wedded bliss: "My dear Copperfield . . . she is, without any exception, the dearest girl! The way she manages this place; her punctuality, domestic knowledge, economy, and order; her cheerfulness, Copperfield!'" (p. 836). This intertwining of the workaday virtues (punctuality, order) with the affective power of cheer offers us the Dickensian vision of domestic labor, carefully distributed by gender. It takes us back to Samuel Smiles's account of "cheerful work" with which I began this chapter. Traddles's exclamation, "her cheerfulness, Copperfield!" is perhaps the purest expression of cheer in the novel, spreading cheer as it announces it.

David Copperfield begins his story wondering if he will be its hero "or whether that station shall be held by anybody else." It is no accident that it should be Traddles who gives voice to a central emotional and psychological value of the ambitious hero: "Her cheerfulness, Copperfield!" Traddles names the quality that Copperfield himself can never acknowledge in himself — or that he can speak only through his account of the actions of others.

The economy of Dickens's novel is built on an ideology of talent and hard work. Copperfield rises through society because of intelligence, persistence — and the material support of his wealthy aunt. Dickens borrows an old romance plot line — the "found" child who turns out to be a prince — and updates it for the new capitalist economy of nineteenth-century England. In Dickens's world, the high bourgeois virtue of cheer, which we saw both embodied and parodied in Austen's depiction of John Willoughby, can no more be linked to the hero than can the embarrassing theme of money be discussed in good company. Indeed, as Adam Smith reminded us, the consequences of a "cheerful" economy for the individual are overwork and exhaustion. So cheer must be deflected onto other characters. Austen has already told us that cheer is a characteristic that can be counterfeited, a surface value that circulates in small societies, a form of deception. The cheer of *David Copperfield* is not merely the obverse of melancholy. It is a central, positive source of power that circulates throughout the novel, but that can be named only outside of the most cheerful of all of the characters, the narrator himself. And so Dickens locates cheer in Agnes's face, in the conversion of Mrs. Gummidge, in Tommy Traddles's axioms about what makes a desirable mate.

Yet if cheerfulness emerges in response to adversity, and if love and ambition hover around Copperfield's tacit cheer, we finally see him "converted" to cheer not as an ambitious writer, but as a lover. Following the death of Dora, he returns to visit his aunt. She questions him and comments on the struggles and rewards of literary creations ("ambition, love of approbation, sympathy, and much more, I suppose? Well: go along with you!" p. 848). He, by contrast, asks about Agnes, who, he has heard, has an attachment to another man. Upon learning that the news is true, we see one of the few moments in the entire novel at which Copperfield seems completely overwhelmed and confused. He can return his aunt's gaze only with difficulty. He knows which affect to display, but it is a struggle: "I summoned the stronger determination to show her a perfectly cheerful face." Upon learning, a second later, that Agnes's marriage is imminent, he summons yet more determination: "'God bless her!' said I, cheerfully" (p. 848). Here we see Copperfield as a more sympathetic version of John Willoughby, struggling to keep up cheer in the face of disaster. And he sets off to find Agnes. Only now, at the moment of potential catastrophe, may he "speak plainly" (p. 850) to her. His response to his aunt has made legible the risk before him. "Cheer," in this moment, is the expected response to crisis. But he puts aside the expected cheerfulness of the jilted lover and finds the voice to express his true desire. Instead of simply cheering up, as Mrs. Crupp has suggested, he declares love to the one who loves him in return. And from this moment of felicity, he can write back cheerfully on his life.

Cheerfulness emerges in *David Copperfield* as an important cement in the life of small communities. While Austen projected cheerfulness into time, as an ideal against which female behavior could be measured, Dickens confronts the problem of how small communities are established and broken apart, either through intrusions from other social groups (the wealthy Steerforth's seduction of Emily) or through the energy of the capitalist-professional class itself (Copperfield as famous barrister). Against this dynamic and even violent world, Dickens presents a constellation of small communities that live in juxtaposition or in opposition to each other. As Hume has taught us, cheerfulness can lend character to a communal experience, zooming around the room like a flame, touching everyone in sight. Dickens's vision of community is more complex than Hume's. He shows us a set of small communities under pressure. The relationship between cheer and community is depicted in the conversion of Mrs. Gummidge from melancholic complainer to cheerful helper. The little community of the boathouse, with its simple, lower-class characters, stands as an allegory of an earlier social world and an earlier affective regime in which melancholy and idleness can turn to cheer and industry whenever the community is threatened. This figure is then expanded and developed in the main narrative thread as Agnes's early "tranquility" converts into a generalized "cheerfulness" that informs the emotional life of the male protagonist. No longer simply a witness to the emotional struggles of characters in crisis (as was, say, Austen's Elinor Dashwood observing Willoughby and Marianne), Agnes becomes, through her role as witness, a crucial force in Copperfield's own self-definition. Ambition and cheer *can* coexist, it would seem, but only through the mediating presence of a figure who is not the ambitious male hero.

"A Cheerin' Reflection"

It is instructive to set Dickens's view of cheerfulness next to a less artistically expansive American version of the same rags-to-riches plot that we saw in *David Copperfield*. This is Horatio Alger's 1868 novel *Ragged Dick, or Street Life in New York with the Boot-Blacks*. Here, as in Dickens, we follow an ambitious male protagonist. Yet if

Dickens seems keen to elide discussions of such embarrassing topics as money and professional struggle, Alger takes them head-on, only to resolve the problem of social and economic inequality through a parable of generosity in which the well-born and wealthy rescue the poor and deserving.

We first meet Ragged Dick waking up for a hard day on the streets of New York. He is roused from sleep by a porter, who, in the course of their conversation, asks him if he has ever stolen anything. "No, and I wouldn't. Lots of boys does it, but I wouldn't," says Dick. "I believe there's some good in you, Dick, after all," answers the porter.[6] And from there we are off. Yet given the porter's last comment, "after all," we might ask, "after what?" Has Dick done something that would suggest that he is to be suspected of not having "some good" in him? What Dick has, in fact, "done" is, of course, to have been born poor.

David Copperfield's scenes of struggle and poverty are the consequence of evildoers (the hero's stepfather). In Alger's novel the social hierarchy is also a moral hierarchy. Those on the bottom of the social ladder must have done something "after all" to explain why they suffer. Within this moral economy, we can ask the same question we asked at the outset of this chapter: Where lies cheerfulness for the ambitious man who rises through the ranks? The reason Dick won't steal is not because he doesn't need to, but because *not* stealing establishes his moral superiority to those around him. His honesty marks him out as worthy of advancement, as unlike the rest of the poor boys among whom he lives.

Yet the depiction of Dick as "honest" raises a problem for the novelist. Alger's world, like the world of Dickens, is a socially dynamic world, marked by mobility as characters rise and fall. The honest man is the man who tends to his own business, remaining in his place. The merely honest have no role in an entrepreneurial social order. So Dick must distinguish himself from his fellows in some other way.

He does so by his wit. We can see this illustrated in the depiction of coats. At the moment of his greatest need, when he has run away from his evil stepfather and set out on foot to find his Aunt Betsey,

Copperfield is robbed and left with nothing. To feed himself, he sells his coat. He is thus stripped, ripe for redemption by his aunt. By contrast, in the opening pages of Alger's novel, we see Dick dress himself and head out onto the street to look for customers. When he stops a prosperous gentleman on the street, they exchange banter about Dick's ragged overcoat. Dick claims that his coat is ragged because it once belonged to George Washington: "When he died he told his widder to give it to some smart young feller that hadn't got none of his own; so she gave it to me" (p. 5). Dick claims a heroic American ancestry for himself not through blood or birth, but through the surface decoration of his own garments, which can transcend time. He goes on to point out that his pants once belonged to Napoleon, who, however, outgrew them (becoming thereby, we surmise, too big for his britches). Thus, it is not Dick's practice of honesty that is his greatest resource in the social dynamics of Alger's novel. It is language. Like Copperfield the writer — and more explicitly — his mastery of words sets him apart. Wit enables Dick to engage with customers and patrons, showing himself through his spirit as something other than he appears to be. In a novel obsessed with surfaces (the first major plot development involves Dick getting a new suit), the way to stand out is through language. And it is not just any language; it is the language of double meanings, of ironic commentary.

Dick's ironic remarks about his situation appear throughout the novel, but they come out most strongly in his greatest moments of trial — which, as in Dickens, is also where cheerfulness appears. Dick's first break involves his friendship with the benevolent Mr. Greyson, who takes him to Sunday school. Along the way, he is attacked by the bully Micky Maguire. Maguire represents perhaps the greatest pressure on the lower-class hero in Alger's world, the pressure to conform. Rising through society involves both the material means to rise (work, thrift) and the psychological strength to break with one's own community and its conventions. Maguire resents Dick for his honesty and success. He believes that Dick is "putting on airs" (p. 102) when he begins to dress well and learns to read. On the first trip to Sunday school (where Dick also meets the lovely Ida, the potential love interest in the novel), Maguire attacks him with a stone. Dick chases him down, and predictably, Maguire trips on another stone — a cobblestone — and falls. Dick confronts him. When Maguire claims that his arm might be broken, Dick responds, "If it's broke you can't fire no more stones, which is a very cheerin' reflection" (pp. 101–102). "I don't want none of yer cheerin' reflections," answers Maguire, as Dick leaves him. But the expression "cheerin' reflection" or "cheerin' thought" becomes proverbial from this moment forward in the novel. A few pages later, Dick encourages his friend Fosdick to pursue gainful employment with the prediction that he will improve his lot, "which is a very cheerin' reflection" (p. 108). And a page farther on, when he is called "impudent" by Fosdick's rival, Dick repeats the phrase.

Here we see what happens when the ambitious novelistic hero lacks a supporting cast of characters to reflect his cheerfulness back to him. Traddles and Agnes Wickfield provide a support team for Copperfield. They supply the moral vocabulary for a hero who is cheerful, but does not comment on that cheerfulness when he looks back on his life. By contrast, Ragged Dick has only himself to rely on, and as such, he speaks his cheerfulness. Yet his expressions of cheerfulness are tinged with sardonic wit. When he is repeatedly challenged, he responds with the claim that each threat generates its opposite, "cheer." In this way, he gives voice to his exceptional nature. Beyond his vaunted honesty, Ragged Dick rises through the society of Alger's novel by virtue not of his cheerfulness, but of his ability to deploy the *language of cheerfulness* at crucial moments. He has mastered the language of cheer and can turn it against itself. Cheer in Alger becomes the indicator of a kind of resilience. It is not the manifestation of a power of the self, but the name that comes to the lips at the moment of powerlessness. It thus frees Dick from the taint of struggle and the whiff of the tragic. The obvious misery that weighs on the lower-class person trying to rise through the ranks is here dispelled with a gesture toward the carefree self-identification of figures such as Montaigne and Shakespeare's Theseus, good-natured aristocrats content with their social status. In Alger's world, "cheer" might be seen as a magic word, a word that, unlike much of the rest of the language of the novel, is not marked by social inequality and misery. The ironic expression of cheer is what passes for cheerfulness. It is the weapon of the man with no weapons, the power of the powerless.

For both Dickens and Alger, cheerfulness involves a relation to language. In Dickens, the ambitious hero can act cheerfully, but he cannot speak his cheer. In Alger's American version of Dickens's story, the poor hero must take cheerfulness upon himself as something that he cannot always practice, but that he can at least speak. In this regard, "cheerfulness" becomes both the mark of moral empowerment and the mark of social disempowerment because, for Ragged Dick, the word can be uttered only ironically, in response to threat or insult. Dick's exclamations both perform cheerfulness for himself and make another claim at the same time—the claim that "I am resilient."

Perhaps here we see one version of the "elasticity" of spirit mentioned by Jane Austen's brother and endorsed by Samuel Smiles, the author of *Self-Help*. The empty time of labor, the time of hoping for success that Smiles suggests we fill up with cheerfulness and "patience," is marked in Dickens by scenes of conversion, of melancholy or tranquil characters who must be brought to cheer through struggle. In Alger's less capacious world, too, the hero struggles with adversity, but he does not use cheerfulness as a weapon of deception, as would the confidence man or dissimulating politician. Rather, he wields it ironically to suggest his own exceptional status.

Our discussion of Dickens and Alger suggests that male social ambition and cheerfulness stand in uneasy relationship to each other. Bourgeois culture is uncomfortable with masculine cheer, which, as we saw in Austen's John Willoughby, sits precariously on the body of the patrician. In the socially dynamic world of expanding capitalism, where fortunes are made and lost by entrepreneurs and glad-handing businessmen, cheerfulness becomes a privileged tool in the arsenal of ambition. Yet one of the literary forms that gives imaginative shape to the new world of modernity — the novel of male ambition — seems less than certain how to engage with the manifestations of cheerfulness. So it links cheerfulness to questions of language and self-expression. In these male-authored narratives, cheerfulness is a defining quality of the ambitious man. Yet it remains an unspoken, even unspeakable resource. In these stories, cheerfulness has migrated from communal experience into the space of the individual subject as a "character trait" that sets the protagonist apart. Because cheerfulness involves power, the linking of cheer with ambition risks turning it into a commodity, something to be circulated and awkwardly displayed.

Yet the commodification of cheerfulness, which, as we will see a bit later, comes to full realization only in the twentieth century, is counterbalanced by another literary and cultural discourse that locates cheer elsewhere, outside of self and society, in the power of nature. If society cannot generate salutary cheerfulness, perhaps nature can.

This rearguard attempt to discover and describe a cheerfulness that would lie outside of the social order has its roots deep in literary history. It takes its most potent form in the tradition of lyric poetry, to which we turn in the next chapter. As we will see, from the earliest days of postclassical European lyric, cheerfulness helped poets conceptualize the healing power of nature. Yet as we move into the modern era, the relationship of poetry, nature, and cheerfulness is transformed. The uneasy, ironic relationship between ambition and cheerfulness that we have seen in the novels of Dickens and Alger becomes, in the lyric tradition, a source of confusion and folly.

CHAPTER NINE

Gay Song and Natural Cheer:

Milton, Wordsworth

Cheering Nature

Previous chapters in this book have studied the social dimension of cheerfulness, often, as in the last chapter, in some kind of relation to language and the presentation or representation of the self. Yet in a society marked by social conflict and competition, social groupings threaten to drain cheerfulness of its authenticity and salutary strength. Fake cheer is no cheer, whether you are ambitious or not. The role of social expectations in alienating the individual from her sense of integrity is, of course, a major theme of much nineteenth-century writing in the West. One powerful description that links it to bodily experience is offered by the American philosopher Ralph Waldo Emerson, whom we will discuss at greater length in our next chapter. Near the beginning of his essay titled "Self-Reliance," Emerson laments that "society is a joint-stock company" in which, in order to succeed, humans trade virtue for conformity.[1] They circulate in "communities of opinion" (p. 264) that require not only intellectual blandness, but certain types of faces:

> There is a mortifying experience in particular, which does not fail to wreak itself also in the general history; I mean "the foolish face of praise," the forced smile which we put on in company where we do not feel at ease in answer to conversation which does not interest us. The muscles, not spontaneously

moved, but moved by a low usurping wilfulness, grow tight about the outline of the face with the most disagreeable sensation. (p. 264)

Emerson speaks here not of specifically "insincere" people (say, Dickens's Uriah Heep, or Austen's John Willoughby), but of anyone caught in a world of good manners and social competition. Fake expressions are part of "the general history." We are all pressured to present faces that are, as he says elsewhere in the same passage, "false in all particulars" (p. 264). Emerson gives us the inverse of Madame de Staël's formulation, seen earlier as part of a discussion of aristocratic wit, whereby a cheerful face works on the soul to lighten it up. Here, the by-product of the foolish face seems to be dyspepsia.

If Emerson suggests that modern society is emptying social relationships of the power to cheer, we should not, perhaps, be surprised to find that he and some of his contemporaries respond to the situation by seeking cheerfulness elsewhere. They look for cheer in nature, as a resource for the sensitive self. Of course, when we speak of natural cheer, we touch on an elemental aspect of cheerfulness: its reach into the basic levels of the instinct for survival. Cheerfulness seems to enliven us at each moment of our engagement with nature. The return of day from the terrifying darkness of the night or the liberation from the cold and hunger of the seemingly endless winter—moments of rebirth, of return to life and fertility—have conventionally been depicted in art as moments of cheer, of the raising of spirit. Cheer resides in nature, in the heavens, in the song of the birds.

The cultural resources available to authors responding to the problems of bourgeois selfhood in nineteenth-century Euro-American society have their roots in the very beginnings of modern European culture. One place to study them is in the tradition of lyric poetry. This chapter will loop back in time and trace the link between nature and cheerfulness from some of the earliest modern European lyrics. This will enable us, in the last sections of the chapter, to discern the pressure placed by modern economic life on poetic representations of cheer. Obviously, it is beyond the scope of this project to offer a comprehensive account of the representations of natural spirit in lyric. What we can do, however, is look at the role played by poetic cheerfulness: where it appears, and what it seems to do. We will see that the appearance of cheerfulness in poetry is often the occasion for confusion or misunderstanding when the contrast between the violence of human events and the rhythms of nature is set in relief. However, the fact that cheerfulness (or gaiety) is such a modest emotion may be what makes it so productive for poets. An ecstatic relationship to nature would place the poet in the realm of the sublime, which imposes its own constraints. And different still would be a melancholic relationship to nature — say, the self-isolating confinement of the aesthete. The limited, but vivifying power of gaiety provides a useful energy field in which poets can explore the transformation of things and people. Cheerfulness wakes things up.[2]

We begin with a poem from the twelfth century, at the very beginning of the modern era of European culture. There the troubadour Bernard de Ventadour celebrates the arrival of spring. He notes that the new season brings flowers of many colors and that this should inspire every lover to be gay and sing, "tuih amador / son gai et chantador," as he says in his beautiful Provençal. Unfortunately, he goes on, because his lady and love have betrayed him, his own "joy" has no flavor — "un jois no m'a sabor."[3] Human weakness, at least in Bernard's case, undermines gaiety.

Bernard's song gives us an early version of the close relationship between gaiety, nature, and song in the Western lyric tradition. A century after Bernard, the Italian poet Guido Cavalcanti writes a song on the same theme, evoking a spring rose, "fresca rosa novella," which later turns into a lady and of whom he sings "gaily," "gaiamente cantando":

Fresh new rose
Beautiful springtime
In the meadow, on the riverbank
Gaily singing
I communicate your worth — to the green world.

Let your great worth
Be renewed with the day
By men and boys
On every pathway
And let the birds sing
Each in his language
At dawn and at dusk
On the green bushes
Let the whole world sing —
For the season has come
When this is the thing to do —
Sing of your rich nobility
For you are an angelic — creature.[4]

What is noteworthy in this scenario is how useful it is for exploring the relationship between poetry and nature, human creation and natural rhythm. Poetry is gay. Nature is gay. Gay nature, which reemerges every spring, inspires gay poetry. The poet draws on the gaiety of nature to shape her or his poems. And so on. Cavalcanti plays with the idea that gaiety is all around, since his poem addresses the rose, describes it/her, and then sets the phrase "gaily singing" in apposition, hinting that the rose is somehow gaily singing, before revealing in the last line of the first stanza that it is he, not the flower, who is in fact spinning out the song, only to return it to nature, whence it came, now in praise of the lady. He then expands this in the second strophe to locate gay singing everywhere, in people and birds.

By the time of the Renaissance, the gaiety of nature and of natural song that I have just pointed to in Bernard and Guido has become a cliché. The imagery is both obligatory for a certain kind of poetic discourse and always in need of renewal. Here are a few examples, though dozens more could easily be adduced: In a sonnet memorized by generations of French schoolchildren, the sixteenth-century poet Pierre de Ronsard urges his rustic, but lazy lover, Marie, to get up in the morning — "Mignonne, levés-vous, vous estes paresseuse" — and greet the song of lark, the "gaye alouette," which is already singing a love song to the heavens. A few poems later, he praises the "gaye et verte nouveaulté," the "gay and green newness," of the month of April. His contemporary, Maurice Scève, praises the "gaie verdure," or "gay greenery" brought by the new spring. Across the English Channel, Edmund Spenser praises the coming of the new year, which will wake up Love sleeping in a "cheerless bower." Some fifty years later, the religious poet Henry Vaughan offers up a poem titled "Cheerfulness" in which he praises God for offering him alacrity: "Lord, with what courage and delight / I do each thing / When thy least breath sustains my wing!" Vaughan sings that the rays of the sun — the old troubadour image for cheer — are the sign of God's presence, according to which he can "make me fair days of every night." A century later, in Thomas Gray, the image is still at work as Gray praises the new morning, which smiles, "the busy race to cheer / And new-born pleasure brings to happier men."[5]

Equally important is how easily the image turns around, becoming a site for evoking lost plenitude: The fourteenth-century Italian poet Petrarch calls to a bird in autumn, who, he notes, is lamenting the "gay months," or "mesi gai," of a spring now long gone. William Shakespeare complains that when his beloved is away, it is like winter: "The very birds are mute; Or, if they sing, 'tis with so dull a cheer, / That leaves look pale, dreading the winter's near." In a more comic register, the Elizabethan poet Philip Sidney celebrates the eyes of his beloved Stella, which warm up the day like the sun, "most freshly gay" — until she turns up the temperature, and they scorch him. And much later, in the mid-twentieth century, in her well-known poem "The Bight," the American poet Elizabeth Bishop offers a modern reworking of the same image, this time blending creation and destruction. She describes the natural rhythms of the ocean wearing down the dockside. After noting how the sounds and colors of the port, the rumble of waves and creak of rotting timbers, create a kind of rhythm, alive with both decay and rebirth, she ends with the memorable lines: "All the untidy activity continues, / awful but cheerful."⁶ As creation or destruction, cheer-fulness inflects change.

Birds, sun, natural rhythms, springtime: all of these elements generate cheerfulness. Gay song results. And yet because the rela-tionship between gay spring and gay song is linked to the returning cycles of nature — there is always another spring — nature's power to cheer us up is also useful for authors who want to think not so much about nature as about *history* — that is, about how human events dis-rupt the gaiety of the natural world. Bernard de Ventadour hints at this when he points out that his lady has destroyed delight by betray-ing him. The contingency of human experience and the dynamism of human action disturb the cyclical gaiety of spring. The seemingly timeless power of nature to cheer us each time the sun comes up is cut short by human behavior. Because it is connected to natural rhythms, cheerfulness seems to bind us to a world beyond human intervention. Yet human events constantly intervene, and those interventions are the stuff of tragedy.

Trouble in Eden

The tension between natural cheer, which returns every spring and even every dawn, and human history, which is shaped by unique, punctuative events, is explored nowhere more compellingly than by John Milton. Milton points to the necessary relationship between humanity and some type of unfallen nature, even as he makes it clear that such an identity can never be unproblematic or unmediated. So we should not be surprised to see him inscribe reflections on cheerfulness, nature, and history into both the imagery and action of his epic *Paradise Lost*. This begins early in the poem, where, in an epic simile, Milton describes the gathering of Satan's minions around him as like the "dusky clouds" that "o'erspread / Heaven's cheerful face." In an ironic reversal of the image of cheerful healing, they end up "rejoicing in their matchless Chief" as when the sun dispels clouds and "the fields revive, / The birds thir notes renew, and bleat-ing herds / Attest thir joy, that hill and valley rings."⁷ Cheer is effaced by bad weather, then reasserts itself in natural cycle, even as the cheering here is for the wrong side in the cosmic war. Milton goes on to link this moment to current human discord in the European wars of religion. The ancient demons, he notes, are in more concord than are his contemporaries.

Milton is of course using language from the fallen world to describe action that took place before the Fall. He turns to the metaphor of the cheerful sun at the very instant that our relationship with nature is about to change, as we face life after the Fall in a world where "Heaven's cheerful face" has become a metaphor. Put differently, after Satan does his work, the cheering sun will be quite different from what it was before. Natural cheer is evoked at the moment that it is about to become the substitute for a lost plenitude.

The loss of cheer in Milton is not merely theological. It is also biographical. A bit later in the poem, Milton applies the crisis of nature to himself. Lamenting his own blindness, he cries out in pain:

> Thus with the year
> Seasons return; but not to me returns
> Day . . .
> . . . .
> But cloud instead, and ever-during dark
> Surrounds me, from the cheerful ways of men
> Cut off. (book 3, vv. 47–50)

The earlier image of cheerful Nature, evoked as it is about to be lost, is recalled in the image of cheerful men, evoked because unreachable, with Milton's own line suggesting the violence by placing "Cut off" at the end of the phrase. Cheerful society is like the return of the day, or the return of spring, but not to Milton, who lives in darkness and solitude.

Milton speaks here for all of those who suffer without change, for those in chronic pain, for those with wounds that will never heal. Nature may have its own rhythm, but for some, such as blind Milton, that rhythm brings no cheer. Rather, it seems to mock his suffering, because all days are the same. By contrast, Satan's first vision of earth is compared to "the break of cheerful dawn" on the "brow of some high-climbing hill" (book 3, vv. 545–47).

It is, predictably, Adam and Eve who are most involved with cheer in Milton, at a crucial moment that recalls the Shakespearean tragic cheer we saw earlier. In book 5 of *Paradise Lost*, in one of the several lyric interludes in the poem, Eve awakens from a dream in which she has tasted the apple and known bliss. Adam corrects her and reminds her that evil thoughts may sometimes enter and leave the mind "and leave no spot or blame behind." He then encourages her to raise her spirits, echoing the figure we have seen linking nature and morning and recalling Erasmus's insistence on the "serene" brow as the ideal face: "Be not disheartened then, nor cloud those looks / That wont to be more cheerful and serene / than when fair morning first smiles on the world" (book 5, vv. 122–24). The reference to "first" smiling is beautifully ironic, since we are on the cusp of a moment that will change human history. Blind Milton never sees this smile, but he paints Eve's cheer as even better than nature's. Indeed, one of the conditions of prelapsarian life may be that the force of gay nature is not particularly needed, since humans are already cheerful.

Here we have an account of the earliest ever instance of social cheer, the very first scene in human history of one person telling another to "cheer up." And cheer up Eve does: "So cheered he his fair spouse, and she was cheered" (book 5, v. 129). The problem, however, is that this very act of cheering leads to a blunder. The "cheer" that Eve finds again after Adam's "cheering" is deceptive. She sheds a tear, but it comes *after* she is supposed to be restored, suggesting that things have not quite been repaired. As Esther Yu has shown, Adam seems unable to accept the basic rhythms of life in Eden. He's too impatient. In his haste to cheer Eve up, he "lulls the conscience into a deceptive state of repair, sapping the demonic dream of its cautionary power."[8] Adam wants things back to normal, and quickly, whereas, after the dream, which prefigures the later Fall, they are not. Adam kisses Eve, "So was all clear'd, and to the Field they haste" (book 5, v. 136).

We've had "cheer," now all is "clear," and everything seems to have returned to normal. Except, of course, that it hasn't, and the very proximity of the two words — "cheer" and "clear" — should put us on alert that all is not well in the fields of Eden. Adam's reflex gesture of cheering Eve up is exactly the wrong thing to do, for it reinstates a condition of cheerfulness that he then completely misreads. Whereas Shakespeare's Player Queen sees her husband's loss of cheer as a danger signal, Adam's confident restoration of Eve's cheer is a catastrophic mistake. It is cheerful reading as bad reading. Milton reminds us that when "cheer" compensates for disappointment, it may lead us astray.[9]

Milton introduces historical contingency into the natural history of cheerfulness. He takes the traditional ideas of nature as a healing force and of cheerful reading as the compensation for discomfort and doubt and turns them inside out. Milton's ironic meditation on cheer in book 5 of *Paradise Lost* suggests that cheer lies at the very origin of misreading. It is both the name of prelapsarian "natural" contentment and the indicator that such contentment is doomed.

Compensatory Cheerfulness

Although Adam and Eve's dream work is unfortunate, Milton is quite clear, elsewhere in his work, about the importance of cheerfulness for community identity. In the final sections of his treatise on censorship and freedom of thought, the *Areopagitica*, Milton praises cheerfulness. But he repurposes the power of the affect. He nationalizes it. He links freedom to the natural cheerfulness of the English people. He claims that it is their "alacrity" that distinguishes them from all other nations. The freedom of the press is the "lively and cheerful presage of our happy success and victory," and the mark, a few sentences later, of "the cheerfulness of the people" that springs up to guard its own freedom and safety.[10]

With this defense of the cheerful English, Milton turns a natural metaphor with theological overtones into a figure of national character. Unlike Montaigne's Brazilian cannibal, whose gaiety emerges

only at the moment of death, turning potential tragedy into mar-
tyrdom and triumph, Milton's cheerful English will triumph in life
through political victory. Milton's formulation suggests the difficulty
of tracing the origins of such cheer. For the troubadours, it erupts
from nature. Here, it seems to come from the fortuitous encounter
of some kind of inherent national character and the new technology
of print, now freely circulated. Are the English cheerful because
they are free to write? Or because they will soon be victorious? Does
cheer come from victory, or vice versa?

   This national dimension of Milton's cheerfulness is replayed and
transformed in the work of one his greatest poetic disciples, William
Wordsworth. Wordsworth brings us back to the nineteenth century,
and we can now build on what we have seen in earlier moments of
lyric cheer. Wordsworth's debt to Milton is well known. In an 1802
sonnet called "London," Wordsworth complains to Milton about the
corruption of England: "England hath need of thee." Wordsworth
paints an England that has lost its spiritual identity ("inward happiness") and given itself over to selfishness. The English risk turning
into grasping merchants and petty tyrants, prey to the "low usurping wilfulness" that inflects Emerson's forced smiles. Wordsworth
praises Milton's poetic voice ("like the sea") and ends the poem celebrating Milton's journey: "So didst thou travel on life's common
way, / In chearful godliness; and yet thy heart / The lowliest duties
on itself did lay."[11] For Wordsworth, Milton's gift lies in his ability to
blend the godly and the humble "in chearful godliness." His godliness
still partakes of the cheerful community of believers evoked by such
biblical commentators as Erasmus and Hooker, whom we met earlier.
And yet he remained blessed with the humility to take on "the lowliest duties," which we might identify here as the scrum of English
politics. As both theological poet and political thinker — as bard of
natural cycles and human events — Milton's voice is still needed, it
would seem.

   The pursuit of "chearful godliness," in Wordsworth's world,
brings us back to the relationship of human beings to nature. We

find this connection explored in what is probably his most famous lyric, "Lines Written a Few Miles Above Tintern Abbey," published in the *Lyrical Ballads* of 1800. From the vantage point of an urban life, Wordsworth casts back to a moment of return to a site of natural beauty, which in turn reminds him of his youth. The sublime moment of watching the river Wye tumble over the rocks, shared with Wordsworth's sister, Dorothy, takes him back to a time "when like a roe I bounded over the mountains" (v. 69).[12] The intensity of the present moment both reminds the poet of his past experiences and points ahead: "In this moment there is life and food / For future years" (vv. 64–65). It is in the power of nature "to lead / From joy to joy" (vv. 125–26). The experience of delight or "joy" extends through time. Nature can "impress / With quietness and beauty" and feed the self "with lofty thoughts" (vv. 127–29). As the poet has matured, he has come to look on nature as something greater than the bounded site where he can hear the presence of "the still, sad music of humanity." It is "a sense sublime" (vv. 92 and 95). "In the mind of man, / A motion and a spirit, that impels / All thinking things, all objects of all thought, / And rolls through all things" (vv. 101–103). This sense of "spirit," as he treads through his beloved mountains, anchors the poet's thoughts and "all my moral being" (v. 112).

Fifty years earlier, Edmund Burke had noted in his *Philosophical Inquiry into the Origin of Our Ideas of the Sublime and Beautiful* that cheerfulness is *not* the province of the sublime and that "cheerful colors," with the possible exception of red, could never generate feelings of sublimity.[13] Here, however, Wordsworth seems to place cheerfulness at the service of the sublime. The moment of intensity is inflected by the voice of the sister. It is through the presence of the other, in her voice, that he connects to his past: "In thy voice I catch / The language of my former heart" (v. 118). In his sister, he hears what he once was. In this moment of spiritual union through voice, Dorothy becomes an earlier version of William. And it is in this moment of union with the beloved "friend" and with nature that the divine manifests itself: so that

> neither evil tongues,
> Rash judgments, nor the sneers of selfish men,
> Nor greetings where no kindness is, nor all
> The dreary intercourse of daily life,
> Shall e'er prevail against us, or disturb
> Our chearful faith that all which we behold
> Is full of blessings. (vv. 129–35)

The moment of sublime experience is a moment at which nature and humanity, past, present, and future, all converge in a "chearful faith." This moment convinces Wordsworth that blessings are all around and up ahead. The dyad of the poet and his sister share the sublimity of the moment.

Cheerfulness emerges as the vehicle through which the momentary experience of the sublime can be reconnected to time. Because cheerfulness involves a nuance of futurity, it inflects the "faith" that Wordsworth and his sister can have in the future, in a future of blessings. Wordsworth appropriates the literary cliché of gay nature that we saw as far back as the troubadours, but now projects it through time, as an article of faith, offering moral guidance. All cheerfulness involves a nanoparticle of faith in the future, in the lightness of the next moment. Here we get not "faith" — which would suggest a theological dimension — but "chearful faith," a belief, through time, in the blessings of natural beauty. The cyclical movement of nature, cheering us each morning or each spring in the lyric tradition, is now absorbed into the narrative of the poetic consciousness, which recasts time and history as a story of blessings. Though human actions may often destroy natural cheer, cheerfulness returns as a memory of a future full of blessings.

Wordsworth's appropriation of the idea of cheerful nature is elsewhere developed in a context that should be familiar to us from our reading of Dickens and Alger, a context involving economic competition and industrial development. This comes in a longer work, the pastoral poem "Michael." "Michael" is the last poem in the expanded collection of the *Lyrical Ballads* that Wordsworth published together with Samuel Coleridge. It was an important poem to Wordsworth, who felt that it revealed the depth of feeling available even to the simplest and poorest of men. And, indeed, the story of Michael is introduced by an unnamed narrator, presumably Wordsworth, who reveals that he learned it when he was young and himself lived without books, close to "the power of Nature," where "the gentle agency / Of natural objects" (vv. 29–30) led him to recognize passions outside himself.[14]

Like *Paradise Lost*, "Michael" is the story of a fall from grace, filtered through allusions to the sacrifice of Isaac by Abraham.[15] It involves the destructive power, not of pleasure and sin, but of money and debt. Michael is a shepherd who lives with his wife, Isabel, and his son, Luke, near Grasmere, in the English Lake Country, where Wordsworth himself resided. Michael lives in a close relationship to the natural world, building his small household across the years through frugality and hard work. Though now over eighty years old, we are told, Michael never fails to love and appreciate "the green Valleyes, and the Streams and Rocks," for it is there that he has lived in harmony, "where with chearful spirits he had breathed / The common air" (vv. 63–64). We might understand "common" in a variety of senses, as implying an air free to all (like the "free land" that Michael will treasure throughout the poem), but also suggesting the humility and simple honesty of the shepherd. Michael's "chearful spirits" are both the consequence of his virtue and hard work and the attribute of a nature that seems to reward and strengthen that virtue. There, in the "common air," upon the hills, we learn, Michael has been through events of "hardship, skill or courage, joy or fear." "These hills," Wordsworth asserts, "were his living Being, even more / Than his own Blood" (vv. 74–75). So great was the virtue and constancy of Michael's estate that his house was taken as a landmark and guidepost by neighbors and travelers, led by the light that unvaryingly shone through the window each evening. It relies on an economic steady state, a chthonic relationship between the laboring shepherd and what Wordsworth calls a bit later "English Land" (v. 325).

Our reading of natural cheer in earlier poets, from the troubadours to Milton, should alert us that the close link between Michael's
spiritual life and the "chearful spirits" of the land involves something more than the ideologies of nature commonly associated with
European Romanticism. The connection goes very far back in the
history of poetry. Wordsworth draws on that tradition and turns it
into narrative to update traditional scenarios of cheerful inspiration.
"Tintern Abbey" activated cheer as the defining feature of the poet's
"faith" persisting through time. In "Michael," though, cheerfulness
is marked by social class. Michael's life is not the cheerful life of
poets such as Bernard de Ventadour, Guido Cavalcanti, or even William Wordsworth, who absorb gaiety from the spring to sing their
lyrics. Here, cheerfulness involves work. It resides in the land and
links the peasant to nature. Beyond that, it is not readily available
to the workingman. The cycle of the years, says Wordsworth, "left
the Couple neither gay perhaps / Nor chearful, yet with objects and
with hopes / Living a life of eager industry" (vv. 123–25). The poet in
"Tintern Abbey" gets a "chearful faith" in the future. The peasant
gets cheer from the land, but otherwise, only "objects and hopes."

Bernard de Ventadour contrasted cyclical gay cheer with the contingency of human action, specifically, amorous betrayal. History
weighs on Michael, as well, for into this scene of peasant stability
comes the disruptive power of debt. We learn midway through the
poem that there is a claim on the land and that Michael needs money.
He considers two options: One is that he might sell part of the land,
thereby destroying both his livelihood and the legacy for his son,
Luke. This would constitute a break in the cycle of productivity, in
the relationship to the land. The other solution is for Luke to leave
the country and seek employment in the city, presumably to return
later. The danger there, of course, is that he might not return or that
his simple country virtue might be corrupted by urban life. The
poem mentions the precedent of the tellingly named Richard Bateman who left, found employment, went abroad to "foreign lands"
and became wealthy. Michael proposes "a chearful hope" (v. 255) that

Luke do the same: "Let us send him forth" (v. 290), says Michael in biblical cadences, proposing a "scheme" whereby a child would be, in effect, exchanged for the preservation of the steady-state economy of "cheerful spirits" and "the common air." This, he says, is his "chearful hope" (v. 254). Whatever seems "natural" or metaphorically prelapsarian about Michael's situation can be preserved only by the sacrifice of the son.

And indeed, no sooner has this idea been proposed than Isabel has reservations. "Thou must not go, / We have no other Child but thee to lose" (vv. 307–308), she complains to Luke. The adventurous Luke, however, brushes aside her objection: "The Lad made answer with a jocund voice, / And Isabel, when she had told her fears, / Recovered heart" (vv. 310–11). The image of the heart is a key figure in the poem, because it registers the emotional connections of the family members, as well as the level of their courage or hope. Isabel seems persuaded by her son, and cheerfulness returns to the world of the poem: "Next morning Isabel resumed her work, / And all the ensuing week the house appeared / As cheerful as a grove in Spring" (vv. 314–16).

And yet, as in Adam's "cheering" of Eve in Milton, something is wrong. Luke's "jocund" answer to Isabel's worries has drowned out her well-founded solicitude. The disruption is signaled by the reversal of the very rhetorical trope that we have been tracing. No longer is the relationship to nature cheerful. Now the house, a human construction threatened by debt and abandonment, is metaphorically described as a natural site, as "a grove in Spring." The human world is described *as if* it were natural. Isabel generates a kind of domestic cheer to paper over her well-founded worry about her son. She creates a second-order cheerfulness, an artificial gaiety, a simulacrum of normalcy: "The house *appeared* / as cheerful as a grove in Spring" (vv. 315–16, my emphasis). Wordsworth offers up the cliché of natural cheer that we saw as far back as the troubadours, but he overturns it, deploying it to describe the endangered house as if it were a site of natural power. This metaphorical cheer is misplaced, a distraction.

And, indeed, Michael returns from the fields to announce that Luke is leaving the next day:

> To this word
> The House-wife answered, talking much of things
> Which, if at such notice he should go,
> Would surely be forgotten. (vv. 327–30)

Isabel consents, but grudgingly. She points out all the things that would be lost with Luke's departure — things that the poem itself forgets to share. All we know is that despite the cheer of the house, she is worried. "But at length / She gave consent" (vv. 330–31).

Isabel is right to worry. After a male-bonding visit to a sheep-fold that Michael has begun to build, Luke departs. Michael continues in his labors: "Once again / The Shepherd went about his daily work / With confident and cheerful thoughts" (vv. 446–48). But this is a mistake, for two lines after this seeming return to normalcy, we are told, "meantime Luke began / To slacken in his duty, and at length / He in the dissolute city gave himself to evil courses" (vv. 451–54). Before he's done, Luke has to flee the country, not, like Richard Bateman, to make a fortune abroad, but merely to hide.

As we saw in *Paradise Lost*, cheerfulness as the compensatory response to disaster can only be a mistake. At the very moment that Adam cheers Eve up, he is misreading. Similarly, Isabel exudes a kind of prosthetic cheerfulness in response to her son's jocundity. She pretends that everything is fine, and Michael returns to his cheerful ways, in communion with his flocks and the land. In both texts, those who should be wary let their guards down and end up as unwitting fools.

Wordsworth's focus is not on sin, as is Milton's, but on economics, as befits a poet under emerging capitalism. Both poets depict the consequences of cheerfulness as a compensation for some error or mistake in judgment. And Wordsworth goes beyond Milton by giving us competing versions of cheer, the originary cheer of the shepherd (and the youthful poet), at one with nature, and the second, compensatory "cheerfulness" of the household that Isabel generates in response to her son's confident jocundity. Her cheer is generated out of work, as is fitting in the world outside of Eden, and is mobilized to save Michael's elemental relationship to the land.

Wordsworth's use of the same word, "cheer," to refer to Michael's spiritual connection to "English Land," to the limits of the old couple's ambitions (no cheer, but "objects" and "hopes"), and to Isabel's attempt to paper over impending disaster effectively explodes the poetic tradition of cheerful nature that we saw going back to Cavalcanti and the troubadours. The woman fabricates cheer to keep the family on an even keel so that the old man can commune with the cheerful spirits of the place. Isabel's cheerful house provides the supporting frame for Michael's heedless return to the cheerful world of the hills. In the process, it distracts from what should be his legitimate caution regarding the fate of his child. We get two kinds of work (domestic and pastoral) and two kinds of cheer. The son is sacrificed for the father and for the continuation of a close relationship between the shepherd and "English Land."

The idea of natural cheerfulness or gaiety extends back to the very beginnings of vernacular European poetry. The image of a "natural cheer" set forth from the time of the troubadours opens the way to a consideration of the tension between human agency, on the one hand, and the cycles of nature, on the other. For the troubadours, it is linked to the generation of gay song. As we move across the lyric tradition, the language of cheerfulness is increasingly implicated in moments of crisis as human action — haste, foolishness — threatens the relationship to natural gaiety. Milton and Wordsworth will repurpose the vocabulary inherited from early lyric. In Milton's parable of Adam's cheering of Eve, cheerfulness becomes a figure for what must be lost with the Fall. And in Wordsworth, it provides the vocabulary for depicting the disruptions brought on by modern economic forces. The credit economy wreaks havoc on the peasant's relationship to the land. As a response, Wordsworth's peasants take refuge in a kind of prosthetic or counterfeit cheerfulness that is presented "as if" it were the product of a relation to the natural world, but instead masks a crisis of economic life. The poem borrows the language of natural cheer to describe a situation in which natural cheer is precisely what is in danger. Bernard de Ventadour can sing. Michael can only sacrifice his son.

In the preceding chapter, I suggested that in bourgeois society, cheerfulness often appears as the response to some type of crisis of the self. Here, in the midst of a crisis in the relationship between human desire and the land, cheerfulness becomes seriously problematic. It is no longer derived from nature. Rather, it counterfeits the cheer that the cycles of nature might provide. We thus run up against a kind of paradox in the depiction of cheer. On the one hand, new bourgeois pathologies of self-presentation seem to empty cheerfulness of its affective strength, turning it into a mere cliché of selfhood, a kind of signpost of the ambitious character. The resistance to that process involves a turn to the venerable tradition of lyric cheer in nature. Yet poetry is caught up in the same economic processes that haunt bourgeois identity, and a poet such as Wordsworth can respond only by giving us situations in which cheerfulness is artifice, a momentary compensation that leads one into folly.

One possible response to this paradoxical situation is to reinvent cheer, not as a moral resource to be found in the relationship between the bourgeois self and nature, but as a source of generative style, both in writing and in self-construal. For writers such as Emerson and Nietzsche, to whom we now turn, cheerfulness will become a willed force that resides, not in the depths of the self or the natural world, but in the surfaces of art.

PART THREE

Modern Cheerfulness

CHAPTER TEN

The Gay Scientists:

Philosophy and Poetry

Festal Style

Cheerfulness is traditionally a modest thing. It is neither ecstatic nor static. It does not take us out of ourselves. Nor does it leave us mired in the dullness of our material bodies, stuck in what the Middle Ages called *acedia*. It can get us moving. It motivates and is shaped by our engagement with others. It brings a kind of influence, an agency, even when flung against powerful forces such as patriarchy or political treachery. It gives shape to the poet's appropriation of the power of nature. For the citizen under capitalism, cheerfulness inflects the relationship to the future, emerging at moments of struggle or crisis, in the winning and losing of fortunes and the fight for property. In such contexts, it can also falsify our relations with others, leading us to misread events and make foolish decisions as radical as Eve's and as problematic as Isabel's and Michael's. As cheerfulness is absorbed into modern bourgeois culture in these ways, however, a counterargument emerges that reinvents cheerfulness as antibourgeois and strips it of its moralism.

Once cheerfulness is associated with struggle in a culture of capitalist competition, we move quickly into another current of modern writing about emotion. We leave behind bourgeois or provincial life and the anxiety over success and fortune and enter the more rarefied zone of another great theme of nineteenth-century European culture — the fascination with the heroic, with strong individuals. There is an entire current of nineteenth-century writing about heroic personality, from the cult of Napoleon to such writers as Thomas Carlyle, Stendhal, and Dostoevsky. Two of the most insightful writers about the heroic, the American essayist Ralph Waldo Emerson and the German philosopher Friedrich Nietzsche, are also interested in cheerfulness. In this chapter, we will see that these writers work to turn cheerfulness inside out, pushing the idea of a superficial power or emotional energy as far as it can go, to the point where it sheds many of the connotations that have hovered around it since the end of the Middle Ages. For this topic, we must shift genres yet again and turn to the philosophical essay. For the poet Wordsworth, cheerfulness touched on the power of nature and on work. When we turn to the nineteenth-century essay, we can see cheerfulness emerge as philosophical style. Emerson and Nietzsche associate it with aesthetic experience. How do the characteristics of cheer (interaction of body and soul, appreciation for the surface, for the ephemeral, etc.) come to shape writing itself?

Nietzsche links morality and language in the final pages of the last essay he wrote while he was lucid, "Nietzsche contra Wagner" (1888). There, he evokes the question of how one can write philosophy in a state of pain. He recounts his own struggles with his health, which, he says, have made him "deeper." There are two alternatives to suffering, he says: One is to fall silent. The other is "like the American Indian who, however badly tormented, repays his tormentor with the malice of his tongue."[1] Nietzsche is of course recalling Montaigne, who, as we saw in Chapter 5, depicts the Brazilian cannibal tormenting his captors with the "gaiety" of his "countenance" just before he dies. Whereas gaiety is corporeal for Montaigne, residing in the face, what matters for Nietzsche is *language*. Whether or not we read the "American Indian" as a figure for Nietzsche himself, it is clear that he is raising here the question of the relationship between moral life ("deepness") and language ("malice," or mockery).[2] This shift to language will permit Nietzsche to reimagine cheerfulness as deep and violent, over against traditional accounts of bodily gaiety.

The body — so important in virtually every account we have seen of cheerfulness so far — now gives way to the word.

We can best understand the history of Nietzsche's yoking of cheer to style by turning to the American essayist Ralph Waldo Emerson. Nietzsche's admiration for Emerson is well known. In his 1882 book *The Gay Science*, he sets him apart as one of the four "masters of prose" (with Leopardi, Mérimée, and Walter Savage Landor) — because, paradoxically, they all write in ways that bring them close to poetry; they are seen as in a constant war with the poetic.[3] Emerson's 1850 collection of essays, *Representative Men*, puts us in the context of nineteenth-century hero worship. It studies a number of exemplary "types" representing different social functions and intellectual casts of mind: We get accounts of Napoleon, Swedenborg, and even Montaigne (as "The Sceptic"). The most powerful of these essays is Emerson's take on Shakespeare as the embodiment of "The Poet."

Emerson had written earlier about poetry without specific reference to Shakespeare in his second series of *Essays*, published six years prior. There, he stresses the ways in which the poet is a generator of new knowledge for humanity by the way she understands the world as a network of symbols or "emblems." Unlike the troubadour, whose poetry, as we saw in our last chapter, emerges from the cycles of nature, Emerson's poet supplants natural cheer with his genius: "His cheerfulness should be the gift of the sunlight" (p. 461).[4] The imagination that the poet exercises, claims Emerson, is not absent from other men. However, it is the poet who brings this knowledge to us and frees us from our limited imaginations: "Poets are thus liberating gods" (p. 461). The poet turns nature into symbols — that is, into language.

These themes are expanded and developed in the essay on Shakespeare. Emerson notes that two things characterize the poet. One is his ability, just noted, to turn natural phenomena into moral phenomena. It falls to the likes of Dante, Homer, and Shakespeare, he points out, to notice that "a tree had another use than for apples, and corn another than for meal" (p. 724). This "other use" is as an "emblem" of human thoughts. The poet turns things into signs, reading them as conveying "in all their natural history a certain mute commentary on human life" (p. 725). Through the poet's noticing, nature and humans are linked. The poet is able "to explore the virtue which resides in these symbols" (p. 725).

Shakespeare's role in all of this is to have manifested the power of the emblematic in a more general way than anyone else. His genius is such that it cannot be isolated in any one feature. Much as, for Spinoza, cheerfulness is everywhere in the body but nowhere excessive, for Emerson, there is a universal strength in Shakespeare's writing that is everywhere present, but impossible to pin down. One can get into the mind of Plato, says Emerson, but not into the mind of Shakespeare, which manifests itself in "that equality of power in farce, tragedy, narrative, and love-songs" (p. 723) that Emerson calls "incessant . . . merit." And he sums up Shakespeare's broader contribution as follows: "This power of expression, or of transferring the inmost truth of things into music and verse, makes him the type of the poet, and has added a new problem to metaphysics. This is that which throws him into natural history, as a main production of the globe, and as announcing new eras and ameliorations" (p. 723). The poet does not draw on the regenerative power of nature, as does the troubadour. In a much more aggressive way, he makes nature into language; Shakespeare, by virtue of his general genius, offers a language that in itself invents new "eras and ameliorations" that plunge him back into nature — as part of "natural history."

Emerson's formulation is striking for its doubleness: "This power of expression, *or* of transferring the inmost truth of things into music" (my emphasis). Creation, for the artist, involves a gesture of abstraction ("the inmost truth") that is then "transferred" into form, the language of music. Stanley Cavell has used the words "conversion" and "transfiguration" to describe the work of Emerson's language.[5] Those processes seem to be at work in Emerson's description of Shakespeare. But we can be even more precise. Because the poet is close to nature, expression is not a movement from inside to outside, but a movement *across*. He does not write what is hidden in himself. He reinterprets and reinvents the meanings that inhere already in nature, "the inmost truth of things." "No recipe can be given for the making of a Shakespeare," concludes Emerson, "but the possibility of the translation of things into song is demonstrated" (p. 723). Poetry is a form of translation. In this sideways movement, Emerson's account of Shakespeare's writing joins the repertoire of oblique, superficial motions that we have witnessed in our earlier chapters: the gaiety with which Montaigne leaps from passage to passage when he reads, the contagious cheer that zooms around the room in Hume's cheerful company, the slippage from the Godhead to creation in Julian of Norwich's account of a "chearfull" world. Yet here, as it will be for Nietzsche, that flitting is explicitly linguistic, linked to style and language.

For Emerson, the precision of Shakespeare's work involves the manifestation of a kind of complete power not in single lines, but generally, "like the tone of voice of some incomparable person, so this is a speech of poetic beings" (p. 723). Personal character and literary style here merge. Shakespeare is everywhere in his work and yet bigger than the whole opus. The result of this is one of the strong features of his work, which is that it is full of him, and yet it eschews personal reference: "In the poet's mind, the fact has gone quite over into the new element of thought, and has lost all that is exuvial. This generosity abides with Shakespeare" (p. 724). The gift of the poet is to present personal experience in such a way as to elide its personal nature. The poet makes the personal the general: "He knows the lesson by heart. Yet there is not a trace of egotism" (p. 724).

Emerson calls Shakespeare's gift a "generosity," a sense of expansiveness that sets the needs of the self aside in order to benefit the larger public community of readers, viewers, or listeners. Yet this transmutation of experience cannot be poetry unless it is marked by another force, one that frees it from obligation:

> One more royal trait properly belongs to the poet. I mean his cheerfulness, without which no man can be a poet — for beauty is his aim. He loves virtue not for its obligation, but for its grace. He delights in the world, in man, in

woman, for the lovely light that sparkles from them. Beauty, the spirit of joy
and hilarity, he sheds over the universe. The true bards have been noted for
their firm and cheerful temper. (p. 724)

Emerson clearly recalls the ancient link between cheer and the
Latin *hilaritas*. Like his literary hero Montaigne, he takes cheerfulness as a force that frees the self from obligation. Yet he goes beyond
Montaigne, for unlike any other writer we have seen, Emerson links
morality to aesthetics, virtue to poetry. It is the mediating term,
"cheerfulness," that makes this possible. The poet translates the
world into a set of "moral emblems," yet he does this not to create rules, in the manner of moral philosophy, but because virtue
is beautiful — "for its grace." Emerson's Shakespeare takes grace
from things and gives joy back to the universe. Emerson echoes and
corrects Hamlet talking to Rosencrantz and Guildenstern ("man
delights not me, no, nor woman either") when he proclaims that
the poet "delights in the world, in man, in woman." In contrast to
the hesitant tragic hero, unable to take pleasure in the world, the
Emersonian poet sees the universal light in everything. This light is
then converted into beauty in poetry, "things into song." He goes on
to mention Homer, Chaucer, and Saadi before concluding, "Not less
sovereign and cheerful, — much more sovereign and cheerful — is the
tone of Shakespeare. His name suggests joy and emancipation to the
heart of men. . . . He touches nothing that does not borrow health and
longevity from his festal style" (p. 724).

What is remarkable here is what we might call the horizontal
nature of Emerson's thinking. Despite his reliance on the conventional language of "expression" to describe the poet's process, the
poet's cheerfulness seems to come not from some interior genius,
but from his "aim," which is beauty. Having the proper goal generates the proper means. The end generates the event. Art is a form of
translation between zones of experience, a displacement from nature
to language and back. Style lends health to things.

This account of the procedures of the poet unfolds in parallel with

Emerson's description of the healthy life in another of the 1844 essays, "Experience." Here, Emerson focuses on the contingent nature of human experience. He evokes the loss of his young son to assert that even grief is limited in its power over us through time. He stresses the danger of too much reflection, which can lead only to unhappiness, because it mires the self in critical skepticism. It is important to keep touch with the everyday contingencies of experience: "Do not craze yourself with thinking, but go about your business anywhere. Life is not intellectual or critical, but sturdy" (p. 478). This sturdiness can keep us balanced. The key to life, he says, is to remain between the abyss of excessive reflection and the banality of the merely material: "We live amid surfaces," he says, "and the true art of life is to skate well on them." More horizontality. The emphasis on the surface links Emerson's own moral thinking to his account of Shakespeare's poetics, which both takes delight from things and returns light to them without dipping into the abyss of critical thought: "Life is not dialectics" (p. 478).

The activity of "skating well" is given impetus, Emerson goes on to point out, by Shakespeare's ability to see "the splendor of meaning that plays over the visible world" (p. 724). Shakespeare knew that objects were not merely objects. They were emblems, things waiting to become song. Apples and corn are things that bear, as we saw a moment ago, "a second and finer harvest to the mind, being emblems of its thoughts," conveying to it a "certain mute commentary on human life" (p. 725). This commentary, in turn, is made available to "public amusement." In this capaciousness and humility (Shakespeare led "an obscure and profane life," p. 725), Shakespeare was able to move beyond such peers as Moses, Swedenborg, and Goethe, who "beheld the same objects," but derived from them "commandments, all-excluding mountainous duty" (p. 726). For them, life became "ghastly, joyless, a pilgrim's progress." Only Shakespeare, he concludes in the last paragraph, was able to turn his vision of knowledge into play, showing that "right is more beautiful than private affection; and love is compatible with universal wisdom" (p. 726).

Cheerful Considerations by the Way

Emerson returned to these questions of morality and aesthetics a decade after he wrote the Shakespeare essay. In 1860, he published the first edition of his *Conduct of Life*. These texts were written under the shadow of the impending Civil War and then revised sixteen years later for the centennial of the American Revolution. The thematic connections to *Representative Men* are clear enough, in that Emerson — who was generally in favor of the war — dwells here on questions of strength and celebrates the kinds of heroism he expects will emerge from the coming conflict. The heroes of politics and culture (Napoleon, Shakespeare) give way to the American heroes who are about to make their marks. We have seen how Emerson's understanding of poetry constitutes a kind of translation that makes the natural world into song. With *Conduct of Life*, we come explicitly to the question of Emerson's own writing, what he calls "this garrulity of advising" (p. 1079).

The nine essays in *Conduct of Life* focus on different themes ("Beauty," "Power," "Illusions") that might shape a person's life. Two essays before the end, however, he digresses to add a somewhat general essay that both sums up the others and diverges from the whole. This is his "Considerations by the Way." "Considerations" begins with a reflection on the limits of didactic prose. He is perforce a writer of counsel, he notes, yet rarely do others take his advice. Because of this, one should not seek to teach through lessons, but rather to inspire: "What we have, therefore, to say of life, is rather description, or, if you please, celebration, than available rules" (p. 1079). Thus, he is working out a new kind of moral writing that is not prescriptive, but celebratory. He wants a celebration in language that involves a praise of "vigor," which he claims is "contagious." "Whatever makes us either think or feel strongly adds to our power, and enlarges our field of action" (p. 1079), he says, in language that might remind us of Spinoza's fascination with affects and strength. It is souls who inspire us. Society wants amusement: "I wish that life should not be cheap, but sacred. I wish the days to be as centuries, loaded, fragrant" (p. 1080). To achieve this, he argues, we must define ourselves as strong individuals. This involves strength as literary style.

Emerson here appears at his most aristocratic, turning his back on the "masses," who, he says, are "rude, lame, unmade, pernicious" (p. 1081). By contrast, Emerson aims for what he calls "new nobilities of power" (p. 1084), which can emerge only out of challenges — we can surmise, out of the coming war. Yet he also departs from the Shakespeare essay by linking the questions of conflict and challenge to the productions of artists: "What would painter do, or what would poet or saint, but for crucifixions and hells?" (p. 1084). Structuring this push and pull of art and violence, says Emerson, is nature, which "watches over all" and which produces civilization out of barbarism. "Out of Sabine rapes, and out of robbers' forays, real Romes and their heroisms come in fulness of time" (p. 1084). It is a cheering thought — though not particularly comforting for the Sabines or the robbed.

In the final pages, Emerson ventures to offer what he calls "the first obvious rules of life" (p. 1088). First is that one must maintain oneself — that is, earn a living. Second is that one must "get health." Like Montaigne, Emerson argues that the soul is shaped by the body. For him, moral life follows health. The sick man cannot be heroic in the way Emerson desires. What follows from health is "a fine disposition" (p. 1089) which is more important than talent. "Nothing will supply the want of sunshine to peaches, and, to make knowledge valuable, you must have the cheerfulness of wisdom. Whenever you are sincerely pleased, you are nourished. The joy of the spirit indicates its strength. All healthy things are sweet-tempered" (p. 1089).

Here, Emerson swirls together his vision of natural order (sunshine) with psychological power and morality — all underpinned by an aristocracy of spirit. The cheerfulness of wisdom comes from grasping the larger order of things — that all events tend toward nature's plan. It leads to a kind of self-producing dynamic: "And so of cheerfulness, or a good temper, the more it is spent, the more of it remains. . . . It is observed that a depression of spirits develops the germs of a plague in individuals and nations." And he goes on to link the heroic to the psychology of the self when he proclaims, "Power dwells with cheerfulness; hope puts us in a working mood, whilst despair is no muse and untunes the active powers" (p. 1089).

Emerson is here working out a model of the self as creator — as artist or hero — that moves against the old cliché of the poet as a figure of melancholy. And just as in the Shakespeare essay cheerfulness was the term that links individual genius to the social world, here, in a more political/moral vein, the notion comes up again as a way of linking nature's plan for bringing good out of all things to the specificity of human endeavor. If cheerfulness is linked to physical health and vigor, it is what can make us heroic.

It is also a motivating force in the social world, through conversation. Conversation brings us into a situation where we can make ourselves useful. "Make yourself necessary to somebody" (p. 1095), notes Emerson. And he concludes the essay by returning to the interaction between individual and group. Nature, earlier seen as the leveler of all events, is now replaced by "the race." "The race is great, the ideal fair, but the men whiffling and unsure." Only "the hero" endures, as "he who is immovably centered" (p. 1096). And the last lines of the text stress the few "great points" of culture: escape from falsity, courage to be ourselves, love of the simple and the beautiful, "independence, and cheerful relation," added to the "wish to serve" (p. 1096). These are the rules for life according to Emerson, the American sage, in 1860.

"My Cheerful Strokes"

The link posited by Emerson between writing and cheerfulness finds an echo and a development in his disciple Nietzsche. Whereas Emerson has spoken of cheerfulness as a kind of power, Nietzsche, who rejects Emerson's Yankee optimism about the smooth course of history, unpacks the violence at the heart of different forms of cheer. Emerson's emphasis on horizontality and lightness provides an opening, of sorts, for Nietzsche's reinvention of cheerfulness. Emerson still resides within a traditional notion of the cheerful as social. Nietzsche turns that notion inside out.

Nietzsche had tackled one notion of cheerfulness as early as his 1871 book *The Birth of Tragedy*. There, he takes issue with an Enlightenment image of Greek art as "cheerful" (*heiter*); that is, serene, balanced. Nietzsche calls this affect the "smugness and cheerfulness of theoretical man," which he associates with the decadent Apollonian taming of the earlier Dionysian impulse he connects to music.[6] Only by looking truly into the "inner, terrible depths of Nature" linked to the figure of Dionysos, he says, can one grasp "the serious and significant concept of 'Greek cheerfulness.'" This is what has been replaced by a "misunderstood notion of . . . 'cheerfulness' . . . identified with a condition of unendangered ease and comfort" (p. 4).[7] True cheerfulness is dangerous, and this danger is linked to the violence of the predatory warrior classes. As he notes in the *Genealogy of Morals*, "the 'boldness' of noble races . . . their hair-raising cheerfulness and profound joy in all destruction" came together in the image of the Goth, associated with the Germanic tribes of old.[8] Next to the Gothic delight in destruction, the "serenity" of the Greeks looks inauthentic.

As his work unfolds, Nietzsche connects the violent cheerfulness celebrated here back to art by moving away from the Goths and the Greeks. In his later writing, he locates it in the southern European culture of Provence, Spain, and Italy. It is the Mediterranean culture of the Romance languages that can offer the antidote to the deep and gloomy obsessions of the Germans as they misread the Greeks. In *The Case of Wagner*, he locates this cheerfulness in the music of Bizet and in the culture of the Mediterranean. He writes that one must "Mediterraneanize" music. Then he expounds: "The return to Nature, health, cheerfulness, youth, *virtue*!"[9] And in a way that is even more explicit than Emerson's juxtaposition of cheer and style, Nietzsche associates this cheer with his own writing. He describes his own style, "my cheerful strokes" (*meinen heitern Strichen*) (p. 20,

p. 624), as what has exposed the decadence of the music of Wagner and of German culture. Cheer and writing are thus intertwined. Whereas Emerson had stood outside of cheerfulness and projected it as characteristic of Shakespeare at a moment of oncoming civil war, Nietzsche takes that war into himself, and along with it, writing as a cheerful practice.[10]

Nietzsche's philosophy is a philosophy of transformation, of what Richard Schacht has called a "new approach to the question of human worth."[11] His 1882 book *The Gay Science* (*Die Fröhliche Wissenschaft*), offers a way into some of his most important ideas while weaving a picture of his own travels and sufferings. The book is bracing and beautiful. It marks Nietzsche's break with much of his earlier insistence on gloom and critique and offers an attempt to imagine the transformation of humanity, a blast toward the future. Indeed, he recalls earlier discussions of cheerfulness when, toward the end of the third book of *The Gay Science*, in aphorism 239, he discusses the "contagion" of emotion: "One single joyless [*Freudlos*] person is enough to create constant sullenness and dark skies for an entire household," he writes. "Happiness [*Glück*] is not nearly as contagious a disease." He here overturns Hume's claim that it is cheerfulness that is contagious.[12] The opposition of contagious "joylessness" and uncontagious "happiness" opens up a space for a cheerfulness that would be not contagious, but willed. And that is what Nietzsche offers us.

Scholars of *The Gay Science* have often dwelt on the last word in the title, the idea of what a "science" or "knowledge" (*Wissenschaft*) would be for Nietzsche at the moment that he seems to turn to the future. Yet no less important is the concept of gaiety.[13] The book features a subtitle, in Italian, "La Gaya Scienza," as if he wanted to free himself from the Teutonic traditions of philosophy and aesthetics.

What, exactly, is a "gay science"? On May 1, 1323, a group of seven poets from Toulouse, in southwestern France, sponsored a contest to promote poetry composed in the Occitan language. The idea was to revive the culture of the troubadours, who had flourished in the previous century.[14] Though the contest continued into modern times as a commemoration of the culture of old Provence, it generated little in the way of important or original verse. Yet the organizers were diligent. They produced extensive guides to writing poetry, listings of the laws of versification — how to use syllables correctly, the importance of the twelve-syllable line, the different kinds of rhyme, and so on. These texts were collected in the nineteenth century under the title *Las flors del gay saber o Las leys d'amors* (The flowers of the gay science or laws of love). As guides, they are striking for their dryness, for their lack of poetry. Yet what matters is the title, which suggests a cheerfulness linked to knowledge and to poetry — the very intersection of concerns touched on by both Emerson and Nietzsche.

We should not be surprised, given Nietzsche's grounding in the study of philology, that he seeks out a historical origin or embodiment of cheerfulness. The Goths and the Greeks give way to the Mediterraneans. In *Beyond Good and Evil* (1886), where he introduces the crucial notions of the "master morality" and the "slave morality," he concludes with the assertion that love as passion, which is the specialty of Europe, is noble in origin. He credits it to "the Provençal knight-poets, those magnificent and inventive human beings of the 'gai saber' to whom Europe owes so many things and almost owes itself" (p. 398).[15]

It is worth pointing out that the phrase "gai saber," or "gay knowing" that is so important for Nietzsche is not, so far as I can determine, ever actually used in the corpus of troubadour poetry. This matters, since the troubadour corpus is limited and our knowledge of their language in some measure reconstructed after the fall of Cathar culture in the early thirteenth century. The troubadours, as we noted in the previous chapter, link "gay song" to the beauty of spring and nature. But the phrase "gai saber," which sums up everything for Nietzsche, appears to be a kind of branding gesture. It seems to be an invention of the late-coming festival organizers I mentioned above. In *Las flors del gay saber*, poetry, the technical construction of verse, is assumed to be linked to emotional and psychic transcendence through love. But the "knowledge" or "saber" presented is the body of didactic rules for writing. Nietzsche's idea does not, in other words, come from the troubadour poets themselves, but from commentary, from a text by the latecomers, the historians eager to maintain a tradition that was already in decline. This is nicely ironic, when we recall Nietzsche's status as a theorist of artistic decadence.

The moral and psychological implications of the thematic blending of poetry, love, and nobility seem to have been Nietzsche's own addition. They are certainly not central to the text of *Las flors del gay saber*, which posits anything but a new morality. But we can see why the troubadours are useful for Nietzsche. They bring his interest in warrior culture (the predatory German tribes) together with art (the misunderstood Greeks). Emerson turned to the soldiers of the American Civil War to connect his idea of cheerful writing to some type of heroism. His "heroic" poet Shakespeare led an obscure and "generous" life, burying his ego. To turn cheerfulness inside out, Nietzsche looks elsewhere. Through his caricature of the work of the troubadours, Nietzsche finds a seeming historical proof that in southern Europe, moral transcendence, emotional lightness, poetry, and warrior identity were one.[16]

The key discussion of cheerfulness in *The Gay Science* comes in book 5. Originally, *The Gay Science* had ended with the autobiographical excurses of book 4, in which Nietzsche speaks of his illness and his joy at having survived another year and where he closes with the phrase "Incipit tragoedia," "The tragedy begins." After this moment, Nietzsche had turned away from the text to write the prophetic fiction *Thus Spake Zarathustra*. He added book 5 of *The Gay Science* somewhat later, in 1887. In the added book, he turns immediately to the spiritual situation of European civilization. "How to understand our cheerfulness" (*Was es mit unserer Heiterkeit auf sich hat*) is the opening tag to book 5.[17] How, he asks, can one be cheerful after the most important recent event, the death of God? Surely, he notes, this new knowledge should bring with it despair, since "our entire European morality" (p. 199) (*unsre ganze europäische Moral*, p. 255) is now in ruins. Why are we not worried?

Nietzsche answers this question with one of his characteristic oblique questions that is also an assertion: "Are we perhaps not still too influenced by *the most immediate consequences* of this event?" (p. 199, his italics). These consequences, he says, are experienced "much like a new and barely describable type of light, cheering, relief, amusement, encouragement, dawn."[18] That is, we are not worried because that thing we feel is relief and new possibility. We experience cheerfulness as the consequence of an absence, not, like the characters in Dickens, as the response to a struggle. Any terror at the consequences of the death of God will have to wait. We are in a kind of middle moment, between a dead bourgeois aesthetics and morality (with their distorted idea of cheerfulness as "unendangered ease and comfort") and some new turn to the tragic. To describe this moment, he adds a striking metaphor: "Finally the horizon seems clear again . . . finally our ships may set out again . . . maybe there has never been such an 'open sea'" (p. 199).[19] It is striking that Nietzsche slips from a language of theology into a language of time, climate, light, and movement. The break with a theological past is enacted in his own sentence. It is powered by the idea of cheerfulness, which can drive humanity forward. And cheerfulness is in turn figured poetically, by the image of the open sea.

The word *Fröhlichkeit* in the German title of the *Gay Science* unmistakably echoes Luther's Bible and the "cheerful giver" of the Second Letter to the Corinthians — "einen fröhlichen Geber hat Gott lieb" (9:7) — to recall again Luther's famous phrase. Immanuel Kant had used the term *Fröhlichkeit* extensively in his 1803 treatise *On Pedagogy* to refer to the happiness that students should derive from a combination of correct religious instruction and play.[20] Yet the value of the term in this specific context may also be linked to its etymology. The words *Fröhlich* and *Froh* come from a Proto-Germanic stem suggesting "quick" or "glad." We might think here of the Dutch word *vrolijk* and the English *frolic*, which suggest a kind of energetic gaiety and movement.[21] The term suggests an ephemeral dimension, a "quickness" that is here and then gone, which seems appropriate to

Nietzsche's claim that we are now in the first flush of our liberation from the old morality.

In *The Gay Science*, Nietzsche thus rewrites Luther's Christian vocabulary. The answer to the death of traditional morality is the metaphor of the dawn. The answer to moral confusion is the image of the sea, with the philosopher as seafarer, like Odysseus. We can see here why Emerson's description of Shakespeare offers a kind of opening for Nietzsche. For the poet, says Emerson, everything natural becomes a symbol bearing moral meaning. He uses the image of light, which Shakespeare transfigures, as his imagination plays across the surface of things. Nietzsche picks up on the horizontal movement of Emerson's image. For Nietzsche, the crisis of European morality produces a new cheerfulness that implies a deep violence, but that can be described only poetically, in the literary images of the dawn and the surface of the open sea. In contrast to Emerson's comfortable assurances about Shakespeare's "festal style," Nietzsche takes account of the violence and will required for a new cheerfulness. Nietzsche appropriates Emerson's metaphors of light and horizontality and links them to a new image of a heroic journey, inverting them and reinventing them. It is, we note, an epic or romance journey on the sea. It is not the rambling and raging of tragedy, as if the "tragic" ending to book 4 of *The Gay Science* had now been suspended for a moment and the movement forward required a return to literary journeying. Violence is refracted into poetry.

Given the central role of art, music, and poetry in Nietzsche's conception of human development, it is worth locating the intersection between cheerfulness and artistic creation. It is one thing to try one's hand at writing troubadour lyrics, as Nietzsche does in the appendix to *The Gay Science*. It is quite another to provide an aesthetic for the new ethos of moral cheerfulness that he advances.

If we understand ourselves only through art, then our new cheerfulness, after the death of God, must involve a new type of art. Nietzsche locates this new art either in the music of Bizet's *Carmen* (that Mediterranean fiction) or in the poetry he has written himself.

Yet it is only in his very last works that he offers a full account of what he has in mind. The troubadours had been important in Nietzsche's earlier writing for their *historical* status and for the *thematic* content of their art. In the closing passages of "Nietzsche contra Wagner" (the final paragraphs of his career, in effect), Nietzsche links cheerfulness to the *medium* of art. He focuses on the "new" art needed for the new age of posttheological cheerfulness. It is "another kind of art — a mocking, light, fleeting, divinely untroubled, divinely artificial art" (*eine andre Kunst — eine spöttische, leichte, flüchtige, göttliche unbehelligte, göttlich künstliche Kunst*). The "mocking" dimension of his thinking may already be seen in description of this posttheological art as "divinely" artificial. And for this art, "what is first and foremost needed . . . is cheerfulness — any cheerfulness, my friends!" (*die Heiterkeit, jede Heiterkeit, meine Freunde!*).[22]

We can't help but notice that the term mentioned earlier, *Fröhlichkeit*, has given way to a different German word, *Heiterkeit*, which Nietzsche originally associated with the bourgeois distortion of Greek culture, back in *The Birth of Tragedy*. He uses both terms across his writing, so we need to be careful about drawing grand conclusions from this shift. Yet the implications of the vocabulary are worth noting. *Heiterkeit* takes Nietzsche away from the temporal and somatic connotations of *Fröhlichkeit* — as well as the Kantian resonances of a kind of cultivated equipoise. Now the connotations are visual. *Heiterkeit* takes us back to etymological roots suggesting "bright," "clear," "shining."[23] The earlier metaphorical interest in light and the surface of the sea is now incorporated, as it were, into Nietzsche's very language, because *Heiterkeit* contains brightness in itself. And, indeed, he goes on to describe the cheer of this new art in the final sentences, where he praises the surface, rejecting the will to truth that drives one to see what lies beneath the veil of surface ornament. Instead, he advocates stopping, "bravely at the surface, the fold, the skin; to worship appearance, to believe in shapes, tones, words, in the whole *Olympus of appearance!*" (p. 282).[24] This powerful formulation echoes and refines Emerson's idea that effective life consists of "skating well" on "surfaces." Emerson sets his skating metaphor against the "critical" faculty, which, he avers, leads only to "dialectics" and depression. Nietzsche leaves us with a vision of art that links the surface specifically to artistic form. Cheerfulness, which has always involved surfaces, is now located in the surface of art. The human face recedes. The turn to surface has both moral and artistic consequences. It involves — in contrast to Emerson — the violence of forgetting and the willful imposition of form on the material of art. Nietzsche evokes the technical materials of writing and representation — the fold, the skin, the musical note. Here, cheer plays only on the surface. Through our engagement with that surface, cheerfulness is both enacted and produced. The aesthetic violence of the rejection of depth becomes the violent morality of a new form of cheer.

Cheerful Stone

In Nietzsche, the metaphysics and bourgeois psychology that informed representations of cheerfulness in earlier moments are now gone. Nietzsche stretches the concept of cheerfulness about as far as it can go. He retains its salutary, generative dimension while dispensing with its psychological depth. What remains is art, surface. We are cheerful because we skate on that surface.

This modernist cheer promises a new aesthetics. It is taken up again, some forty years after "Nietzsche contra Wagner," in one of William Butler Yeats's late lyrics. This is the 1937 poem "Lapis Lazuli," dedicated to his friend Harry Clifton, who had given him the stone carving that appears in the poem. Yeats's situation, on the threshold of the Second World War, mirrors Emerson's in "Considerations by the Way." And like Emerson, Yeats rejects a response to the coming conflict that would lose sight of the imperatives of poetry. Here is how the poem begins:

> I have heard that hysterical women say
> They are sick of the palette and fiddle-bow,
> Of poets that are always gay,

> For everybody knows or else should know
> That if nothing drastic is done
> Aeroplane and Zeppelin will come out,
> Pitch like King Billy bomb-balls in
> Until the town lie beaten flat.[25]

Something "drastic" must be done to alleviate historical catastrophe, it would seem. Yeats evokes the opinion of what Emerson called "the Masses" with his canny claim that "everybody knows or else should know." A new war is coming, with the image of bombing raids blending into a vision of a pummeling, "Until the town lie beaten flat."

Just as Emerson implicitly distinguishes Shakespeare, the poet who "delights" in "men and women," from his tragic character Hamlet, Yeats turns to questions of representation. "All perform their tragic play," he continues, before evoking Shakespeare's tragic heroes and heroines: "There struts Hamlet, there is Lear, / That's Ophelia, that Cordelia." Yet he notes that when tragedy strikes, these characters "do not break up their lines to weep." Weeping is for the "hysterical women" of the first lines. The figures of literature, who have been created by the literary style that Emerson praises so highly in Shakespeare, are given the strength to continue their play despite the catastrophe: "They know that Hamlet and Lear are gay; / Gaiety transfiguring all that dread." Just as for Nietzsche art is seen to lie in the surface of representations, in the "fold" or the "note," here, it is the performer/performance, not the "real" actor behind the performance, who holds things together. In this account, gaiety — cheerfulness — is linked to the form of art, tragic or otherwise, to the power of structure, "trans-figuration" — to form a bulwark against "King Billy" and the disaster of war.

From here, Yeats expands his vision through time to consider the rise and fall of entire peoples. In the third stanza, he evokes "Old civilisations put to the sword." Against this historical tragedy, he praises the work of the Hellenistic sculptor Callimachus, whose delicate work "stood but a day." Then he comes to the heart of his

Nietzschean/Emersonian argument: "All things fall and are built again / And those that build them again are gay." Emerson argues that history is a "rag-merchant" who makes good things out of bad. Yeats, following Nietzsche's antimetaphysical gaiety, turns to the specific role of the poet as maker of forms. The "power" that Emerson linked to cheerfulness is here located in a specific figure, not the generalized hero, but the poet or troubadour as builder. "Those that build them again are gay."[26]

In Nietzsche, the moment of cheerfulness that emerges against darkness is shaped by the metaphors of the dawn and the open sea. Yeats gives us a different sort of allegory in the form of an ekphrastic description of a stone carving, to which he turns in the last movement of the poem:

> Two Chinamen, behind them a third,
> Are carved in Lapis Lazuli,
> Over them flies a long-legged bird
> A symbol of longevity;
> The third, doubtless a serving-man,
> Carries a musical instrument.

Here Yeats steps back from the tragedy of history, having moved from the local history of interwar Europe, through the "Old civilisations," now to China. He offers an account of the "Chinamen" as separate from everything that has gone before. The poem concludes with a scene of music making:

> There, on the mountain and the sky,
> On all the tragic scene they stare.
> One asks for mournful melodies;
> Accomplished fingers begin to play.
> Their eyes mid many wrinkles, their eyes,
> Their ancient, glittering eyes, are gay.

And with this triumph of art as the response to historical catastrophe, the poem ends. The three "Chinamen" stand as the alternative to tragedy and "dread." Their gaiety and cheer offer the figure of "those that build . . . again" on the ruins of history.

So far, so good. This is Emerson's and Nietzsche's heroic figure, now associated with the poet. The *Heiterkeit* of the Nietzschean philosopher and the "cheerfulness" of the Emersonian sage/hero have mutated into the triumph of Yeats's wise, wrinkled "Chinamen." Yet given the interest of both Nietzsche and Emerson in the role that surfaces play in the making of art, we cannot fail to notice the interpretive moment when Yeats confronts the materiality of the stone on which the "Chinamen" are carved. Just before the triumphant conclusion cited above, he muses:

> Every discolouration of the stone,
> Every accidental crack or dent
> Seems a water-course or an avalanche,
> Or lofty slope where it still snows
> Though doubtless plum or cherry-branch
> Sweetens the little half-way house
> Those Chinamen climb towards, and I
> Delight to imagine them seated there.

Here we see in action the process described by both Emerson and Nietzsche of the poet turning natural phenomena into emblems of the mind. Yeats constructs a setting for the Chinese sages by reading *into* the stone, turning each blemish into landscape. The surface itself is *already* art. Yet his own language points to the tentative nature of the exercise: "Every accidental crack or dent / *Seems* a water-course or an avalanche" (my emphasis) in winter, before he acknowledges that what we *should* be looking on ("doubtless") is a spring scenario of "plum or cherry-branch." The tension between what the generic convention of stone carving leads us to expect (spring) and what the stone *actually* looks like (snowy winter) sets into relief Yeats's own process of reading the world and transfiguring it into art. He is staging the transformation of raw material into form. But it also lends a tentative note to the triumphant conclusion, for from this revelation we might wonder if the "many wrinkles" of the wise eyes of the gay Chinese sages are not themselves already in the stone, rather than nuances produced by the artist's skill. Is wisdom itself nothing but an "accidental crack or dent"? As Nietzsche showed us, cheerfulness becomes art when it skims the surface, attending to the play of appearance, of "stopping bravely at the surface, the fold, the skin." The use of cheerfulness here mobilizes its ability to power and give shape to a moment of shimmering or wavering, between winter and spring, between the darkness of the death of God and the new light of dawn, between the cracks in the raw stone and the wrinkles in the faces of the wise. Nietzsche shifts cheerfulness away from its traditional location in the human face, setting it instead in the surface of the artwork. Yeats restores the face — but as art.

At the same time, however, the poem leaves open the status of the poet himself. Is he gay? We watch him in process as he constructs meaning by moving across the surface of things, yet he leaves us with the possibility that meaning inheres in nature itself, in the folds of the stone. The shift from the grand vision of civilizational collapse set up early in the poem to the focused account of the aesthetic object that ends it also suggests that the creation of art can come only through an act of the will, a deliberate forgetting or shutting out of the catastrophe around us. We recall that Yeats does not praise the *actors* in the play for not breaking up their lines "to weep" at the fact of tragedy. He praises the fictional creations, Hamlet and Cordelia. Only, it would seem, by willfully pushing aside the fact of historical catastrophe can the poet in Yeats embrace the redemptive character of art.[27]

Emerson, Nietzsche, and Yeats develop a strand of cheerfulness that locates it not in individual psychology or group dynamics (say, Dickens, or Hume), but in the medium of art itself, in the violence of form. A moment ago, I called this "modernist cheer." These writers embrace a heroic vision of cheerfulness that takes us out of the bourgeois culture of capitalism, with its ambitious strivers and economic crises, even as their own turn to a kind of aristocratic aestheticism might be seen as the reactionary response to those same struggles. The barely disguised conceptual violence that haunts their work — the images of war, death, and panic — suggests the strenuous effort of the will required to imagine a version of language and a vision of artistic form that would project energy and lightness while stopping bravely at the surface.

The language of art, however it is conceived, is constituted by some kind of relationship with the experience of life as it is or can be lived, and its formal aspects are one way in which this experience is conveyed. It need not be used in this way. As we will see next, the discourses of cheerfulness also can be used to repurpose old forms for new uses in a commodity culture where old ideals can be made to serve new ends.

CHAPTER ELEVEN

It Is Amazing!:

Self-Help and Self-Marketing

"A Sunshine-Maker"
In modern marketing culture, cheerfulness becomes an empty form. It provides a language that can mimic community experience while empowering a culture of the isolated self. It functions rhetorically to evoke earlier values for new communities of consumers and employees that those values no longer serve. This emptying out of cheerfulness follows on the developments we have seen across the nineteenth century. We have seen cheerfulness, threatened in the patrician society of Jane Austen's England, return, spread across the multiple characters who support the rise of Dickens's hero David Copperfield, only to be turned inside out in Nietzsche's heroic effort to reimagine morality aesthetically, in the surface, in the fold. Each of these forms of cheerfulness is, of course, distinct from the others. But all embody a flicker of power, a blink of confidence in the brighter instant about to arrive. "Finally, the horizon seems clear again," says Nietzsche. As this story moves into the twentieth and twenty-first centuries, the energizing force and practical utility of cheerfulness become themes in much modern popular culture.

Given the rise to international prominence of American lifestyles after World War I, it is to them that we turn. "Spectroscopic gayety" is the phrase used by F. Scott Fitzgerald in the quintessentially American modern novel *The Great Gatsby* to describe the brilliance of the parties thrown by his protagonist on his Long Island estate. A spectroscope is a super prism, a tool for splitting white light into the various colors of the rainbow. This is gaiety radiating in all directions. Fitzgerald's novel uncovers the darkness beneath the colors. His tragic heroine, Daisy Buchanan, speaks with the voice of cheer: "There was an excitement in her voice that men who had cared for her found difficult to forget: a singing compulsion, a whispered 'Listen,' a promise that she had done gay, exciting things just a while since and that there were gay, exciting things hovering in the next hour."[1] Daisy is the American descendent of Jane Austen's privileged cheer-expectant heroines. Gatsby's inability to bring her private gaiety into line with his "spectroscopic" cheer is at the center of his tragedy. Yet the mere fact that we see here a proliferation of different types of gaiety reminds us that cheer was generally in the air during the so-called Jazz Age. The year after *The Great Gatsby* was published, 1926, saw the formation of the first squad of female "cheerleaders," at the University of Minnesota.

The terrain was cleared for a popular explosion of cheerfulness even before the Great War. In 1911, the Boy Scouts organization published its first *Scouts Handbook*. The book combines advice about such practical skills as how to build a fire in the woods with moral encouragement toward a better life. The development of the self is governed by a "Scout Law," consisting of twelve virtues. The eighth of the twelve is cheerfulness. Here is how the Scouts define it: "Another scout virtue is cheerfulness. As the scout law intimates, he must never go about with a sulky air. He must always be bright and smiling, and as the humorist says, 'Must always see the doughnut and not the hole.' A bright face and a cheery word spread like sunshine from one to another. It is the scout's duty to be a sunshine-maker in the world."[2] Here, in a breathtaking bundle of clichés, the Scouts bring cheerfulness into everyday life for boys. No more of Ragged Dick's ironic "cheerin' thoughts" — these thoughts are without irony and are intended to turn every Ragged Dick into a successful David Copperfield.

We've seen this language before: the idea of contagion, the old metaphor of the cheering sun (now located inside the body of the scout),
the rapid leap from "sulky" to "bright and smiling," as if there were no
middle ground. The only new detail here is the strange reference to
"the humorist," whose words don't seem, in this context, at least, to
be humorous at all. But also interesting is the reference to the "Scout
Law," of which these sentences are an excerpt. "As the scout law intimates," suggests some kind of vague cloud of obvious meaning beyond
the specifics of each precept. A scout should have got it by now that
cheerfulness is called for. "The duty of always being cheerful cannot
be emphasized too much," continues the manual. The law authorizes
itself as it goes along, a rhetorical procedure that we will see repeated
in several forms of modern self-help throughout this chapter.

The Scouts go on to locate this cheer in a larger historical frame:
"A good scout must be chivalrous. That is, he should be as manly as
the knights or pioneers of old . . . . He should be cheerful and seek
self-improvement, and should make a career for himself."[3] The Scouts
skillfully tie together a knot of examples that we have seen through
our story — the chivalry of Chaucer's knights, the conversational
cheer of Hume's philosophers, and so on. In the process, the passage
slides easily from self-presentation, to upright morals, to professional
ambition. Montaigne's sage cheerfulness included an escape from
convention. Here, cheerfulness is the very quality that will turn the
boy into the king of conformists.

In the twentieth-century expansion of consumer and mass experience, cheerfulness circulates as a useful concept that can bring the
ethos of capitalist ambition into phase with older ethical concerns.
The Scouts' emphasis on skills of woodcraft and survival are intended
to prepare a new, mostly male class of consumers and producers, each
looking out for himself, for life in the rough world of the market-
place. Capitalism pits individuals against each other in a duel to the
death for resources and money. It is a lonely business. Scout cheerfulness gives it a heroic cast. The external diffusion of cheerfulness
will lead to professional success as the salesman or junior executive

brightens up the office. Now, however, actions that might appear to be self-serving or unctuous are recast as echoes of a heroic past. Each fledgling organization man, we learn, is, at heart, a wandering knight or a rugged trapper. He is helping society at large by seeing the doughnut instead of the hole. Cheer makes woodcraft ethically uplifting. Woodcraft grounds cheer in the practical world.

The rise of consumer capitalism, as the sociologist Arlie Russell Hochschild has shown, brings with it a new form of affective life.[4] Our most intimate emotions are repackaged as bits of information that shape our presentation of ourselves. We are remade as tokens of exchange. In a social and economic system that consumes and produces selves as commodities, the performance of cheerfulness becomes a value in itself. Gone now are the metaphysical shapings of early modern Christianity; gone the social cohesion of Enlightenment conversation; gone even the clear focus on the discrete individual, destined for distinction, that we saw in *David Copperfield*.

Yet there is a larger ideological mission here. For the Boy Scouts, cheerfulness does important mediating work to bind up the wounds caused by social and economic disruption. The terms set out above — survival in the forest and the pursuit of a career — obviously reflect two different stages of American cultural development set in juxtaposition and opening onto a new world of industrial and commercial expansion. One of the keys to the popularity of the Scouts and any number of subsequent "outdoors" and "youth" movements evolves from the way Scouting could make sense of a world in which mechanized labor and salesmanship were pushing aside older, agrarian modes of being. "Cheerfulness," in the Scout formulation, can hold these worlds in suspension. It is an abstract quality that — because of its abstraction — can bridge the space between woodcraft and market competition.

Moreover, the emphasis on youth culture, offset with the constancy of the "virtue" of cheerfulness, turns the disruption of pastoral values by capitalism into a natural narrative movement. The movement from the campfire to the office suite is a movement from youth to maturity for both the individual and the country. Learn the old ways, the ways of the knights and the pioneers, and carry them forward "naturally" as you grow up and into a "career." In this way, your very development will mark out a continuity between older ethical structures and modern economies — even as, objectively, the machine of capitalism is rendering those older forms of life obsolete. Of course, the rare Boy Scout who leaves the campfire long enough to read some history will quickly realize that the "chivalrous" knights of old and the pioneer trappers were, in fact, generally sociopaths. But as we have seen in our earlier discussions of literary works, cheerful communities often work to bring aliens — Amazons, skeptical older sisters, melancholy widows, street urchins — into their ambit. Eventually, like Shakespeare's Hippolyta, we must all be brought to cheer.

The new Scoutlike version of cheerfulness, which aims not at charity or art, but at professional success, is traced by the philosopher William James, writing in 1902 — at virtually the same moment as the Scouts — to what he calls the "Mind-cure movement." He sees it as a new phenomenon: "The deliberate adoption of an optimistic turn of mind thus makes its entrance into philosophy." And he locates it particularly in the psychology of the Americans, calling it "their only decidedly original contribution to the systematic philosophy of life."[5] He tracks it back, as we have, to Emerson, but also to the Gospel texts and to the poetry of Walt Whitman. No less important, though not mentioned by James, is the voluminous work of the turn of the century "inspirational" writer Orison Swett Marden, whose many books on self-motivation were widely distributed. We might think, for example, of *Cheerfulness as a Life Power* (1899), *The Optimistic Life (or, in the Cheering Up Business)* (1907), and *Thoughts about Cheerfulness* (1910). Marden was a disciple of Samuel Small, whose *Self-Help*, we noted earlier, was important for Dickens. Marden's volumes are largely lists of "wise sayings" and clichés about the advantages of being upbeat. These advantages are seen to be both personal and professional. They will make you happy and help you make money.

For Marden, the need for cheer is national. In *Cheerfulness as a Life Power*, he calls cheerfulness "the Cure for Americanitis."[6] The book is laced with reflections on how hard Americans work, on how little time they have to enjoy themselves, on how materialistic they are. Marden's goal is not only to get Americans to relax, but to get them to become more productive and richer at the same time. This miracle is to be achieved through the spread of cheerfulness. And yet as his book unfolds, cheerfulness changes meaning. It modulates from the Scoutlike spreading of sunshine to a willingness to stop complaining about the conditions of labor. The cheerful are "the true peacemakers and worth a regiment of grumblers," he says.[7] This is good propaganda, blending emotional health, political quietism, and religious beatitude. Colleagues who might be militating for decent working conditions on the assembly line are a "regiment" of the unpleasant, relegated to the dark side of emotion. The "true peacemakers" recall the blessed in Jesus's Sermon on the Mount: "Blessed are the peacemakers, for they will be called Children of God," says Matthew 5:9. Marden goes on to praise singing on the job, good hygiene, and a pleasant demeanor. He ends with quotations from Goethe and Longfellow, who sang, "'It is always morning somewhere.'"[8]

This type of writing, which, as James points out, is peculiarly American, is noteworthy for the ideological work it does in injecting an earlier moral and emotional vocabulary into the fabric of everyday life under capitalism. Because capitalism induces a culture of selling, it disjoins the power of cheerfulness from the contexts and discourses we studied in earlier chapters — early modern theology, Enlightenment sociability, modernist aesthetics. Cheerfulness is now a form of self-consolation, an affective tool that can reconcile you to drudgery. Yet it is figured by Marden, as by the Scouts, as the character trait of the rugged individualist. The individualist or nonconformist — the brave American — is the cheerful subject, someone who is worth more than "a regiment of grumblers." When all of the other workers on the factory floor are complaining, the cheerful voice is the voice in the wilderness, like the chivalrous knight or the resolute trapper. To be different, be cheerful.

Going Metaphysical

The patriotic nuance in the new cheerfulness is important, since it inflects much modern inspirational writing. We find it again in what is probably the masterpiece of modern American self-help literature, the 1956 book by clergyman Norman Vincent Peale titled *The Power of Positive Thinking*. Like Marden's work, Peale's book (or books, for they are legion) blends commonplaces about keeping one's spirits up with promises of practical success. "Power dwells with cheerfulness," we recall Ralph Waldo Emerson saying. Peale attempts to literalize that insight, turning it into a marketing tool. And he, like Marden, frames it in terms of a national crisis. He opens with the language of post–World War II popular psychology: "It is appalling to realize the number of pathetic people who are hampered and made miserable by the malady popularly called the inferiority complex." With impressive verbal virtuosity, Peale mobilizes several meanings of "pathetic," suggesting at once the suffering, or pathos, of the "inferior" person and his own negative judgment of their "pathetic" state of mind. The helpful comment that the topic under discussion is "popularly called" the inferiority complex suggests Peale's own professional expertise in matters of emotional health. It hints that he has mastery of a more technical vocabulary, to be called upon if needed. Everywhere he goes, says Peale, he is met by people who are miserable because they think of themselves as inadequate. His book will help these people live better, work better, and be successful. This is an American problem, and one of his first techniques is to remind his interlocutors that they live in the United States, "the land of opportunity" (p. 9).

The Power of Positive Thinking is built out of a set of exhortations disguised as scientific truths intertwined with exemplary anecdotes. The anecdotes are particularly interesting since, like Dickens's communities in *David Copperfield*, they divide the world into actors and observers. The book is peopled by a shadowy group of unnamed persons, some of them uncomfortably strange: "I was on the stage greeting people when a man approached me with a peculiar intensity of manner" (p. 1), recounts Peale.[10] These people are miserable, and they come to Peale after his various speeches. Lonely and uncertain, they have been driven to seek new solutions for their problems. We watch as Peale consults with the many strangers who approach him out of nowhere. He consoles them (and us) with anecdotes about some of his close friends, who, unlike the anonymous sufferers in the shadows, are generally named and all of whom seem to be successful business people or media stars ("a group of us consisting of Lowell Thomas, Captain Eddie Rickenbacker, Branch Rickey . . . ").[11] Thus, the movement of the community in the book is from anxiety to success, from hesitation in the shadows at the edge of the crowd to the light of confidence, from anonymity to implicit inclusion in the group of the positive thinkers. Peale's book moves between the nameless suffering ones, who approach him in search of help, and his celebrity crowd, who seem to have gotten his message.

The uncertainties that bother Peale's sufferers have their roots in the massive corporate expansion of the postwar economy. The memory of the recent war — and the possibility of trauma in many of these characters — is never mentioned. It lurks as the unspoken background to the action. Peale's miserable clients often seem to suffer from the fear that they are undereducated, unprepared for challenges, or that they cannot conform to the cultures of their corporations. In other words, Peale is placing us right in the midst of a set of social transformations analogous to what we saw with the Boy Scouts, where an earlier, agrarian economy was refigured for the modern world via woodcraft. In Peale, we meet a class of workers in the midst of a new economy for which they are spiritually and emotionally unprepared.

Peale is an easy target for criticism. His book is a transparent hodgepodge of clichés and fake anecdotes, presented through the sober "case study" tone of the midcentury social sciences. But the larger implications of his description of the American malaise are worth noting. Peale's answer to the misery of his subjects is to translate their *objective* dilemmas, rooted in economic uncertainty and a changing job market, into *subjective* problems. You are pathetic not because you've been fired in a corporate restructuring and are too old to be rehired, but because you have the wrong attitude. Thus, the very first example mentioned is of a man who says he has come to town "to handle the most important business deal of my life" (p. 1). If he fails, he says, "I'm done for." Peale is not impressed. He tells the man to calm down, that if he fails, "tomorrow is another day" (p. 2). What he needs is a positive outlook. A page later, we meet a man who approaches Peale to tell him that he is in despair because the business he has worked his entire life to build has been destroyed: "I have nothing left at all. Everything is gone. There is no hope, and I am too old to start over again" (p. 8). Peale persuades the fellow to cheer up and remind himself that he's an American, he believes in God, and he has a family: "Faith swept away his doubts, and more than enough power to overcome all his difficulties emerged from within him" (p. 10).

We are never told if the first man succeeded in his business deal or if the second one did, in fact, "overcome all his difficulties." Was positive thinking the elixir that could make him young enough to be rehired? All we know is that both men now have renewed emotional resources. Again and again, Peale recasts *objective* economic misery, the overwhelming depredations of American capitalism, as simply a problem of attitude. This is important, for though it is cleverly packaged here in the language of *positive* affect and problem-solving, Peale is giving voice to a tenet of the modern conservative movement's approach to *negative* situations. Peale's message is that you alone are responsible for your success. If things go bad, it could not possibly be because objective market conditions need to be regulated or because corrupt corporate behavior needs to be reined in. It is your own fault. It follows from this that the government bears no responsibility for your failure and that it has no obligation to help you. All it can do is cheer you on. Already, in 1956, this is Reaganism in a nutshell. The policy implications are massive. My point is that they are enabled by a rhetoric of cheer. Cheerfulness acts as a kind of switching mechanism through which Peale turns objective economic life into a matter of personal emotion. Once cheerfulness is located in the self, away from community, Peale can cleverly give spiritual and psychological cover to an ideology of economic warfare.

Central to Peale's message is the chapter called "How to Create Your Own Happiness." Here, he sets us on a train with a group of businessmen, including himself. They seem to be strangers, beset by the awkwardness that comes from unfamiliarity. This is not the community of friends we saw in Jane Austen, but the lonely crowd. As they shave awkwardly together in the men's lounge (the metaphors of hygiene and self-revelation are themselves revealing), "there was little conversation." Suddenly, into this taciturn, anonymous crowd comes "a man . . . wearing on his face a broad smile. He greeted us all with a cheery good morning." When someone complains ("Why all the cheer?"), he reveals his secret, "I make it a habit to be happy."[12] The nameless intruder, like a messenger from the gods in some ancient epic, brings crucially important information. Yet it is not information about the destiny of peoples or divine will. It is an individual confession, an emotional message that, as it turns out, grates on the rest of the group. It is Hume's idea of cheerfulness as contagion, except that here the contagion seems not to catch, for we learn that no one else in the group cheers up. Nevertheless, Peale comments that he is certain that every man left the train "with those interesting words in mind." One step at a time, I guess.

Marden advocated for cheerfulness as a form of individual resistance to the grumbling of the industrial proletariat, but Peale goes him one better. He argues that cheerfulness does more than provide levity and better attitudes at work. Attitude shapes happenings in the world: "Such thoughts will help cause events to turn out that way." This magical thinking — for it is simply that — gives way to a more modulated reformulation a page later: "Affirm happy outcomes at the start of every day, and you will be surprised at how often things will turn out so. . . . It is amazing."[13] Herein lies the magic of Peale's rhetoric. The fake anecdotes and empty promises of success aim to locate us in such a way that we measure our lives against his platitudes. We are readers and witnesses not of someone else's gaiety, but of our own reactions. When there is concurrence between us and Peale, we can be "amazed" that we were right to be so positive. When things don't work out, we pay no mind, since failure is just noise that gets in the way of our positivity.

This is the structure of modern self-help cheerfulness. We are readers not of the Bible or our friends, but of ourselves. We generate for ourselves not "happiness," which is simply a red herring in Peale's argument, but a kind of constant amazement when things fall into place — when we land a new account, publish an article, don't get food poisoning. Our cheerfulness is generated out of the blips of pleasure we experience from the occasional overlapping of Peale's platitudes and events in our world. And since clergyman Peale is thinking positively for his own professional advancement, it is a small step from these affirmations to religious doctrine: "Think positively, for example, and you set in motion positive forces which bring positive results to pass. Positive thoughts create around yourself an atmosphere propitious to the development of positive outcomes." This technique, he asserts a page later, constitutes the channeling of "God's power into personality."[4]

Peale builds on the old tradition of Christian hermeneutics that we saw earlier, in which all events and texts are to be taken "in the best sense" — as Rabelais said, "en perfectissime partie." Yet here, charitable reading is not the reading of the acts of others. It is the reading of one's own actions. We no longer take energy from the hilarity of Rabelais's giants or Shakespeare's festal style. We work on ourselves. This is a hermeneutic practice linked to an affective regime of improvement. Saint Augustine advocated placing one's interpretive practice in line with the rule of charity, which binds God's church together. Yeats reads gaiety in the surface of stone, as art. By contrast, Peale wants us to read ourselves. Our charity is self-charity; it turns our deeds into markers of our own power, which, in a brilliant gesture of self-idolatry, is identified with God's power.

We stand here at the polar opposite of Saint Paul's famous dictum that "God loveth a cheerful giver" with which we began our story. In that phrase, we were able to read the metaphysical presence of the deity in the construction of community through the practice of charity, generosity, even sacrifice. For Peale, working in a world where all human activity is a commodity, cheerfulness generates itself, like a kind of repeated echo. Specific examples are not required, nor are the mediations of community, history, or art. Be cheerful, and you will be successful, which will make you more cheerful, since success is all that matters. Cheerfulness is now pure marketing technique, swept up into the language of motivation and "optimism."

Cheerios

This repurposing of a language of cheer beyond the networks of ethical and aesthetic activity in which it traditionally circulated may be seen, writ small, in yet another cultural detail from the mid-twentieth century — a detail that can help us understand the material manifestations of cheer in modern economies. In 1941, on the threshold of yet another world war, the General Mills Corporation introduced Cherioats, a ready-to-eat breakfast cereal. The name brings the affective force of cheerfulness into conjunction with the idea of a nourishing grain. "He's feeling his Cheery-oats!" was the initial promotional slogan. Packets were shipped to service members fighting overseas. However, after a complaint from a competitor objecting to absorption of generic material — oats — into a brand, the name was altered and became Cheerios.[15] This brilliant innovation would appear to have been generated by the sound of the name itself — *oats* become *o*'s. But it also brought the shape of the name — the O — into harmony with the shape of the object itself, which is a small, circular, hollow bit of cooked dough. A tiny doughnut, in effect. The material object becomes its own message; it is both thing and sign. It is an O that embodies physically its name and separates name from thing (O from oats), retaining only an outline of material presence (the O shape). As the Boy Scouts noted, the cheerful scout sees the doughnut, not the hole. In the process, the product enters into a dialogic relationship with us as consumers, for the name calls to us — Cheerio! — even as it avoids, in its plurality, turning into a mere Anglicism: not "Cheerio!" but Cheerios, which, however, contains and replicates "Cheerio!" Saint Paul had pointed to cheerfulness as the mediating affect that defines our relationship to the mystical body of Christ in the community of the new church. General Mills responds by calling to us, "Cheerio!" as we walk by, inviting us to join the community of consumers, consuming not the bread of the Eucharist, but the O of the oats.

To promote the product, the company associated it, for sixteen years, with the radio serial and television program called *The Lone Ranger*. The contrast between the name of the product and the character, a sociopathic do-gooder rambling across the landscape of the Old West, suggests the blending of community-oriented "sunshine" and solitary "chivalric knights" and "trappers" extolled by the Boy Scouts back in 1911. The protagonist was once a member of a community — a "ranger" — but he now works as a free agent, accompanied only by his faithful companion, Tonto. He has absorbed the ethics of the ranger life, but cannot tolerate its social structure, like a Scout who's gone into business for himself. Each episode of the Western series ended with a set of moral lessons about honesty and integrity. Thus, the program offered heroic deeds coupled with cheerful maxims. It replayed the pairing of Old West courage and modern marketing values promoted first by the Boy Scouts. In both of these instances, a balancing act is set up between the exploitation of cheerfulness for commercial ends and the atomized social experience that an economy based on endless innovation enables and demands.

I have been suggesting here that the power and energy associated with cheerfulness by earlier thinkers as diverse as Montaigne and Nietzsche migrates, in the modern era, from the realm of high literature and aesthetic thought to popular advice literature and advertising jargon. Cheerfulness functions as a key mediating term that can bring the values and experiences of an earlier moment in American history — the moment of a rural, agrarian economy based in physical labor and craft — into relationship with a new economy of buying and selling, of factory production and salesmanship. For the Boy Scouts and General Mills, a reach back to an earlier moment of mythical heroism lends ethical gravitas to a culture of self-advancement. The more devious Norman Vincent Peale turns his attention to the collateral damage of capitalist competition, reaching out to those who did not get the message that no matter how domesticated by the office routine, we are all really knights and cowboys at heart. His characters are lonely and disheartened, lurking in the darkness at the edge of the stage when he speaks. To brighten their outlook, he reimagines objective economic relationships as if they were problems of emotional outlook. Then he reworks the biblical image of cheerful community as a theology of the self. Self-empowerment becomes self-reading; adherence to Peale's counsel becomes a manifestation of God's will. The key, he tells us, is to act with a cheerful intention and then to read what we have done cheerfully, connecting successful undertakings to previous intention and disregarding the rest. In this way, we can achieve both success and emotional integrity. It is amazing!

The counsels of cheerfulness we have just explored occur within the classic American genre of self-help: acting cheerful is the way for the individual thrown back on their own resources to succeed in an impersonal society and competitive economy, a way simultaneously to market oneself and possibly to preserve a sense of personal integrity in a world that violently threatens it. It is performative: to act cheerful is what it means to be cheerful. However, as we will note in the next chapter, performativity is a characteristic of many of the forms of cheerfulness we have studied, and while it has been a way to affirm or create or enter into a community, or even to induce conformity, as in the texts we have just studied, it also can be used to subvert and disrupt oppressive social and economic forces.

CHAPTER TWELVE

"Take It, Satch!":

Cheer in Dark Times

Vibrating Art

"Is Art Cheerful?" "Is die Kunst heiter?" asked the cultural critic
Theodor Adorno in the title of an essay for his collection *Notes to
Literature*, first published in 1974. Adorno's target is both the style of
certain artworks and the uses of art. He begins by comparing the
Latin poet Ovid and the German court poet Schiller. Ovid calls his
muse "jocosa." Schiller proclaims that "life is serious, art is cheerful."
Ovid's phrase is an instance of "Latin cunning," says Adorno, aimed
at protecting himself from a political establishment that could, as it
eventually did, banish him from Rome. Ovid downplays the seriousness of art to save himself. By contrast Schiller was never in danger,
and his maxim simply trivializes art. It becomes "pure ideology" and
enters into the jargon of a bourgeois culture willing to limit itself to
entertainment. It is this tradition of a "lighthearted" art that Adorno
takes as his target.

Adorno claims that any notion of cheerfulness or gaiety in art
originates, as we have in fact shown, in the processes through which
modern art disentangles itself from myth and metaphysics in the
early modern period. (He mentions Cervantes, Rabelais, and Boc-
caccio.) By the mid-twentieth century, however, any gaiety in art is
false, for it implies an avoidance of the pain of history. The explosion of popular marketing, as we saw in the preceding chapter, has

emptied cheerfulness of the power it had for Nietzsche and Yeats. Any serious art thus has a duty to register the misery brought on by economic and political violence. It cannot simply be "gay," as if gaiety were not a suppression of surrounding suffering. Yeats had hinted at the violence underpinning gay art in his evocation of the tragedy that art must brush aside. For Adorno, this hinting becomes a full-scale paradox that underpins art conventionally understood to be "cheerful." (Adorno's example is Mozart.) The contradiction lies in the fact that the more art projects lightness and gaiety, the more it discloses the social and economic disharmonies that it must obscure in order to come into being: "Contradiction vibrates through its most remote mediations, just as the din of the horrors of reality sounds in music's most extreme pianissimo," he notes.[1]

For Adorno, cheerfulness persists only in a refracted form. It flashes up between the harmony of a form that projects cheer and the acknowledgement of the pain that it cannot name in its structure. "As something that has escaped from reality and is nevertheless permeated with it, art vibrates between this seriousness and cheerfulness. It is this tension that constitutes art." The only legitimate art, he claims, is what "embodies something like freedom in the midst of unfreedom." This constraint is tied to the definition of art: "The fact that through its very existence it stands outside the evil spell that prevails allies it to a promise of happiness, a promise it itself somehow expresses in its expression of despair." Adorno's hedgings — "something like," "somehow" — suggest his difficulty in offering anything specific that could link art to cheer. Even then, Adorno is clear that he is not talking about specific works, only about an abstract idea of art in general — "art as a whole . . . not individual works" (p. 250). It is only in a "tension" between seriousness and cheerfulness that art can find its existence. And within its structure, cheerfulness can only vibrate, pointing to both misery and the freedom from misery.

To see the limitations of this powerful critique, we might remind ourselves that cheerfulness, as we have traced it throughout this history, is implicitly and often explicitly performative. Nietzsche, exceptionally, located it in the "surface" of art — even as Yeats offered us a poetic application of Nietzsche's ideas that stressed the *process* of art making as much as the material. We can acknowledge the importance of Adorno's argument as a response to the trivialization of art in the twentieth century, exemplified, to be sure, in the bourgeois elevation of Mozart as an exemplar of lightness and gaiety. But we could also suggest that some forms of performance move past the terms of Adorno's argument. As we have seen in previous chapters, cheerfulness does not necessarily function as a "characteristic," or a "structural law," to use Adorno's language. It is manifested through action. It emerges through contingent moments of affect, activated in the doing.

To explore this question, we might turn to a figure contemporaneous with both Adorno and Norman Vincent Peale. This is Louis Armstrong, the founding figure of modern American popular music and the most influential jazz musician in the world during the middle years of the twentieth century. Armstrong performs cheerfulness in ways that take us back to Nietzsche's interest in art as *Heiterkeit* — the power of which lies in "the surface, the note, the fold." Yet where the Boy Scouts and Norman Vincent Peale point to cheerfulness as a presentation of the self to others for the purpose of manipulation and, in the end, profit, Armstrong's cheerfulness is more complex and involves a dialectical model of self-presentation.

Armstrong's performances, his broad smile and his willingness to place himself in less than dignified situations to transmit his music, made him a somewhat controversial figure. By the early 1960s, many people thought his swing-based music was hopelessly old-fashioned, given the innovations of bebop. At the same time, with the rise of the civil rights movement, his accommodating spirit was sometimes seen as a sellout to a racist social system. Yet the high spirits of Armstrong's performances are generated not only through the unprecedented virtuosity of his trumpet technique, but through the disruptive ways in which he used that technique against the very vehicles through which he was presenting himself. This playful dimension to Armstrong's work, which was commented on at the time, functions like the ironic comments of Ragged Dick on the assertions of his enemies.

Armstrong's work can be seen against a long tradition of African American performance. It is a tradition of misuse and misprision. As Saidiya Hartman has noted, nineteenth-century descriptions of the slave coffle written by white authors and reporters often stress the presence of some form of "cheerfulness" in the comportment of the slaves. This was often manifested through the performance of music. Indeed, in many slave market contexts, "cheerful" performance became one way in which slaves made themselves more "appealing" while for sale. Singing by slaves was heard by many white observers as "cheerful" and taken as evidence either that slavery was not so bad after all or that gaiety is a universal trait, even of the miserable. Thus, we witness Abraham Lincoln commenting on an encounter with a group of captives:

> Yet amid all these distressing circumstances, as we would think of them, they were the most cheerful and apparently happy creatures on board. One whose offence for which he had been sold was an over-fondness for his wife, played the fiddle almost continually; and others danced, sang, cracked jokes and played various games with cards from day to day.[2]

Against this tradition of hideous misreading of the suffering of others, we can note the importance of the conclusion of the first major theoretical text in the history of African American nation building. This is W. E. B. Du Bois's *The Souls of Black Folk*, from 1903. Du Bois ends his book with a chapter titled "Sorrow Songs" in which he celebrates the importance and power of traditional African American song. He admonishes his Caucasian readers, reminding them of the three great gifts of Black Americans: story and song, sweat and brawn, and "a gift of the Spirit." And he ends with a powerful set of questions: "Our song, our toil, our cheer, and warning have been given to this nation in blood-brotherhood. Are not these gifts worth the giving? Is not this work and striving? Would America have been America

without her Negro people?" He evokes the last of the numerous spiri-
tuals that he has quoted and transcribed throughout the book. "My
children, my little children, are singing to the sunshine," he avers.
Then he quotes the words and transcribes the music of the song:

Let us cheer the weary traveler,

Cheer the weary traveler,

Let us cheer the weary traveler

Along the heavenly way

"And the traveler girds himself," concludes Du Bois, "and sets his face
toward the Morning, and goes his way."[3]

Du Bois's version of cheerfulness responds to the misreadings of
slave sorrow as "cheerful." Here we do not get images of white observers passing judgment on Black performance. Rather, we get the new
performance of cheer by an emerging community. The location of the
spiritual in a tradition of ancient "sorrow songs" acknowledges the
pain that Adorno calls for in the presentation of art, yet the lyric and
the performance depicted here gesture toward some type of utopian
moment as a newly emerging African American nation both acknowledges its past and comes together in and through art. The song is about
cheer, and the singing of it cheers those who sing. The insertion of a
musical transcription of the song reminds us that African American
performance is difficult to convey in traditional European-based musical notation, even as it makes oral tradition at least partly available to
the same audience that Du Bois is admonishing in the paragraph just
preceding. Music as performance and text — the intersection of action,
writing, and sound — offers a vision somewhat different from the dialectical "vibrating" between cheerfulness and seriousness called for by
Adorno. Armstrong builds on this.

"Dig, Man!"

Central to Louis Armstrong's self-presentation on stage was his
continual projection of himself as playing some type of a role, as if,
like "Hamlet" and "Lear" in Yeats's poem "Lapis Lazuli," he were

not only Louis Armstrong, but a character of gaiety, "transfiguring all that dread." This ironic performance strategy made Armstrong exceptionally difficult to pin down. He was always both himself and beside himself as an ironic commentator on his own performing self. We have noted throughout this book the ways in which cheer seems to radiate between persons in the interplay of social relations. If Cheerios absorbs the concept of cheer into a single object, Armstrong opens it up again, generating gaiety out of the distance between himself and himself, between his dead-serious virtuosity and his performing persona.

We can see the power of Armstrong's innovations by turning to several of his most "cheerful" songs. His 1931 recording of the 1910 tune "Shine," for the short film *A Rhapsody in Black and Blue*, offers an exemplary instance of his approach. "Shine" features a lyric by Cecil Mack about someone whose "teeth are pearly" and "hair is curly." It is a condescending characterization of an African American, playing into the cliché of the smiling, submissive Black man. Armstrong takes it apart. "Oh, chocolate drop, that's me," he murmurs at the outset. Then he rambles through the first verse until the punch line, "That's why they call me 'Shine,'" which would complete the thought and impose the racial cliché. However, just before he is to pronounce the final word — the moment of naming that would effect closure on the demeaning lyric — Armstrong bursts into scat singing and never enunciates the name. He then takes the verse again, now almost incomprehensible, with whoops and nonsense syllables, only then hitting the concluding line as it was written. In other words, he quite literally inserts himself and his extraordinary original singing style into the syntax of the lyric, breaking it up into nonsense, splitting the last pronoun ("me") and its antecedent ("Shine") apart with an entire chorus of improvised lyric. Then, for good measure, he takes an extended solo that recasts the melody as a series of leaping intervals and glissandi until he hits the final high C. In live performances of the tune, this final stretch often contained literally dozens of leaps up to the highest note (counted by his sidemen, in astonishment).[4]

No less impressive, if less dramatic, is Armstrong's reworking of the Jimmy McHugh and Dorothy Fields tune "On the Sunny Side of the Street" — the unavoidable theme song for any history of cheerfulness. Armstrong recorded it multiple times, beginning in the 1920s. The official song lyric begins by telling the listener to get up and go: "Grab your coat and get your hat," it urges, "Leave your worries on the doorstep. / Just direct your feet / To the sunny side of the street."[5] Cheerfulness is here a "life power," as Orison Swett Marden might say, something we can all use to make ourselves less pathetic and more successful. But Armstrong is not interested in cheering us up. "Grab your coat and get your hat, baby," he says, before continuing, "Just direct your feet, babe / On the sunny side of the street." He repeats the term of endearment, "baby," after almost every line. This changes the song completely. It makes what appeared to be a song about generalized cheerfulness into a song of seduction. It is about two lovers, not about the Boy Scouts or anxious American workers. This is reinforced with a detail: Armstrong urges his partner to direct her feet not "to" the sunny side of the street, but "on" the sunny side; the cheerfulness resides in their pairing, not in the symbolic geography. They will flourish not because of where they walk, but because they are in love. Armstrong makes the lyric into a beguiling come-on: walk with me, and everything will be OK. For good measure, he turns the original lyric's pallid Depression-era consolation that high spirits are as good as cash — "I'll be rich as Rockefeller" — into the vanquishing of an invented amorous rival, "If I never have a cent, mama / I'll be rich as Rocky Fellow." Love, not cheerfulness, is where the wealth is in Armstrong's version. Through the distortion of the lyric, Armstrong absorbs the clichéd message of generalized cheerfulness into an urgent, sweet song of seduction set in a small community of lovers.

Armstrong's ironic version of cheerfulness is laid out spatially, as it were, in a 1932 Betty Boop animated short titled *I'll Be Glad When You're Dead, You Rascal, You!* It shows Betty Boop captured by cannibals. Her companions seek to rescue her and engage in fantastic chase scenes with the cartoon captors, who are caricatured as black-skinned Africans. The scene unfolds over Armstrong's performance of one of his signature tunes, in which he admonishes a man for fooling around with his wife. Yet because of Armstrong's joking, growling presentation of the lyric, the love triangle is here built around Betty, her protectors, and the cannibals. Armstrong overcomes the racist tenor of the entire production by making it clear that his wish of death may be directed toward the "white" protectors of Betty, more than her "African" captors. And, indeed, midway through the cartoon, the face of Armstrong himself appears at the top of the screen space, singing in disembodied glory, occasionally merging with the head of the cannibal king. The identification is only momentary, and Armstrong emerges again. But it sets him on the side of Betty Boop's captors. Armstrong is identified with the characters in the cartoon at the same moment as he establishes himself as an ironic commentator on the cartoon. He performs against and around any number of possible positions he could take within the world of the story.

These multiple position-takings reach an apogee, of sorts, in Armstrong's 1956 hit recording of "Mack the Knife." The tune, which recently had been translated and adapted by Marc Blitzstein, had originated in Berlin in the 1928 *Threepenny Opera*, composed by Kurt Weill and scripted by one of Adorno's most frequently discussed exemplars of artistic modernism, Bertolt Brecht. Indeed, at the very same moment that Weill was composing his innovative "jazz-inspired" score to the *Threepenny Opera* (for a small group of seven musicians), Armstrong was busy recording the groundbreaking "Hot Sevens" sessions that would go on to shape much subsequent jazz. When Armstrong first encountered the story of the criminal Macheath, he noted that back home in New Orleans, he had known men just like him. This wasn't a Marxist fable; it was personal history. He took to Blitzstein's adaptation of the tune, which became his first mainstream hit. And while it might seem that Armstrong's up-tempo reworking of the song constitutes exactly the type of "cheerful" art that Adorno condemned, it must be noted that what Armstrong is doing is in fact remaining completely true to the Brecht/Weill composition: Its jazzlike character (complete with strummed banjo), while innovative in 1928, was hopelessly outdated by 1956. To have sung it as written would have been the equivalent of playing Mozart only on period instruments. Thus, Armstrong made the song into the jazz it had always wanted to be by updating it. There's even a banjo, though it soon disappears in the mix.[6]

This dynamic engagement with history is made clear in the arrangement. Whereas the original features one of the *Threepenny Opera*'s main characters, Polly Peachum, calling out after the song ends that Macheath is on the prowl. Armstrong identifies him before we begin: "Dig, man, there goes Mack the Knife!" Then he plays the melody straight with a muted trumpet, over slurred woodwind lines, as if introducing us into the story with a modicum of seriousness. From there, he launches into the vocal. Yet rather than taking on the melody as written, through an upward-moving melodic figure based on a major sixth chord (E-G-A), Armstrong jettisons the melodic buildup and begins on the top note, the A, as if he were already in the middle of the story, which he is. And, in effect, he sings the verse mostly on that single note, rather than working his way back up with each new phrase. This means in effect that Armstrong sings not a melody, but a rhythm — the matter of jazz itself. He offers the kind of countersong, independent of melody, that Brecht himself had pointed to as important to generating critical reflection on the material of art.[7] Each verse unfolds in dialogue with a different instrument from his band, even as another trumpeter, presumably Billy Kyle, offers a counter line in the background.

The key moment comes following the verse. When the vocal stops, he turns to himself, as it were, and murmurs, "Take it, Satch." He then plays an ornamented jazz solo, muteless, now backed by his All Stars, who play a Dixieland-influenced last verse, letting themselves go into multiple interlocking lines. Armstrong offers a virtuoso version of the jazz that Kurt Weill's original had only gestured toward. In the process, we see Armstrong's disruptive self-depiction. His cheery vocal parodies, in its way, countless depictions of African Americans in literature and the movies as "cheerful" Black servants or helpers. He follows it with a demonstration of technical virtuosity that blows such clichés aside.[8] At the moment of transition, he urges himself on, "Take it, Satch," reminding us that his performing persona is at the very least double. He has just "taken it," in the vocal. Now he takes it again. The urging speaks to itself, about itself. It performs its own cheer and comments on it all at once.

The multiple layers of the performance are what take us past Adorno's idea of art as vibrating form. If the effect came only through Armstrong's lively trumpet, we could place him in the company of the "cheerful" Mozart mentioned and dismissed by Adorno. But the unique character of the work comes through the *interplay* of song, vocalese, commentary, rhythm, and sound. Much of the energy, in fact, comes through the shifts, the jumps between one level of performance and another. Armstrong's performance recalls, in his vocal, the sorrow of the blues, even as his virtuosity and pleasure transfigure that dread into gaiety. Whether such a performative transmutation would have qualified as the "something like freedom," or "something like pleasure" that Adorno sought in art, we can never know. This is in part because Adorno locates cheer in style and structure, following, in a sense, Nietzsche's violent relocation of traditional cheer in the surface of art. For Armstrong, by contrast, cheer emerges from the ephemera of the single performance. Moreover, because Armstrong is both cheerful and playing someone who is cheerful, it is impossible for us to dismiss his cheer, treating it as either essential or as mere consolation. He offers the salutary alternative to Peale's "How to Create Your Own Happiness," where we are enjoined to watch ourselves and be amazed. Because it is performance, and not merely form, it moves away from Adorno's structurally rooted negative dialectic toward some more dynamic version of cheerfulness as subversive self-delight. Against a world in which cheer is monetized as a force for manipulating one's customers, Armstrong plays with his own overwhelming enthusiasm, seeming to marvel at its intensity as he goes.⁹

Armstrong's ironic amusement at his own persona enables a variety of postures through which he can assert himself without risking pathos. This is made clear in his last important film appearance in the 1969 spectacle *Hello, Dolly!* starring Barbra Streisand. Streisand plays a turn-of-the-century widowed matchmaker who is looking to find herself another man. In the climactic scene, she makes her return to society at the Harmonia Gardens Restaurant, prancing onstage in a bustle, singing the title song. She turns to the conductor of the café orchestra, who stands with his back to the camera, but soon reveals himself to be none other than Louis Armstrong. Armstrong's career had been somewhat in decline for the previous decade, and he had been out of action not only because of changing tastes, but because of health problems. Thus, when Streisand sings Jerry Herman's lyric, "It's so nice to be right back where I belong," it is clear that it is not Dolly who is "back," but Armstrong. He had often complained, "White folks call me Louie."¹⁰ Here, he names himself with his opening line, as he jumps into the song: "Well, hello, Dolly, / This is Louisss, Dolly."

The moment brings forth the performative paradoxes in Armstrong's personality. For one thing, he is back as himself, "Louisss." Yet he appears in a context where the person simpering next to him is pretending to be a woman from nearly a century earlier. So he is Louisss playing an old-time bandleader, or vice versa. The juxtaposition of "authentic" jazz musician proclaiming his real-life self and the cabaret star pretending to be from another century points to the ways in which Armstrong's self-presentation — his cheerful demeanor — is linked to a performative self-consciousness that doubles his identity. Armstrong is both there and not there, both a character and a self. In the constant interplay between the two, we find the generation of cheerfulness, a gay amusement at one's representation of one's own self. This is self-reading not as Peale envisioned it, but as Armstrong reinvented it.

Cheer in Pandemic Days

The Germans won the victories. By God they were soldiers. But they were cooked too. We were all cooked. I had to go, I said. I had to get back to the hospital. "Good-by," he said. Then cheerily, "Every sort of luck!" There was a great contrast between his world pessimism and personal cheeriness.

— ERNEST HEMINGWAY, *A Farewell to Arms*

Since the Renaissance, moral philosophers, religious advisers, and psychologists have worried about negative emotions. They have tried to cure us of depression, to heal trauma, to mitigate nostalgia, to dispel melancholy. Even optimism, as Lauren Berlant has shown recently, has become an affective trap, destined, in an unequal society, to doom us to frustration.[1] But no one, so far as I can tell, wants to cure us of cheerfulness. Even the careful philosopher Spinoza, as we saw, suggests that you can't have too much of it. Perhaps this is because, as I suggested earlier, cheerfulness is a modest thing. It never overwhelms us. Rather, it radiates between people and shapes their interactions and selves. It presents a form of power or energy that we can harness in the work of managing our emotional lives.

This book has studied two aspects of cheerfulness. We have looked at what writers and philosophers have said about it and at how it has functioned as a key term or concept in stories and philosophical arguments. We have looked at what people think it *is* and what it *does*.

The historical arc of our argument reflects both of these aspects of the project.

We have seen cheerfulness take many roles and serve many masters across the past five centuries. At times, cheerfulness is a theme. At other times, it is a metaphor, offering a conceptual link between distinct zones of experience, such as, for the troubadours, between song and nature. It takes many forms, interacting with actions, bodies, and faces. For Julian of Norwich, "cheer" is a rhetorical resource, an image for representing absolute presence. For Montaigne, cheerfulness it is a modality of acting, for Rabelais, a way of reading that would heal the body. For religious thinkers, from Erasmus of Rotterdam to John Donne, it is a kind of emotional supplement that both intensifies and completes the practice of charity. In Shakespeare, it is a poetic device that helps harmonize the formal conventions of literary genres with the politics of an emerging court society. In the novels of Jane Austen, it gives emotional content to the future, shaping the trajectory of a young woman — for better or worse — into maturity and conformity. For Dickens, it is an atmosphere, a glimmer in the glances of the women who empower the ambitious male protagonist. For Nietzsche, it is the violent refusal of the art of depth for the art of the surface, "the whole Olympus of appearance." For Louis Armstrong, it is an aside: "Take it, Satch!"

The emotional life of our modernity may be read as much in the ways that cheerfulness works as in the ways it is described. Early on, it envelops the self within a web of cheerful community. It heals the body. It shapes the relationship between characters and literary plots. As we move into the Enlightenment, it offers an ideal to the world of conversation and economic exchange. In the culture of emerging capitalism, it takes root in the individual as an attribute of personality. Yet it circulates uneasily in the world of bourgeois individualism, coming to rest uncomfortably on the shoulders of ambitious low-born heroes. In the twentieth century, it mediates between new forms of professional life and obsolete social practices. It retains its spiritual power, perhaps, only in the field of performance, in the work of a figure such as Louis Armstrong, in the ironic improvisation and hilarity of an art that both registers the misery of life and points to its own capacity, for the moment of a song, to deflect that misery.

Cheerfulness has been largely overlooked by literary critics and intellectual historians. Yet as we have seen in the previous pages, accounts of cheerfulness, evocations of cheerful attitudes, and discussions of gaiety are consistently present in novels, poems, plays, and philosophical essays. The story of cheerfulness is bound up with the story of bodies, with how we control and inhabit our faces and gestures. But it is also bound up with the story of communities, with the small communities that dot the landscape of the Western imagination. And as those communities are erased and reimagined in the developing world of industrial and now postindustrial capitalism, cheerfulness is both evoked endlessly and drained of its power to bind humans to each other. The more you call on it, the less power it seems to have. Yet throughout this story, the *language* of cheerfulness—its metaphors and images—remains remarkably consistent. The virtue of the Boy Scouts harks to the generosity of the medieval knight; the "hilarity" evoked by Emerson points us back to the Latin vocabulary of Erasmus; Nietzsche's *Fröhlichkeit* is clearly in dialogue with Luther's. In other words, there is a *tradition* of cheerful reflection, and of reflection on cheer, which our story has brought forth. And cheerfulness today evokes the ghosts of earlier cheerful scenes. We walk among the ruins of theological and natural cheer. We live among the phantoms of cheerful communities. Contemporary cheer—the gaiety of networking apps and cheer squads—mimics the spirituality of communities that no longer exist.

These days, cheerfulness may be a blinking light on a screen. In 1963, a publicity agent named Harvey Ball designed a round yellow smiling face to improve morale at the State Mutual Life Assurance Company. "A smile is contagious. It is entertainment and medicine. It is food for friendship," proclaimed the internal magazine of State Mutual Life.[2] Ball's brilliant reduction of the human face to a single circle—bolder in color than the *O* of the Cheerio—has become emblematic of our own cultural/historical moment. The smiley face prepares us, through its reduction of the human to the electronic, for the emergence of online networks such as Facebook in which people are digits. In contrast, say, to the little boat community in Yarmouth, where David Copperfield joins the family circle of the Peggottys, the digital network is endless and without center. One need not practice charity to enter it. It has made possible the self-creation of humans, not through Peale's positive thinking, but through homogenous "positive" representations, through the piling up of "likes." The emoji renders useless the type of dialectical play with self-representation that Armstrong found so productive. It removes the "countenance" from cheerfulness and leaves us with a face — in the reduced sense of the word, that is, a surface, like a rock face or the face of a watch.

I began thinking about cheerfulness as a way of trying to understand the effect on cultural life of the new digital technologies. The 2008 financial crisis had been in large measure brought on by cheerful economists selling financial products of no value. Digital culture responded by eliminating dignified work and promoting the hyped-up "gig" economy, by replacing community with shapeless social networks, and, as I have noticed in my own teaching, by supplanting serious reading with tweets. I conclude this book in a state of lockdown as the planet succumbs to a wave of panic over the COVID-19 disease. On the last day of March 2020, as I was revising my work, the president of the United States, an avowed disciple of Norman Vincent Peale, went on national television to promote a set of fake medications that he falsely claimed could cure the sick and dying. When challenged by the press about his comments, the president took no responsibility, but declared, "I am a cheerleader for America."[3] Such is the status of cheerfulness at the beginning of the twenty-first century. Whatever happens next, something has changed.

Yet one of the consequences of life in the pandemic age is that it demands cheerfulness and, in the process, transforms the impersonality of digital connection. Because we can communicate only from a distance, the vacuity of emoji culture has given way to genuine, if often fleeting expressions of community identity. Indeed, in a mediated, slow-motion world, the ephemeral character of cheerfulness now becomes an advantage. The pandemic, which cruelly mimics the Enlightenment celebration of conversational "contagion" as the incubator of cheerfulness, imposes a reinvention of cheer. Hume's idea of cheerful affect as a kind of fever that can transform the emotional tenor of a community is turned inside out. The mere practice of self-discipline, of social distancing and proper hygiene, now becomes a reaffirmation of community. We can remain cheerful only because we do *not* contaminate, because we remain separate. And cheerfulness bridges the distance imposed on us by our fear of contamination. It can circulate because the disease does not. Because we can both control cheerfulness and cultivate it through our conversations—digital or otherwise—it is part of what still makes us human. The digital tools, lethal to genuine cheer under normal circumstances, make expressions of cheer possible in pandemic days. So from a distance and despite digital mediation, cheerfulness may reemerge in expressions of care and concern, in offers of help from afar. These are only small gestures, but they are gestures nonetheless—like the biblical practice of the "cheerful giver." They imply care and empathy. They counterbalance public claims that lies don't matter if one is a "cheerleader." Moreover, the cautious relationship to time imposed on humans by the pandemic—I am safe for now, my family survives for today—generates an affect of cheer that may be one of the few emotional resources we can mobilize. In this reaffirmation of cheerfulness against virulent nature, we approach something like the idea of the "elastic" cheer that Jane Austen is said to have demonstrated on her deathbed. Across cyberspace, perhaps, we may become elastic.[4]

Debased and overlooked, cheerfulness provides an instant of solace, a flash of support. Its vital usefulness emerges at moments of crisis. Beyond the commercialization of our cheery culture and the fake gaiety of our politics, cheerfulness is a tool that, as Montaigne's gay cannibal knew, frees us from our bonds by asserting affective freedom in the very face of oblivion. Even in its modern iteration, cheerfulness may be one of the forms of emotional power that should not be overlooked. It is not the "hope" of the messianic, or the "optimism" of the cheap politician. It makes more modest promises — to get you through the next few hours, to connect you to a neighbor. You can't build a politics on it. But you probably can't rebuild a world without it.

Acknowledgments

Two portions of this book have been published elsewhere. An early version of a section of Chapter 5 appeared in *Montaigne Studies* 30 (2018), in a special issue edited by Todd Reeser. A section of Chapter 3 may be found in *Positive Emotions in Early Modern Europe*, edited by Brad Irish and Cassie Miura, published by Manchester University Press in 2021. My thanks to these publications for permission to reprint this material.

This critical expedition has in many ways been a group undertaking, and many colleagues and friends have helped me think about its elusive topic and define my themes and focus. All mistakes and infelicities are, of course, my responsibility.

For their support of my work, here and elsewhere, I would like to thank Meighan Gale, Kyra Simone, and the staff of Zone Books. Their collaborative spirit is rare and much appreciated. Thanks as well to Bud Bynack for his editorial and critical sagacity. I am lucky to have benefited from Ramona Naddaff's exemplary editorial guidance and scholarly friendship.

Early work took place at the Institut d'Études Avançées in Paris, to which I extend my thanks. Also in Paris, members of the *Transitions* study group at the Sorbonne, under the genial direction of Professor Hélène Merlin-Kajman, welcomed me for a very early presentation of some of this work and offered generous and helpful commentary.

Fellows in the Doreen B. Townsend Center for the Humanities at Berkeley listened to several bits of this work and helped me gather my wits as I was working. Thanks to C. D. Blanton, Brandon Callahan, Penny Edwards, Eric Falci, Jacob Gaboury, Cecil Giscombe, Priya Kothari, Christopher Kutz, Hans Sluga, and Sophie Volpp. Thanks, as well, to my colleagues in the Center, Rebecca Egger, Colleen Barroso, Diane Soper, Eric Kotila, and Alex Brostoff, for their friendship and encouragement.

I am deeply grateful to Katherine Ibbett and Alan Tansman, who read a first version of the manuscript and offered many comments, suggestions, and criticisms. James Porter and Esther Yu were valued readers and interlocutors who made suggestions and helped me clarify arguments on various chapters. They have my sincere thanks. Thanks as well to Kathryn Crim and Rupinder Kaur, who took time from their own important work to serve as research assistants and thought partners along the way. My Berkeley colleagues Oliver Arnold, Albert Ascoli, Suzanne Guerlac, Victoria Kahn, Jeffrey Knapp, Leslie Kurke, Niklaus Largier, Anthony Long, Michael Nylan, Nicholas Paige, Joanna Picciotto, Peter Sahlins, Debarati Sanyal, Ethan Shagan, and Linda Williams offered helpful information and suggestions as I formulated this project. Further afield, I would like to thank Martin Harries, Paul Holdengräber, Virginia Jackson, Seth Lerer, Jane Newman, and David Quint for their friendship, encouragement, and suggestions. Thanks as well to Henry A. Sauerwein Jr. who many years ago told me about the troubadours and the gay science.

My parents, Gertrude and Ralph Hampton, and my sister, Kathy Lujan, who passed away unexpectedly during the time I was finishing this book, taught me in different ways about both cheerfulness and work. I honor their memories.

My last, and first, thanks go to Jessica Levine, Sophia Hampton, and Emily Hampton, without whom my world would be cheerless indeed.

Notes

INTRODUCTION: A CONTAGION, A POWER

1. Robert Burton, *Anatomy of Melancholy*, ed. Floyd Dell and Paul Jordan-Smith (New York: Tudor Publishing, 1951), p. 525. The epigraph from Montaigne to this chapter is translated by me. Montaigne uses the term *esjouissance*, the capacity to take pleasure in things—not unconnected to the Latin-derived "jocund" or the Italian *giocosa*.

2. Baruch Spinoza, *Ethics*, trans. Edwin Curley (London: Penguin Books, 1994), pp. 138–39.

3. David Hume, *A Treatise of Human Nature*, ed. Ernest C. Mossner (Harmondsworth: Penguin, 1969) p. 661. This is in book 3, "Of Morals."

4. For an interesting account of happiness in the Western tradition, see Daryl Mac-Mahon, *Happiness: A History* (New York: Grove Press, 2006). As will be clear, my work takes a quite different approach, focusing on language and nuances of meaning, rather than the general history of an idea. The marginality (or, more properly, the absence) of discussions of cheerfulness in discussions of emotion may tell us as much about how emotions are categorized and weighted (more or less arbitrarily) as it does about the emotions themselves. Thus, Amélie O. Rorty comments: "Emotions do not form a natural class. A set of distinctions that has generally haunted the philosophy of mind stands in the way of giving good descriptions of the phenomena. We have inherited distinctions between being active and being passive; between psychological states primarily explained by physical processes and psychological states not reducible to nor adequately explained by physical processes." With each distinction, she notes, certain phenomena fall away and escape analysis. See Rorty, "Explaining Emotions," in *Explaining Emotions*, ed. Amélie O. Rorty

(Berkeley: University of California Press, 1980), p. 104. Certain currents of recent affect theory have tried to counter these distinctions. On optimism, see Lauren Berlant, *Cruel Optimism* (Durham: Duke University Press, 2011).

5. The bibliography here is, of course, vast. See, for an introduction, Noga Arikha, *Passions and Tempers: A History of the Humours* (New York: Harper, 2007). On the passions, see, in particular, Susan James, *Passion and Action: The Emotions in Seventeenth-Century Philosophy* (Oxford: Oxford University Press, 1997); Victoria Kahn, Neil Saccamano, and Daniela Coli, eds., *Politics and the Passions, 1500–1850* (Princeton: Princeton University Press, 2006); and Gail Kern Paster, Katherine Rowe, and Mary Floyd-Wilson, eds., *Reading the Early Modern Passions* (Philadelphia: University of Pennsylvania Press, 2004). For discussions of passion and rhetoric, see Gisèle Mathieu-Castellani, *La rhétorique des passions* (Paris: Presses Universitaires de France, 2000), and Daniel M. Gross, *The Secret History of Emotion: From Aristotle's "Rhetoric" to Modern Brain Science* (Chicago: University of Chicago Press, 2006).

6. Here is the original French: "Le désir de paraître aimable conseille de prendre une expression de gaieté, quelle que soit la disposition intérieure de l'âme; la physionomie influe par degrés sur ce qu'on éprouve, et ce qu'on fait pour plaire aux autres émousee bientôt en soi-même ce qu'on ressent." Madame de Staël, *De l'Allemagne*, ed. Simone Balayé (Paris: Flammarion, 1968), vol. 1, pp. 103–104. My translation.

7. The meditational connection with cheer and self-healing is most popularly seen, perhaps, in the work of Thích Nhất Hạnh. See Nhất Hạnh, *The Miracle of Mindfulness: A Manual on Meditation* (Boston: Beacon Press, 1975), pp. 79–85. On the importance of facial attitudes for the ecology of the self, see Bryan Kolb and Laughlin Taylor, "Facial Expression, Emotion, and Hemispheric Organization," in Richard D. Layne and Lynn Nadel, eds., *Cognitive Neuroscience of Emotion* (Oxford: Oxford University Press, 2000), pp. 62–83. I will say more about modern self-help literature below, in Chapter 11.

8. See Michel Foucault, "Technologies of the Self," in *Foucault: Ethics*, ed. Paul Rabinow (New York: New Press, 1997), pp. 223–53.

9. Melissa Gregg and Gregory J. Seigworth, "An Inventory of Shimmers," introduction to Gregg and Seigworth, eds., *The Affect Theory Reader* (Durham: Duke University Press, 2010), p. 1. On the "betweenness" of affects, see Gilles Deleuze's discussion of affective images in *Cinema 1: The Movement-Image*, trans. Hugh Tomlinson and Barbara Habberjam (Minneapolis: University of Minnesota Press, 1986), pp. 61–65.

10. Sara Ahmed, "Happy Objects," in *The Affect Theory Reader*, p. 29. See as well Ahmed's

fuller exposition of her approach in *The Promise of Happiness* (Durham: Duke University Press, 2010). Also, Antonio Negri, "Value and Affect," trans. Michael Hardt, *boundary 2* 26.2 (1999), pp. 77–88.

11. Ruth Leys, "The Turn to Affect: A Critique," *Critical Inquiry* 37.3 (2011), p. 465. Leys's essay, while not unproblematic in some ways, offers a strong engagement with several scholars of affect. See also the ensuing debates in later issues of the same journal.

12. See David Hume, *An Enquiry Concerning the Principles of Morals*, in *Enquiries Concerning Human Understanding and Concerning the Principles of Morals*, ed. P. H. Nidditch (Oxford: Clarendon Press of Oxford University Press, 1975), section 7, p. 250. For the Pascal passage, see Blaise Pascal, *Pensées*, trans. Honor Levi (Oxford: Oxford World Classics, 1995), no. 78, p. 17. Here is Pascal's French, in all of its gloomy glory: "Les habiles par imagination se plaisent tout autrement à eux-mêmes que les prudents ne se peuvent raisonnablement plaire. Ils regardent les gens avec empire, ils disputent avec hardiesse et confiance, les autres avec crainte et défiance. Et cette gaieté de visage leur donne souvent l'avantage dans l'opinion des écoutants, tant les sages imaginaires ont de faveur auprès de leurs juges de même nature." Blaise Pascal, *Pensées*, ed. Philippe Sellier (Paris: Garnier, 1991), p. 174. For Emerson, see Ralph Waldo Emerson, "Considerations by the Way," in *The Conduct of Life*, in *Essays and Lectures*, ed. Joel Porte (New York: Library of America, 1983), p. 1089.

13. See *Curiosities in chymistry, being new experiments and observations concerning the principles of natural bodies* (London: H. C. 1691), s.v. "Volatile Alcali." See, for similar recommendations, Henry Dodwell's *A Treatise Concerning the Lawfulness of Instrumental Musick in Holy Offices* (sic) (London: William Haws, 1700), p. 36. These are commonplace formulations in both medical and moral writing.

14. Herman Melville, *Billy Budd, Foretopman*, in Melville, *Bartleby the Scrivener, Benito Cereno, Billy Budd, Foretopman* (New York: Quality Paperback Book Club, 1996), p. 220. Critical reception of this story often focuses on either the sexual attraction of Claggart to Billy or the politics of the ship community. So far as I am aware, no one has noticed that Billy is consistently and repeatedly singled out for his cheerfulness, and no one has studied the disruptive power of that cheerfulness in the world of the story.

15. Seneca, "On the Tranquillity of Mind," in *Moral Essays, Volume II*, trans. John W. Basore, Loeb Classical Library 254 (Cambridge, MA: Harvard University Press, 1951), 2.4, p. 215. The Democritus quote is from Diogenes Laertius, *Lives of Eminent Philosophers, Volume II*, trans. R. D. Hicks, Loeb Classical Library 185 (Cambridge, MA: Harvard University Press, 1991), p. 455. See, as well, Seneca's discussion of the virtue of the wise man in his essay

on constancy, "De Constantia": "Virtue is free, inviolable, unmoved, unshaken, so steeled against the blows of chance that she cannot be bent, much less broken. Facing the instruments of torture she holds her gaze unflinching, her expression changes not at all whether a hard or a happy lot is shown her." It is this resolution that leads to the "elation" (*laetus*) of the Stoic in the face of adversity. He directs his life "neither towards hope or towards fear." Seneca, "On Firmness," in *Moral Essays, Volume I*, trans. John W. Basore, Loeb Classical Library 214 (Cambridge, MA: Harvard University Press, 1928), 5.5, p. 61; 9.3, pp. 75–77.

16. On the methodological difficulties of writing the history of emotion as a way of understanding "how we got modern," see Peter N. Stearns, "Modern Patterns in Emotions History," in Susan J. Matt and Peter N. Stearns, eds., *Doing Emotions History* (Urbana: University of Illinois Press, 2013), pp. 17–40. My project, as will become clear, is a more modest one and aims to describe the various forms that cheerfulness takes at different moments, as well as its interaction—how it shapes and is shaped by—with other types of discourse. For *hilaritas* as a characteristic of lively conversation, see Seneca, "On the Tranquillity of Mind" 7.3, p. 239.

17. See Michael Nylan, "Lots of Pleasure But Little Happiness," *Philosophy East & West*, 65.1 (2015), pp. 196–226, as well as her measured discussion in *The Chinese Pleasure Book* (New York: Zone Books, 2019), p. 39: see, on the Yogic tradition, *The Yogic Aphorisms of Patanjali*, trans. R. Mitra (Calcutta, 1883), pp. 40–42. I am grateful to conversations with Michael Nylan, Priya Kothari, Anthony Long, and James Porter for help in distinguishing modern ideas of cheer from Chinese, Yogic, Roman, and ancient Greek notions.

18. Obadiah Walker, *Of Education, Especially of Young Gentlemen* (Oxford, 1673), p. 239.

19. Madeleine de Scudéry, *Clelia, An Excellent New Romance* (London: H. Herringman, 1678), book 4, p. 491. The French original has the terms *gay, enjouement*, and *joye*. See, *Clélie, histoire romaine*, published under the name of Scudéry's brother, "Mr. de Scudéry," 10 vols. (Paris: Augustin Courbé, 1658), vol. 8, part 4, book 2, pp. 751–52. More will be said about the French vocabulary of cheer below in Chapters 3 and 5.

20. For the study of literature as a way into the "meaning world" or *mundus significans* of earlier cultures, see the classic study by Thomas M. Greene, *The Light in Troy: Imitation and Discovery in Renaissance Poetry* (New Haven: Yale University Press, 1982), pp. 1–3. Also suggestive to me has been Owen Barfield, *History in English Words* (London: Faber and Faber, 1953).

21. Thus, John Florio's *A World of Words*, the first Italian-English dictionary (London, 1598), lists "mirth," "joy," "solace," "pastime," "glee," and "sport" to define *allegrezza*. Then

he adds that an *allegrezza* is also a victory march, featuring a trumpet and drum, suggesting a shading away from the modesty of cheerfulness.

CHAPTER ONE: BODY, HEAVEN, HOME

1. See Johnson's account at https://johnsonsdictionaryonline.org/views/search. php?term=cheer. Joan Corominas's *Diccionario crítico etimológico de la lengua castellana*, 4 vols. (Madrid: Gredos, 1954), vol. 2, p.661, acknowledges the uncertainty that hovers around the origins of the Spanish word *cara*, which first appears in the *Poem of the Cid* in the eleventh century. Presumably there is a "low Latin" term whereby the Greek *kara* turns into a Latin *cara*, though he provides no examples. Wilhelm Meyer-Lübke's *Romanisches Etymologisches Wörterbuch* (Heidelberg: Carl Winter, 1992) simply lists the Greek *kara* as the origin of *cara*, bypassing the putative Latin mediation. *Le grand Robert de la Langue Française* (Paris: Robert, 1985) lists the first French use of *chiere* from 1080. Italian also activates the word *cera*, as a version of *chiere*. Through metonymic contamination, it links to the word for wax and suggests the wax imprint of a face, as in a sculpture. See Christian Joseph Jagemann, *Dizionario italiano-tedesco* (Leipizig, 1791), s.v. "cera." I am indebted to Professor Sergius Kodera of the University of Berlin for this reference.

2. Geoffrey Chaucer, *The Riverside Chaucer*, ed. Larry D. Benson et al. (Boston: Houghton Mifflin, 1987), p. 88, v. 97.

3. Ibid., p. 56, v. 2295; p. 60, v. 2586.

4. Ibid., p. 89, v. 180.

5. Chrétien de Troyes, *Romans*, ed. Michel Zink (Paris: Livre de Poche, 1994), p. 572, v. 2516. The blushing maiden is in *Cligès* (vv. 2967–68), and the suffering face is in the same poem at v. 5614.

6. William Shakespeare, *The Sonnets and Narrative Poems*, ed. William Burto (New York: Alfred A. Knopf, 1992), p. 136, vv. 89–91.

7. Julian of Norwich, *Revelations of Divine Love*, trans. George Tyrrell, S. J. (London: Kegan Paul, 1902), p. 56. I have occasionally modified the translations to eliminate archaisms. Here is the original: "Then I saw him ryally reigne in hys howse and all fulfyllyth it with joy and myrth hym selfe, with mervelous melody in endelesse love in hys awne feyer, blessydfulle chere, which glorious chere of the Godhede fulfyllyth alle hevyn of joy and blysse." Quoted from *The Showings of Julian of Norwich*, ed. Denise N. Baker (New York: Norton, 2005), p. 55.

8. See Dante Alighieri, *Paradiso*, ed. and trans. Robert M. Durling (Oxford: Oxford University Press, 2011), canto 33, vv. 115–32, p. 634.

9. Julian of Norwich, *Revelations of Divine Love*, trans. Tyrrell, p. 95. Here is the original, from Baker's *The Showings of Julian of Norwich*, p. 55: "Then hope we that God has forgevyn us oure synne. And it is true. And than shewyth our curtesse Lorde hym selfe to the soule mereley and of full glad chere, with frendfully welcomyng as if it had been in payne and in preson, seyeng thus, 'my dere darlyng, I am glad thou arte come to me in alle thy woe.'"

10. Julian of Norwich, *Revelations of Divine Love*, trans. Tyrrell, p. 141; Baker's *The Showings of Julian of Norwich*, p. 81. On the importance of the return to good as characteristic of the human, see Joan M. Nuth, "Human Nature: The Image of God," in *The Showings of Julian of Norwich*, p. 178.

11. *The Showings of Julian of Norwich*, p. 108: "The blessydfull chere of oure Lorde God werkyth it in us by grace." The last sentence is missing from Tyrrell's translation, p. 191. I have translated it here.

12. Margery Kempe, *The Book of Margery Kempe*, modernized by W. Butler-Bowdon (Oxford: Oxford University Press, 1940), p. 54. On the similarities and differences between Julian and Kempe, see Nicholas Watson, "The Middle English Mystics," in David Wallace, ed., *The Cambridge History of Medieval English Literature* (Cambridge: Cambridge University Press, 2002), pp. 539–65.

13. Kempe, *The Book of Margery Kempe*, p. 153.

14. Kempe, *The Book of Margery Kempe*, p. 133.

CHAPTER TWO: AMONG THE CHEERFUL

1. Myles Coverdale, *Biblia: The Bible, that is, the Holy Scripture of the Olde and New Testament, faithfully and truly translated out of Douche and Latyn in to Englishe* (London, 1535). I have consulted the online version at https://archive.org/details/CoverdaleBible1535_838/mode/2up. For Tyndale's version, http://textusreceptusbibles.com.

2. I have worked with the Latin Bible in the edition of Alberto Colunga and Laurentio Turrado: *Biblia Sacra* (Madrid: Biblioteca de Autores Cristianos, 1977). For Greek passages, I have used *The Greek New Testament*, ed. Kurt Aland et al. (Stuttgart: United Bible Societies, 1977). Lexical help comes from Charlton T. Lewis and Charles Short, *A Latin Dictionary* (Oxford: Oxford University Press, 1996), and H. G. Liddell and R. Scott, *An Intermediate Greek-English Lexicon*, based on the seventh edition of Liddell and Scott's *Greek-English Lexicon* (Oxford: Clarendon Press of Oxford University Press, 1986).

3. The Geneva and King James versions differ here only in that the Geneva version

says "as every man wisheth in his heart," whereas the King James has "purposeth." For the Geneva Bible, I have consulted the online version available at https://studybible.info/ Geneva. The King James is from *The Reader's Bible* (London: Oxford University Press, 1951). For Luther, see *Neues Testament und Psalmen* (Stuttgart: Württembergische Bibelanstalt, 1968), p. 281.

4. See *La Bible en françoys: Sensuyt la Bible diligemment translatee de latin en françoys, au plus pres du vray texte, pour les gens qui nentendent latin, avec les sept Aages* (Lyon: O. Arnoullet, 1550). Calvin's account of gaiety may be found in *Commentaires de M. Jehan Calvin sur toutes les Epistres de l'Apostre S. Paul* (Geneva: Badius, 1557), p. 135. This text may be found online at https://www.e-rara.ch/gep_g/content/titleinfo/1751526 via the initiative of the Library of Geneva. See also *La Saincte Bible contenant le Vieil & Nouveau Testament* (Lyon: Sebastian Honorat, 1566) as well as *La Bible, qui est toute la saincte Escriture du Vieil et du Nouveau Testament* (Geneva: Berjon, 1605).

5. From the paraphrase of the passage in Romans: "Hilaritate gratiam officii conduplicet, ut quicquid facitis, velut ex alieno et ex animo facere videamini." Erasmus, *Opera omnia: emendatiora et auctiora ad optimas editiones, praecipue quas ipse Erasmus postremo curavit, summa fide exacta, doctorumque virorum notis illustrata*, 10 vols. (Hildesheim: Georg Olms, 1962), a reprint of the 1706 Amsterdam edition, vol. 7, p. 818. Elsewhere, in the paraphrase of the Second Letter to the Corinthians, he stresses that "charity" must come from the heart, "ex pectore." See ibid., vol. 7, p. 931.

6. First published in 1508, Erasmus's *Adagia* was the scholarly best seller of the age. I have consulted the bilingual edition of Jean-Christophe Saladin, *Les adages*, 5 vols. (Paris: Les Belles Lettres, 2013), 1.8.91.

7. *The seconde tome or volume of the Paraphrase of Erasmus upon the Newe Testament*, trans. Myles Coverdale (London, 1548). The same vocabulary appears in Erasmus's recasting of the canonical passage from Corinthians that I quoted earlier. Erasmus renders the notion of God's love for a "happy giver" as "atqui hilarem datorem amat deus," and Coverdale faithfully provides "God loveth a cherefull giver," a phrase that will be picked up verbatim in the King James Version. Erasmus adds the reflection that in God's eyes the one who complies with his duty grudgingly does not comply at all. For Calvin, that God's-eye projection will become a human discrimination.

8. The nuance of a seemingly excessive gloss in which Coverdale gives us two terms in lieu of one ("cherefulness," "a mery looke") is an instance, noted above, of what linguists call a binomial. But it is also a common Renaissance rhetorical technique, known as the

practice of *copia*, or a copious style. This is important, because as I show, Coverdale's *copia* does more than add in more words. It shifts the focus of cheerfulness away from a more conventional notion of charity or generosity onto the face, inflecting it with a dynamic of sociability. To be cheerfully charitable is to present a certain kind of face.

9. Except where otherwise noted, the English versions of Calvin in what follows will come from John Owen's translations (Edinburgh: Calvin Translation Society, 1849), available online at the Library of Liberty https://oll.libertyfund.org. In this instance, I am translating from the French version, to be found in *Commentaires*, p. 393. This text may be found online through the www.e-rara.ch initiative of the Library of Geneva at https://www.e-rara.ch/gep_g/content/zoom/239677. The Latin will come from the *Ioannis Calvini opera exegetica: Commentarii in secundam Pauli Epistolam ad Corinthios*, ed. Helmut Feld, 16 vols. (Geneva: Droz, 1994). I here cite volume 15, p. 153. Calvin's texts circulated in both French and Latin. To see both the overlap and difference between languages in key passages, here is the French of the bit just quoted, with the Latin interspersed: "Quand il dit que Dieu aime celuy qui donne *joyeusement* il signifie au contraire que Dieu rejette ceux qui donnent à regret et en chichete: [Nam quum *docet hilarem* datorem a Deo diligi, exadverso malignos et coactos respui significat] car il ne veut point dominer sur nous comme un tyran [neque enim instar tiranni vult nobis imperare, sed sicuti patrem nobis se exhibet]: mais tout ainsi qu'il se demonstre nous estre Pere, aussi requiert-il de nous une obeissance filiale, qui soit prompte et franche."

10. John Calvin, *Commentary on the Epistles of Paul to the Romans*, 12.1, https://oll.libertyfund.org/titles/calvin-commentaries-on-the-epistles-of-paul-to-the-romans, 449; Calvin, *Opera exegetica*, vol. 13, p. 255. The French version uses the phrase "une amour de justice, fraiche, volontaire et alaigre" to describe the believer's behavior. See *Commentaires*, 131.

11. My translation from the French version. "Il veut que le service qu'ils feront selon leur charge, soit avec liesse et alaigreté, de peur que s'ils y procedent avec chagrin ou quelque contenance desdaigneuse, cela ne face perdre toute grace a leur service, comme souvent il en advient." Calvin, *Commentaires*, p. 135. We note yet another instance of doubling down on the translation as *hilaritas* is rendered by "liesse et alaigreté" — this latter a beautiful, but short-lived (in French), invention, linked to such terms as the Latin *alacritas*, the Italian *allegrezza,* and the Spanish *alegría.*

12. Richard Hooker, "A Learned Sermon of the Nature of Pride," in *The Works of That Learned and Judicious Divine Mr. Richard Hooker*, ed. John Keble, 7th rev. ed., 3 vols. (Oxford: Clarendon Press of Oxford University Press, 1888), vol. 3,

p. 631, accessed online via Library of Liberty at https://oll.libertyfund.org/titles/ hooker-the-works-of-richard-hooker-vol-3.

13. Richard Hooker, "A Sermon, Found Among the Papers of Bishop Andrews," in *The Works of That Learned and Judicious Divine Mr. Richard Hooker*, vol. 3, p. 702, https://oll. libertyfund.org/title/keble-the-works-of-richard-hooker-vol-3.

14. My translation. "Je prens icy joye, non pas comme elle est prise au 14 des Romains, ch. 17, mais pour une façon de faire joyeuse, ou une alaigreté que nous démontrons envers notre prochain laquelle est contraire à chagrin." This passage of Calvin may be found in *Commentaires*, p. 476. Calvin's influential commentaries to Paul's letters stress the active practice of cheerfulness.

15. John Donne, *A Sermon of Commemoration of the Lady Danvers, late Wife of Sir John Danvers. Preached at Chilsey, where she was lately buried. By John Donne Dean of St. Pauls, London. 1 July 1627.* Accessed through the Digital Collection of the Brigham Young University Library, https://contentdm.lib.byu.edu/digital/collection/JohnDonne/id/3240/. I am indebted to Ethan H. Shagan's book, *The Rule of Moderation: Violence, Religion and the Politics of Restraint in Early Modern England* (Cambridge: Cambridge University Press, 2011) for pointing me to this text.

16. John Donne, Sermon on Psalm 38.2, delivered at Lincoln's Inn in 1622, in *The Sermons of John Donne*, ed. by George R. Potter and Evelyn M. Simpson, 10 vols. (Berkeley: University of California Press, 1953–1962), vol. 2, p. 50.

CHAPTER THREE: MEDICINE, MANNERS, AND READING FOR THE KIDNEYS

1. See Michel Foucault, *Security, Territory, Population: Lectures at the Collège de France, 1977–1978*, trans. Graham Burchell (New York: Picador, 2007).

2. This is from book 30 of the *Problems*, 953b1, trans. E. S. Forster, in *The Complete Works of Aristotle: The Revised Oxford Translation*, ed. Jonathan Barnes, 2 vols. (Princeton: Princeton University Press, 1984), vol. 2, pp. 1499–1501. For a succinct history of the humoral tradition see Noga Arikha, *Passions and Tempers: A History of the Humours* (New York: Harper Books, 2007). For a useful expansion of the problem of the humors in Renaissance literature, see Gail Kern Paster, *Humoring the Body: Emotions and the Shakespearean Stage* (Chicago: University of Chicago Press, 2004).

3. Timothy Bright, *A Treatise of Melancholy: Contayning the causes thereof, and reasons of the straunge effects it worketh in our minds and bodies* (London: John Windet, 1586), p. 38.

4. Ibid., p. 160.

5. Ibid., pp. 241 and 247.

6. Levinus Lemnius, *Touchstone of Complexions*, trans. Thomas Newton (London, 1576), p. 156, accessed through the University of Oxford Text Archive, https://ota.bodleian. ox.ac.uk/repository/xmlui/handle/20.500.12024/A05313. The Latin original repeats the phrases we have seen: "hilaritas," "omnia hilariter tan facta sunt," "magna alacritatis indi-cia." See Lemnius, *De habitu et constitutione corporis* (Antwerp: Guilielmum Simonem, 1561), p. 144. Newton's translation nicely expands the range of cheer by spelling the unre-lated verb "cherish" (from the French word *cher*, meaning dear or darling) "cheerish." On the meterological causes of good cheer, see, as well, Robert Burton, who notes, quoting Lemnius, that "if the western winds blow, and that there be a calm, or a fair sunshine day, there is a kind of alacrity in men's minds; it cheers up men and beasts." Robert Burton, *The Anatomy of Melancholy*, ed. Floyd Dell and Paul Jordan-Smith (New York: Tudor Pub-lishing, 1951), p. 30. The literature on early modern melancholy is, of course, massive and ranges from deeply historical accounts of medical theory to psychoanalytically inflected accounts of the origins of poetry. For a balanced recent study that privileges melancholy as a dominant sensibility of the period, see Barbara H. Rosenwein, *Generations of Feeling: A History of Emotions, 600–1700* (Cambridge: Cambridge University Press, 2016), chapter 8.

7. William Salmon, *The Family Dictionary, or Houshold Companion* (London: W. Rhodes, 1696), s.v. "Powder to Create Cheerfulness." I am grateful to Katie Kadue for pointing me to this reference, as I am indebted to her forthcoming work on the material labor of humanism, *Domestic Georgic: The Poetics of Preservative: Labors of Preservation from Rabelais to Milton* (Chicago: University of Chicago Press, 2021).

8. "Mentem sibi bene consciam, et ingenium liberale prae se serens." Erasmus, *De civilitate morum puerilium* (Basel: Froben, 1534), p. 3, verso. For thinking about Erasmus's book and its influence, I am indebted to Norbert Elias's classic study *The Civilizing Process*, trans. Edmund Jephcott (New York: Pantheon, 1982), as well as, more recently, Harry Berger Jr.'s *Fictions of the Pose: Rembrandt against the Italian Renaissance* (Stanford: Stanford University Press, 2000). A century later, the French doctor Cureau de la Chambre is less certain than is Erasmus about the meaning of the "serene" forehead. He associates it with joy. He notes that a smooth forehead seems to expand: "Il semble qu'il s'ouvre et s'etende de tous costez." This might seem to suggest laughter, he says. But he brushes this idea aside, since laughter is linked to surprise. See Cureau de la Chambre, *Les characteres des passions* (Paris: chez P. Rocolet, 1660), s.v. "Joye."

9. See Erasmus, *Opus Epistolarum Des. Erasmi Roterdami*, ed. P. S. Allen, 12 vols. (Oxford: Clarendon Press of Oxford University Press, 1906–1958), vol. 2, p. 576. The letter is from May 30, 1517. There is a discussion of this anecdote in Simon Goldhill, *Who Needs Greek?: Contests in the Cultural History of Hellenism* (Cambridge: Cambridge University Press, 2002), pp. 17–21. Lemnius makes a similar point in the *Touchstone of Complexions*, p. 36: "The head not aslope cornered, but rounde and globewyse fashioned, the hayre of fayre aburne or chesten colour: the forhead smoth, cheerefull and vnwrynckled, beautifyed wyth comely eyebrowes, and greatly honoured wyth a paire of amyable eyes, not holow, but delightfully standinge out. The colour freshe, sweete and pleasaunte."

10. Here is the entire phrase: "à plus hault sens interpreter ce que par adventure cuidiez dict en gayeté de cueur." François Rabelais, *Gargantua*, in *Oeuvres complètes*, ed. Pierre Jourda, 2 vols. (Paris: Garnier, 1963), vol. 1, 7. All translations of Rabelais are by me.

11. Ibid., p. 9.

12. Saint Augustine, *On Christian Doctrine*, trans. D. W. Robertson Jr. (New York: Bobbs-Merrill, 1958), book 1, section 36, p. 30. Later in the book, Augustine addresses the thorny question of how to read the often confusing metaphors in the Bible with this recommendation: "Therefore in the consideration of figurative expressions a rule such as this will serve, that what is read should be subjected to diligent scrutiny until an interpretation contributing to the reign of charity is produced." See book 2, section 15, p. 93.

13. Ibid., book 3, sections 2 and 3, pp. 79–83. The concept of interpreting events "for the best" is also, of course, a Stoic commonplace. See Seneca's "On the Tranquillity of the Soul," in *Moral Essays, Volume II*, trans. John W. Basore, Loeb Classical Library 254 (Cambridge, MA: Harvard University Press, 1951), 14.2, p. 269. Seneca speaks of interpreting kindly "even adversities"—"etiam adversa benigne interpretetur." Plutarch makes a similar point in his essay "On Tranquillity of Mind," Plutarch's *Moralia, Volume VI*, trans. W. C. Helmbold, Loeb Classical Library 469 (Cambridge, MA: Harvard University Press, 1962), p. 191. I'm assuming that Saint Augustine is building on this moral tradition, which he turns into a hermeneutic gesture aimed at written text, even as Rabelais is building on Augustine.

14. The French of the *Third Book* is "Une forme specificque et propriété individuale, laquelle nos majeurs nommoient Pantagruelisme, moienant laquelle jamais en maulvaise partie ne prendront choses quelconques ilz congnoistront sourdre de bon, franc et loyal courage." See Rabelais, *Oeuvres complètes*, vol. 1, p. 401. I note in passing that the actual etymology of "gay" is unstable. While noting the Latin cognomen Gaius (from *gaudeo*, to

take pleasure), most etymologists trace it to the Old High German *wahi*, meaning "beautiful." On the shifting relationship between community and fiction-making in Rabelais, see Timothy Hampton, *Literature and Nation in the Sixteenth Century: Inventing Renaissance France* (Ithaca: Cornell University Press, 2000), chapters 2 and 3.

15. Rabelais, *Oeuvres complètes*, vol. 2, p. 14.

16. Ibid., p. 12.

17. Ibid., pp. 232 and 233. The scene unfolds over chapters 64 and 65.

18. Rabelais, *Oeuvres complètes*, vol. 2, p. 239. On the relationship of this episode to larger questions of reading and travel in the sixteenth century, see Wes Williams, *Monsters and Their Meanings in Early Modern Culture: Mighty Magic* (Oxford: Oxford University Press, 2011), chapter 1.

CHAPTER FOUR: SHAKESPEARE, OR THE POLITICS OF CHEER

1. *The Courtyer of Count Baldessar Castilio* (London, 1561), n.p., accessed through the University of Oregon online resources at https://scholarsbank.uoregon.edu/xmlui/bitstream/handle/1794/671/courtier.pdf. This is Magnifico's assertion at the very outset of book 3 of the *Courtier*. For the Italian, see the edition of Carlo Cordié in his *Opere di Baldassare Castiglione, Giovanni Della Casa, Benvenuto Cellini* (Milan: Ricciardi, 1960), p. 214. In considering the relationship between cheer and sociability, we might note that in French Renaissance colloquies, female characters frequently turn to address their interlocutors, "d'un visage riant." (My thanks to Ullrich Langer for this insight.) Obviously, the gendering of cheerfulness is an important facet of the topic. I will deal with it at more length a bit later, in my discussion of Jane Austen.

2. Dissimulation can be both negatively and positively weighted. Stefano Guazzo's *La civil conversazione* (Venice, 1574), a late contribution to the European vogue for courtly handbooks, offers the example of a certain Margherita Stanga, whose "gentile spirito in persona" conforms to social expectations while hiding her much more spiritually oriented interior. Guazzo cites poems written in her honor stressing the disjunction between her face and her soul. George Pettie's influential 1581 English version of the text makes references to her "cheerful" eyes and countenance to render the Italian. See *The ciuile conuersation of M. Steeuen Guazzo . . .* (London: Richard Watkins, 1581), p. 20. I have accessed this text through the Early English Books Online digital partnership at https://quod.lib.umich.edu/e/eebo/A02291.0001.001?view=toc.

3. Word searches tell us that the Shakespeare play in which the term "cheer" appears most frequently is the early farce *The Comedy of Errors*. There, we see Antipholus of Ephesus refused entry to his own home, where "cheer" (as food) resides. The broader implications of cheer, however, are, as I will suggest, explored only in Shakespeare's later work. On Shakespeare's engagement with the early modern theory of the humors, see Gail Kern Paster, *Humoring the Body: Emotions and the Shakespearean Stage* (Chicago: University of Chicago Press, 2004).

4. William Shakespeare, *King Richard III*, ed. Antony Hammond (London: Routledge, 1994). All scene and line numbers will be indicated in parentheses.

5. Holinshed's *Chronicles*, in the Oxford World Classics edition of *Richard III*, ed. John Jowett (Oxford: Oxford University Press, 2000) p. 330.

6. David Scott Kastan argues that plot and history are articulated through the body in *Richard III*, that "Richard's deformity can be taken . . . as the sign of history itself, the distortion that history works upon the past." Within this materialist account, we might want to look, I am suggesting, at the shifting vocabulary of emotions, at the appearance and disappearance of a language of feeling (itself linked to the body) as a way of thinking about genre. See Kastan's insightful essay, "Shakespeare and English History," in Margreta de Grazia and Stanley Wells, eds., *The Cambridge Companion to Shakespeare* (Cambridge: Cambridge University Press, 2001), p. 180. Stephen Greenblatt argues that the scene of Richard's self-contemplation illustrates the "absolute loneliness" of the tyrant figure. The loss of cheer may have something to do with this, as Macbeth's example below suggests. See Greenblatt, *Tyrant: Shakespeare on Power* (London: Bodley Head, 2018), p. 92.

7. William Shakespeare, *Macbeth*, ed. Kenneth Muir (London: Methuen, 1980), 3.4.32–36.

8. William Shakespeare, *Hamlet*, ed. Harold Jenkins (London: Methuen, 1982), 1.2.115–17.

9. Ibid., 3.2.157–59.

10. William Shakespeare, *As You Like It*, ed. Agnes Latham (London: Routledge, 1994).

11. William Shakespeare, *Romeo and Juliet*, ed. Brian Gibbons (London: Methuen, 1980), 2. 3. 3.

12. William Shakespeare, *A Midsummer Night's Dream*, ed. Harold F. Brooks (London: Methuen, 1979).

13. Sara Ahmed, *The Promise of Happiness* (Durham: Duke University Press, 2010), pp. 41–42.

14. See Northrop Frye, *Northrop Frye on Shakespeare* (New Haven: Yale University Press, 1986), p. 172. And see as well Seth Lerer's more recent description of *The Tempest* as

a play "attempting to retell its pasts" in Lerer, *Shakespeare's Lyric Stage: Myth, Music, and Poetry in the Last Plays* (Chicago: University of Chicago Press, 2018), p. 59.

15. William Shakespeare, *The Tempest*, ed. Frank Kermode (London: Methuen, 1989), 1.1.5.

CHAPTER FIVE: MONTAIGNE, OR THE CHEERFUL SELF

1. References to Montaigne come from *The Complete Essays of Montaigne*, trans. Donald Frame (Stanford: Stanford University Press, 1958). I alter his version here, replacing "sociable" with the more accurate "social." The French is from Michel de Montaigne, *Oeuvres complètes*, eds. Albert Thibaudet and Maurice Rat (Paris: Gallimard, 1962). When relevant, I will include the customary letters *a*, *b*, and *c*, to refer to different "levels" of Montaigne's text. The book was constantly being added to and appeared in different versions in 1580, 1588, and 1594. John Florio's translation, which I will dip into as a way of suggesting the broader implications of Montaigne's formulations, is from *The Essayes of Montaigne* (New York: Modern Library, n.d.).

2. Here is the French: "Ce que je ne voy de la premiere charge, je le voy moins en m'y obstinant. Je ne fais rien sans gayeté; et la continuation [c] et la contention trop ferme [b] esbloüit mon jugement, l'attriste et le lasse. [c] Ma veüe s'y confond et s'y dissipe" (p. 389).

3. "C'est pitié d'estre en lieu où tout ce que vous voyez vous embesogne et vous concerne. Et me semble jouyr plus gayement les plaisirs d'une maison estrangere, et y apporter le goust plus naïf" (p. 928).

4. "Celuy qui n'y employe que son jugement et son adresse, il y procede plus gayement: il feinct, il ploye, il differe tout à son aise, selon le besoing des occasions . . . il marche toujours la bride a la main" (p. 985b).

5. Richard Leake's concordance to the *Essays* shows that *contenance* is the noun most frequently modified by *gaye* and lists four appearances of the two terms together. Montaigne uses *gaie* twelve times in the *Essays*. Richard Leake, *Concordance des Essais de Montaigne*, 2 vols. (Geneva: Droz, 1981), vol. 1, p. 560. Two excellent discussions of Montaigne's depictions of the body are Jean Starobinski, *Montaigne in Motion*, trans. Arthur Goldhammer (Chicago: University of Chicago Press, 1985), chapter 4, and David Quint, *Montaigne and the Quality of Mercy* (Princeton: Princeton University Press, 1998), chapter 4. I take this opportunity to add a corrective nuance to my own earlier discussions of the Montaignian face in *Writing from History: The Rhetoric of Exemplarity in Renaissance Literature* (Ithaca: Cornell University Press, 1990), chapter 4, which privileged the term *visage*.

6. Jean Nicot's pioneering French/Latin dictionary, *Trésor de la langue françoyse*, published in 1606, defines *contenance* as the general disposition and "maintien" of the body and face. In Latin: "vultus membrorumque corporis compositio, status." Nicot goes on to link it to the Latin *continentia*, or "constancy." Randle Cotgrave's *A Dictionarie of the French and English Tongues* of 1611 expands the network of association further, indicating that the word means "posture" or "form" and that it can denote a mirror that is worn from the belt and used to check one's appearance. See Cotgrave, *Dictionarie of the French and English Tongues*, ed. William S. Woods (Columbia: University of South Carolina Press, 1968). One of the first English/Latin dictionaries, Thomas Thomas's *Dictionarium linguae Latinae et Anglicanae* of 1587, lists "the cheer" and "countenance" as synonyms of the Latin *facies*, or "face."

7. John Florio's influential English version of Montaigne, which I have been including in my quotations of his text, renders *gaieté* for the most part as "cheerfulness(e)." The term, with its implicit reference to the face or *chère*, locates it etymologically precisely where Montaigne locates it thematically, in the "countenance." Florio's translation, like all translations, is semantically imprecise, but it is somatically right on target. It sweeps the easy freedom of the Montaignian subject back into the theologically freighted "cheerful" charity of the English Protestant world. Florio occasionally comes to Montaigne's aid by tempering the more extreme implications of his formulations. Thus, Montaigne celebrates the "gayeté" (p. 165a) of the Athenian youth, which, he says, was the province of the gods; the Protestant Florio renders this as a praise of their "recreation and pastime" (p. 128). These lexical choices show us how Florio tames the disruptive power of Montaigne's own language. Florio's version marks out a freedom from convention and drudgery, but a limited range of movement within the confines of social decorum and political obligation.

8. Jean de la Fontaine, *Fables*, ed. Marc Fumaroli (Paris: Livre de Poche, 1985), p. 7. My translation.

9. Joseph-Antoine-Joachim Cerutti, *Discours sur la question proposée par l'Académie des Jeux floraux pour l'année 1761: La lumière des lettres n'a-t-elle pas plus fait contre la fureur des duels que l'autorité des lois* (Paris: chez Aimé Delaroche, 1761), p. 56. Cerutti was a friend of Mirabeau and the editor of *La Feuille villageoise*, one of the newspapers during the revolutionary years. The pamphlet on character comes early in his career. For more on Cerutti and the theme of gaiety in eighteenth-century Paris, see Colin Jones, *The Smile Revolution in Eighteenth-Century Paris* (Oxford: Oxford University Press, 2014), pp. 88–97.

10. Cerutti, *Discours sur la question proposée par l'Académie des Jeux floraux pour l'année 1761*, p. 56.

11. "Le désir de paraître aimable conseille de prendre une expression de gaieté, quelle que soit la disposition intérieure de l'âme; la physionomie influe par degrés sur ce qu'on éprouve, et ce qu'on fait pour plaire aux autres émousee bientôt en soi-même ce qu'on ressent." Madame de Staël, *De l'Allemagne*, ed. Simone Balayé, 2 vols. (Paris: Flammarion, 1968), vol. 1, pp. 103–104, my translation. On the French obsession with conversation during the ancien régime, see Alain Viala, *La France galante* (Paris: Presses Universitaires de France, 2004), chapter 4.

CHAPTER SIX: SOCIAL VIRTUE, ENLIGHTENMENT EMOTION

1. Teresa Brennan, *The Transmission of Affect* (Ithaca: Cornell University Press, 2004), p. 18. Brennan studies the collective experience of affect via a group-psychology vocabulary of "entrainment," focusing on the late nineteenth century in chapter 3. Colin Jones gives a portrait of the gay life in Paris in the eighteenth century in *The Smile Revolution in Eighteenth-Century Paris* (Oxford: Oxford University Press, 2014), chapter 4.

2. Baruch Spinoza, *Ethics*, trans. Edwin Curley (London: Penguin Books, 1994), pp. 159 and 200. For Spinoza's original Latin, I have used the bilingual French version, *Éthique*, ed. Bernard Pautrat (Paris: Éditions du Seuil, 1988).

3. For an account of Spinoza that stresses the partial or perspectival nature of the affects while also exploring their implications for political and communal experience, see Rosi Braidotti, *Transpositions: On Nomadic Ethics* (London: Polity, 2006), pp. 146–63. Braidotti goes on to offer what she calls "an ethics of joyful affirmation" (p. 198) via Deleuze and Virginia Woolf. Cheerfulness seems not to enter into her thinking in this regard. One of the few commentators to mention Spinoza's interest in cheerfulness is Don Garrett. See "Spinoza's Ethical Theory," in Don Garrett, ed., *The Cambridge Companion to Spinoza* (Cambridge: Cambridge University Press, 1996), pp. 278–82. Spinoza's use of *hilaritas* recalls the vocabulary of the Vulgate Bible. Yet to understand the semantic slipperiness of the concept, it is worth noting that one of the most widely circulated recent Spanish versions of Spinoza's text, the translation by Vidal Peña, *Ética* (Madrid: Editora Nacional, 1984), struggles with the term, alternating between the conventional Spanish word for happiness, *alegría* (for example, p. 245), and the less common *regocijo* (p. 309, where p. 245 is cross-referenced). The latter word stems from the verb *gozar*, to enjoy.

4. Michael McKeon, *The Secret History of Domesticity: Public, Private, and the Division of Knowledge* (Baltimore: Johns Hopkins University Press, 2005), p. 376.

5. David Hume, *Enquiries Concerning Human Understanding and Concerning the Principles of Morals*, ed. P. H. Nidditch (Oxford: Clarendon Press of Oxford University Press, 1975), p. 268, his italics.

6. David Hume, *A Treatise of Human Nature*, ed. Ernest C. Mossner (Harmondsworth: Penguin Books, 1969), p. 661.

7. There is a large literature on the role of sympathy. On the prehistory of Enlightenment fellow feeling, see Katherine Ibbett, *Compassion's Edge: Fellow-Feeling and Its Limits in Early Modern France* (Philadelphia: University of Pennsylvania Press, 2018), especially chapter 3. On sympathy in the literary tradition, see David Marshall, *The Surprising Effects of Sympathy: Marivaux, Diderot, Rousseau, and Mary Shelley* (Chicago: University of Chicago Press, 1988), introduction and chapter 1. On Hume, Smith, and sympathy see Rae Greiner, *Sympathetic Realism in Nineteenth-Century British Fiction* (Baltimore: Johns Hopkins University Press, 2012), chapter 1, and Evan Gottlieb, *Feeling British: Sympathy and National Identity in Scottish and English Writing, 1707–1832* (Lewisburg: Bucknell University Press, 2007), chapter 1. For a less literary account, see Christel Fricke, "Adam Smith: The Sympathetic Process and the Origin and Function of Conscience," in Christopher J. Berry, Maria Pia Paganelli, and Craig Smith, eds., *The Oxford Handbook of Adam Smith* (Oxford: Oxford University Press, 2013), pp. 179–200, as well as Duncan Kelly, "Adam Smith and the Limits of Sympathy," pp. 201–18 in the same volume. For a discussion of political subjectivity and sympathy, see Victoria Kahn, *Wayward Contracts: The Crisis of Political Obligation in England, 1640–1674* (Princeton: Princeton University Press, 2004), chapter 9. Alasdair MacIntyre locates sympathy in both Hume and Smith as the force that is presumed to bridge the gap between general moral rules, on the one hand, and our "fluctuating, circumstance-governed desires, emotions and interests," on the other. "But the gap of course is logically unbridgeable, and 'sympathy' as used by Hume and Smith is the name of a philosophical fiction." See his discussion in *After Virtue: A Study in Moral Theory* (South Bend: Notre Dame University Press, 1984), p. 49. The important distinction between the two figures is that sympathy seems to be involuntary for Hume, whereas for Smith, it involves a moral agency on the part of the observer.

8. On the relationship between the passions of others and the individual sensibility in Hume, see Elizabeth S. Radcliffe, *Hume, Passion, and Action* (Oxford: Oxford University Press, 2018), pp. 155–76. Radcliffe's larger argument, however, focuses more on the individual constitution of the subject than it does on social interactions.

9. We find a somewhat later, more moderate account of this same process in Louis-Nicolas Bescherelle's 1851 book, *L'art de briller en société*, where Bescherelle distinguishes

between two kinds of gaiety. One, he says, is loud and obnoxious (it might correspond to what we have elsewhere called "mirth"). The other, sweeter, version "insinuates itself" into the company, and "each person participates and contributes to expanding it." See the edition of Bescherelle's popular guide to success in society by Pierre Assouline (Paris: Flammarion, 2014), s.v. "Gaieté," my translation.

10. David Hume, *Selected Essays*, ed. Stephen Copely (Oxford: Oxford World's Classics, 2008), p. 79.

11. Hume refers to Castiglione and "Gratian." However, it is clear that he is thinking of the Spanish Baroque moralist Baltasar Gracián, whose books on virtue, *The Hero*, *The Man of Judgment*, and *The Art of Worldly Wisdom* were extremely popular in seventeenth-century and eighteenth-century Europe, rather than Gratian, the twelfth-century compiler of canon law.

12. Adam Smith, *The Wealth of Nations*, ed. J. C. Bullock (New York: Barnes and Noble, 2004), p. 69.

13. The reference is to Bernardino Ramazzini, whose book on occupational diseases, *De Morbus Artificium Diatriba*, had appeared in 1700.

14. Adam Smith, *The Theory of Moral Sentiments*, ed. Ryan Patrick Hanley (London: Penguin Books, 2009), p. 59.

15. It is interesting that writers about Smith generally note his attention to the "martial spirit" without focusing on the several moments where the military activity becomes a figure for communal or labor activity. Spiros Tegos offers useful comments on the tension between commerce and military ideals in "Adam Smith: Theorist of Corruption"; see the *Oxford Handbook of Adam Smith*, pp. 353–71.

16. We might think here of the extraordinary and disturbing scene in Preston Sturges's 1942 film *Palm Beach Story* in which a group of wealthy men on a hunting holiday — lubricated by alcohol — begins shooting up the dining car of their train. So great is their energetic gaiety that the African American barman is soon ducking bullets. The scene offers the prototype for any number of scenes in cinema of "good-humored" cruelty visited by small groups on outsiders.

CHAPTER SEVEN: JANE AUSTEN, OR CHEER IN TIME

1. Quoted in Jane Austen, *Northanger Abbey*, ed. Marilyn Butler (London: Penguin Books, 1995), p. 4.

2. On the impossible rhetoric of Austen's novels, which both include and exclude us, see

the different analyses of D. A. Miller, *Jane Austen, or, The Secret of Style* (Princeton: Princeton University Press, 2003) and Alex Woloch, *The One vs. the Many: Minor Characters and the Space of the Protagonist in the Novel* (Princeton: Princeton University Press, 2003), chapter 1.

3. Jane Austen, *Sense and Sensibility*, in *The Complete Novels of Jane Austen*, 2 volumes (New York: Modern Library, 1992), vol. 1, p. 114.

4. Jane Austen, *Pride and Prejudice*, in *The Complete Novels of Jane Austen*, vol. 1, p. 422.

5. Jane Austen, *Emma*, in *The Complete Novels of Jane Austen*, vol 2, p. 162.

6. Jane Austen, *Northanger Abbey*, in *The Complete Novels of Jane Austen*, vol. 2, p. 445.

7. Jane Austen, *Persuasion*, in *The Complete Novels of Jane Austen*, vol. 2, pp. 638 and 639.

8. Nancy Armstrong has stressed the way that the marriage contract structure offers a kind of narrative paradigm for women writers, or writers about domestic experience. I am arguing for something extracontractual. See her discussion in *Desire and Domestic Fiction: A Political History of the Novel* (Oxford: Oxford University Press, 1987), chapter 1. David Kaufmann traces the shifting notions of propriety in the novel between some sense of public law and individual agency in "Law and Propriety, *Sense and Sensibility*: Austen on the Cusp of Modernity," *ELH* 59.2 (1992), pp. 385–408.

9. *The Polite Lady; or, A Course of Female Education in a Series of Letters, from a Mother to a Daughter* (Philadelphia: Mathew Carey, 1798), p. 243. This is from letter 38. I cite the American edition. The text first appeared in London in the 1760s. For useful background on domestic cheerfulness, see Christina Kotchemidova, "From Good Cheer to 'Drive-By Smiling': A Social History of Cheerfulness," *Journal of Social History* 39.1 (2005), pp. 5–37.

10. On the ideological work done by narrative voice in Austen as a compromise between bourgeois sensibility and public vision, see the interesting analysis by Franco Moretti in *The Bourgeois: Between History and Literature* (New York: Verso, 2013) pp. 96–98.

11. Armstrong, in *Desire and Domestic Fiction*, pp. 150–52, notes that Austen's heroines generally reject fiction-making and, presumably, the fictions of romance. Her examples are Emma and Elizabeth Bennet. Here, by contrast, we see an indication that the situation is not necessarily cut and dried as we watch a debate over fiction between two generations. In an essay on embarrassment in Austen that circles around Willoughby's humiliation without landing on it, David Southward points out, nonetheless, that "*Sense and Sensibility* presents Austen's most exhaustive treatment of impression management." See Southward, "Jane Austen and the Riches of Embarrassment," *Studies in English Literature, 1500–1900* 36.4 (1996), pp. 763–84.

12. On the importance of witnessing for a new type of "ascetic" ethics in the postmodern context, see Rosi Braidotti, *Transpositions: On Nomadic Ethics* (London: Polity, 2006), pp. 179–82. Jane Austen, *Mansfield Park*, in *The Complete Novels of Jane Austen*, vol. 2.

CHAPTER EIGHT: CHEERFUL AMBITION
IN THE AGE OF CAPITAL

1. On the complex relationship between Dickens's career as a writer and his depiction of the labor of literature, see the insightful discussion by Alexander Welsh in *From Copyright to Copperfield* (Cambridge, MA: Harvard University Press, 1978), especially chapter 8. A somewhat different account that sees the domestic in "perpetual struggle" with the economic is offered by Matthew Titolo in "The Clerk's Tale: Liberalism, Accountability, and Mimesis in *David Copperfield*," *ELH* 70.1 (2003), pp. 171–95.

2. Samuel Smiles, *Self-Help: With Illustrations of Character and Conduct*. I cite the 1864 Boston edition, accessed through the libertyfund.org website at https://oll.libertyfund.org/titles/smiles-self-help-with-illustrations-of-character-and-conduct. I have just quoted from pages 74 and 378. It is worth pointing out that Smiles describes cheerful work as essentially English. He says of Josiah Wedgwood, "it is the glory of our country that men such as these should so abound.... They furnish proofs of cheerful, honest working, and energetic effort to make the most of small means and common opportunities" (p. 27). For an account of Dickens's debts to Smiles, see *"Great Expectations* and *Self-Help*: Dickens Frowns on Smiles," by Jerome Meckier, *Journal of English and Germanic Philology* 100.4 (2001), pp. 537–54.

3. Charles Dickens, *David Copperfield* (New York: Random House, 2012), p. 3.

4. On the relationships between these various female characters, though without reference to the psychological vocabulary used by Dickens, see, again, Welsh, *From Copyright to Copperfield*, chapter 9. For an account of Agnes's role in the novel through a discussion of the imagery of angels, though without reference to her cheer, see Alexander Welsh, *The City of Dickens* (Oxford: Clarendon Press of Oxford University Press, 1971), chapter 11.

5. Welsh, *From Copyright to Copperfield*, p. 109. For a careful historical account of the role of time and work in the novel, see Jennifer Ruth, "Mental Capital, Industrial Time, and the Professional in 'David Copperfield'," *NOVEL: A Forum on Fiction* 32.3 (1999), pp. 303–30.

6. Horatio Alger, *Ragged Dick or, Street Life in New York with the Boot-Blacks*, ed. David K. Shipler (New York: Modern Library, 2005), p. 4.

CHAPTER NINE: GAY SONG AND NATURAL CHEER

1. Ralph Waldo Emerson, "Self-Reliance," in *Essays and Lectures*, ed. Joel Porte (New York: Library of America, 1983), p. 261.

2. Of course, the goal of the troubadours is often something they call "joi," a transcendent pleasure, either sexual or spiritual. It is a worthy goal, but often deferred or remembered, whereas gaiety is present and vital.

3. See Bernard's poem, "Lo gens tems de pascor," in Martín de Riquer's anthology, *Los Trovadores* (Madrid: Planeta, 2011), p. 356. For another use of similar terms, see Bertran de Born's "Be'm platz lo gais temps de pascor" on p. 740 in the same volume. On p. 1004, Raimon de Miraval praises the gentle air of spring, "l'aur'es dous'e-'l temps gais."

4. *Poeti del Dolce Stil Novo*, ed. Gianfranco Contini (Milan: Ricciardi, 1960), p. 55, my translation. Here is the Italian:

> Fresca rosa novella,
> piacente primavera,
> per prata e per rivera
> gaiamente cantando,
> vostro fin presio mando — a la verdura.
> Lo vostro presio fino
> in gio' si rinovelli
> da grandi e da zitelli
> per ciascuno camino
> e cantinne gli auselli
> chiascuno in suo latino
> da sera e da matino
> su li verdi arbuscelli
> Tutto lo mondo canti
> po' che lo tempo vene,
> sì come si convene,
> vostr'altezza presiata:
> ché siete angelica — crïatura.

Two more stanzas follow.

5. Pierre de Ronsard, *Les amours*, ed. Marc Bensimon (Paris: Garnier-Flammarion, 1981), pp. 100 and 166; Maurice Scève, *Délie*, ed. by Françoise Charpentier (Paris: Gallimard,

1984), no. 148; for Spenser, see Emrys Jones, ed., *The New Oxford Book of Sixteenth-Century Verse* (Oxford: Oxford University Press, 1991), p. 281; *Henry Vaughan*, ed. Louis L. Martz (Oxford: Oxford University Press, 1996), p. 36; Thomas Gray, "On the Death of Richard West," https://www.poetryfoundation.org/poems/44305/on-the-death-of-richard-west.

6. *Petrarch's Lyric Poems*, trans. Robert M. Durling (Cambridge, MA: Harvard University Press, 1976), nos. 356 and 353; for Shakespeare, see *The Sonnets and Narrative Poems*, ed. William Burto (New York: Knopf, 1992), sonnet 92, p. 51. For Sidney, see *Silver Poets of the Sixteenth Century*, ed. Gerald Bullett (London: Everyman's Library, 1970), p. 201. For the Bishop poem, see Elizabeth Bishop, *Poems* (New York: Farrar, Strauss & Giroux, 2011), p. 59.

7. John Milton, *Complete Poems and Major Prose*, ed. Merritt Y. Hughes (Indianapolis: Bobbs Merrill, 1978), book 2, vv. 487–92.

8. Esther Yu, "Tears in Eden: The Tragedy of the Tender Conscience," *Representations* 142 (Spring 2018), p. 23. I am indebted to this essay and to conversations with Professor Yu for help framing my reading of Milton.

9. On the "clearing" of Eve's misery, see Michael Schoenfeldt, "'Commotion Strange': Passion in *Paradise Lost*," in Gail Kern Paster, Kathrine Rowe, and Mary Floyd-Wilson, eds., *Reading the Early Modern Passions* (Philadelphia: University of Pennsylvania Press, 2004), pp. 59–60.

10. John Milton, *Areopagitica*, in *Complete Poems and Major Prose*, pp. 744–45.

11. William Wordsworth, "London," in *William Wordsworth*, ed. Stephen Gill (Oxford: Oxford University Press, 1984), p. 286.

12. William Wordsworth, "Lines Written a Few Miles Above Tintern Abbey," in *William Wordsworth*, pp. 131–35.

13. Burke mentions the cheerful in passing, quickly to dismiss it. See Edmund Burke, *A Philosophical Inquiry into the Origin of Our Ideas of the Sublime and Beautiful* (London: John C. Nimmo, 1887), part 3, section 15 and part 4, section 15.

14. William Wordsworth, "Michael," in *William Wordsworth*, pp. 225–36. On the context for the poem and its importance to Wordsworth, see the well-known, but still useful commentary by Geoffrey H. Hartman, *Wordsworth's Poetry 1787–1814* (New Haven: Yale University Press, 1971), pp. 260–66, and Marjorie Levinson's important political reading of the poem in *Wordsworth's Great Period Poems: Four Essays* (Cambridge: Cambridge University Press, 1986). The tension between landscape and emotional landscape is explored by Jerome J. McGann in *The Romantic Ideology: A Critical Investigation* (Chicago: University of Chicago Press, 1983), chapter 8. See, as well, Alan Liu's gloss on the readings of Levinson

and McGann in *Wordsworth: The Sense of History* (Stanford: Stanford University Press, 1989), pp. 216–18.

15. The biblical allusions, along with an account of how labor functions in the poem (though without our attention to affective life), have been studied by Marjorie Levinson in *Wordsworth's Great Period Poems*, chapter 2.

CHAPTER TEN: THE GAY SCIENTISTS

1. Friedrich Nietzsche, "Nietzsche contra Wagner," in *"The Anti-Christ," "Ecce Homo," "Twilight of the Idols and Other Writings,"* trans. Judith Norman (Cambridge: Cambridge University Press, 2005), p. 280. Citations of the German of "Nietzsche contra Wagner" are from *Nietzsche Werke: Kritische Gesamtausgabe*, ed. Giogio Colli and Mazzino Montinari, 30 vols. in 8 sections (Berlin: Walter de Gruyter, 1967–), here, section 6, vol. 3. Nietzsche refers to pitting his will against pain, "und es dem Indianer gleichthun, der, wie schlimm auch gepeinigt, sich an seinem Peiniger durch die Bosheit seiner Zunge schadlos hält" (p. 435).

2. We can note in passing that despite his famous interest in questions of diet and health, there are remarkably few actual references to the body in Nietzsche.

3. Friedrich Nietzsche, *The Gay Science*, trans. Josefine Nauckhoff (Cambridge: Cambridge University Press, 2001), book 2, no. 92, p. 90. I have also worked with Pierre Klossowski's French translation, *Le gai savoir* (Paris: Gallimard, 1982).

4. Ralph Waldo Emerson, "The Poet," in *Essays and Lectures*, ed. Joel Porte (New York: Library of America, 1983).

5. See Cavell's discussions of Emerson and Nietzsche in *Conditions Handsome and Unhandsome: The Constitution of Emersonian Perfectionism* (Chicago: University of Chicago Press, 1990), chapter 1, and see Branka Arsic's comments in her *On Leaving: A Reading in Emerson* (Cambridge, MA: Harvard University Press, 2010), pp. 87–89 and 336.

6. Friedrich Nietzsche, *The Birth of Tragedy*, trans Ronald Speirs (Cambridge: Cambridge University Press, 1999), p. 4. I have slightly altered the translation—Speirs here uses "serenity," to suggest the classical equipoise claimed by Enlightenment criticism of Greek art. The German phrase is "Genügsamkeit und Heiterkeit des theoretischen Menschen." Friedrich Nietzsche, *Die Geburt der Tragödie*, in *Nietzsche Werke*, section 3, part 1, p. 6. This is from the prefatory "self-critique."

7. "Den ernsthaften und bedeutenden Begriff der 'griechischen Heiterkeit'... den falsch verstandenen Begriff dieser Heiterkeit im Zustande ungefährdeten Behagens aus allen Wegen und Stegen der Gegenwart antreffen." *Die Geburt der Tragödie*, p. 6. For an

account of the paradoxes underpinning attempts to theorize the "classical" in German philological and classical traditions, see James I. Porter, "What is 'Classical' about Classical Antiquity?: Eight Propositions," *Arion* 13.1 (2005), pp. 27–61. For a broader analysis of Nietzsche's relationship both to philology and to the Greeks, see James I. Porter, *Nietzsche and the Philology of the Future* (Stanford: Stanford University Press, 2000).

8. Friedrich Nietzsche, *The Genealogy of Morals*, trans Walter Kaufmann, in *The Basic Writings of Nietzsche* (New York: Modern Library, 1968), p. 478. Here is the German: "Ihre Gelichgültigkeit und Verachtung gegen Sicherheit, Leib, Leben, Behagen, ihre entsetzliche Heiterkeit und Tiefe der Lust in allem Zerstören." Friedrich Nietzsche, *Zur Genealogie der Moral*, in *Nietzsche Werke*, section 6, part 2, p. 289.

9. Friedrich Nietzsche, *The Case of Wagner*, trans. Walter Kaufmann, in *Basic Writings of Nietzsche*, p. 616. "Die Rückkehr zur Natur, Gesundheit, Heiterkeit, Jugend, Tugend!" Friedrich Nietzsche, *Der Fall Wagner*, in *Nietzsche Werke*, section 6, part 3, no. 3, p. 10.

10. For an extensive account of Nietzsche's relationship to "exemplary" figures, and his debts to Emerson, among others, see James Conant, "Nietzsche's Perfectionism: A Reading of *Schopenhauer as Educator*," in Richard Schacht, ed., *Nietzsche's Postmoralism* (Cambridge: Cambridge University Press, 2001), pp. 181–257. On Emerson's interest in the exemplary see Judith N. Shklar, "Emerson and the Inhibitions of Democracy," in Stanley Hoffmann and Dennis F. Thompson, eds., *Redeeming American Political Thought* (Chicago: University of Chicago Press, 1998), chapter 4. Klossowski's edition of *Le gai savoir* includes Nietzsche's annotations to Emerson written during the period of the *Gay Science*. I send readers as well to Benedetta Zavatta's *Individuality and Beyond: Nietzsche Reads Emerson*, trans. Alexander Reynolds (Oxford: Oxford University Press, 2019), which came to me too late for consultation in the composition of this book.

11. It might be useful to contrast, in passing, Nietzsche's account with the writing of John Stuart Mill, a philosopher whom Nietzsche detested. In his *Three Essays on Religion* (1875), Mill makes an argument for the value of "dwell[ing] on the brighter side of both the present and the future." He asserts that a chief blessing in life is "a cheerful disposition." This means that despite the bleakness of the facts, the cheerful individual will always "keep all the active energies in good working order" through the exercise of the imagination. If death is inevitable, says Mill, we should just not think about it: "The way to secure this is not to think perpetually of death, but to think perpetually of our duties, and of the rule of life." He goes on to suggest that such a "hopeful" vision can help us maintain, in the absence of any clear evidence, the existence of God (that same being who, Nietzsche

asserts, has just died). Much in the same way that the cheerful spirit remains cheerful despite the fact that external reality looks bleak, we must remain hopeful of our salvation and attend to our duties. What is less important for our purposes than Mill's strange logic is his sense that human personalities are fixed, defined by qualities such as cheerfulness. See John Stuart Mill, "On Theism," in *Essays on Ethics, Religion and Society*, ed. J. M. Robson (Toronto: University of Toronto Press, 1985), volume 10 of *The Collected Works of John Stuart Mill*, accessed through the libertyfund.org website, https://oll.libertyfund.org/titles/mill-the-collected-works-of-john-stuart-mill-volume-x-essays-on-ethics-religion-and-society. On Nietzsche and Mill, see Conant, "Nietzsche's Perfectionism." In *Twilight of the Idols* Nietzsche had dubbed Mill "John Stuart Mill: or insulting clarity." My earlier citation of Richard Schacht comes from his essay "Nietzsche's *Gay Science*, Or, How to Naturalize Cheerfully," in Robert C. Solomon and Kathleen M. Higgins, eds., *Reading Nietzsche* (New York: Oxford University Press, 1988), p. 73.

12. For a somewhat different approach to this aphorism that focuses on its relationship to work, see Sianne Ngai, *Our Aesthetic Categories: Zany, Cute, Interesting* (Cambridge, MA: Harvard University Press, 2012), p. 223.

13. Walter Kaufmann notes that in a letter to Franz Overbeck, Nietzsche laments Emerson's lack of a rigorous philosophical training, "a really scientific education." Kaufmann also notes Emerson's self-description in his journals as a "professor of the Joyous Science." See Kaufmann's introduction to his translation of *The Gay Science* (New York: Random House, 1974), pp. 7–13. For an account of *The Gay Science* that explores the "scientific" resonances in depth, see Babette Babich, "Nietzsche's 'Gay' Science," in Keith Ansell-Pearson, ed., *A Companion to Nietzsche* (Oxford: Blackwell, 2006), pp. 97–114.

14. See Laura Kendrick, "The *Consistori del Gay Saber* of Toulouse (1323–Circa 1424)," in Arjan van Dixhoorn and Susie Speakman Sutch, eds., *The Reach of the Republic of Letters: Literary and Learned Societies in Late Medieval and Early Modern Europe*, 2 vols. (Leiden: Brill, 2008), vol. 1, pp. 17–32.

15. Friedrich Nietzsche, *Beyond Good and Evil*, trans. Walter Kaufmann, in *Basic Writings of Nietzsche*. The German is: "Den provençalischen Ritter-Dichtern zu, jenen prachtvollen erfinderischen Menschen des 'gai saber', denen Europa so Vieles und beinahe sich selbst verdankt." Friedrich Nietzsche, *Jenseits von Gut und Böse*, in *Nietzsche Werke*, section 6, part 2, no. 260, p. 222.

16. See *Las flors del gay saber o Las leys d'amors*, ed. M. Gatien-Arnoult, trans. Le Marquis d'Aguilar (Toulouse: J.-B. Paya, 1841), 3 vols. "Gai" is generally used in the troubadour

corpus when speaking of the heart, or "cor." It often appears in proximity to "cortes" (courtly, or courteous) or, as we saw in Chapter 9, in the context of song. So, Raimon de Miraval speaks of "un nou son gai e legier" (a new song that is gay and light); Arnaut de Mareuil praises his lady as "Dompn'ab cors gai, cortes" (Lady with a gay and courteous heart). Betran de Born evokes the "gay, courteous, and pleasing" presence of his lady (E il gai e il cortes e il plazen). "Saber" is used in any number of contexts, occasionally, though not often, to speak of the writing of poetry. So, Gaucelm Faudit: "Mos ferms cors fis, / Movon tuit miei cortes saber- / C'Amors m'ensegna / Cansons far" (My faithful and fine heart is moved by my courtly knowledge [*saber*], for Love teaches me to make songs). I have explored the troubadour corpus through the concordance provided by the ARTFL online search engine at the University of Chicago, https://artfl-project.uchicago.edu. Also of help has been the authoritative anthology by Martín de Riquer, *Los trovadores* (Barcelona: Ariel, 2011). On the linguistic politics underpinning *Las flors del gay saber*, see Catherine Léglu, "Languages in Conflict in Toulouse: 'Las Leys d'Amors,'" *Modern Language Review* 103.2 (2008), pp. 383–96. On one aftermath of troubadour culture, see Roger Boase, *The Troubadour Revival: A Study of Social Change and Traditionalism in Late Medieval Spain* (London: Routledge, 1978). For general commentary on Nietzsche and the "gay science," see Walter Kaufmann's introduction to his translation, pp. 5–6. His account of the troubadours, however, is limited to a reference to the 1955 edition of *The Shorter Oxford English Dictionary*. Nicolas L'Hermitte argues that the troubadour poems offer Nietzsche a model of poetic making that brushed aside the limitations imposed by both Platonic and Aristotelian traditions. See L'Hermitte, "The Troubadours through the Eyes of Nietzsche," *Exemplaria*, 25.2 (2019), pp. 110–29.

17. Friedrich Nietzsche, *Die Fröhliche Wissenschaft*, in *Nietzsche Werke*, section 5, part 22, no. 343, p. 255. A useful history of the terms of the title may be found in Rolando Pérez, "Towards a Genealogy of the Gay Science: From Toulouse and Barcelona to Nietzsche and Beyond," *eHumanista/IVITRA* 5 (2014), pp. 546–603, https://www.researchgate.net/publication/331998035_Towards_a_Genealogy_of_the_Gay_Science_From_Toulouse_and_Barcelona_to_Nietzsche_and_Beyond. For an account that focuses on the legal resonances of the "laws of love" context see Peter Goodrich, "Gay Science and the Law," in Victoria Kahn and Lorna Hutson, eds., *Rhetoric and Law in Early Modern Europe* (Princeton: Princeton University Press, 2001), pp. 95–124.

18. "Stehen wir vielleicht zu sehr noch unter *den nächsthen Folgen dieses Ereignisses* … eine neue … Art von Licht, Glück, Erleichterung, Erheiterung, Ermuthigung,

Morgenröthe." *Die Fröhliche Wissenschaft*, p. 256. I have slightly altered the translation here to catch the "cheerful" dimension of *Erheiterung*, which Nauckhoff skirts.

19. The German is: "Endlich erscheint uns der Horizont wieder frei ... endlich dürfen unsre Schiffe wieder auslaufen ... vielleicht gab es noch niemals ein so 'offnes Meer.'" *Die Fröhliche Wissenschaft*, p. 256.

20. Kant, in fact, associated *Fröhlichkeit* and *Heiterkeit* to describe the joy of children at play. Here is Kant: "Children ought to be open-hearted and cheerful in their looks as the sun. A joyful heart alone is able to find its happiness in the good. A religion which makes people gloomy is a false religion; for we should serve God with a joyful heart, and not of constraint." (*Kinder müssen auch offenherzig sein und so heiter in ihren Blicken wie di Sonne. Das fröliche Herz allein ist fähig, Wohlgefallen am Guten zu empfinden. Eine Religion, die den Meschen finster macht, ist falsch, denn er muss Gott mit frohem Herzen und nicht aus Zwang dienen.*) Immanuel Kant, *On Pedagogy*, trans. Annette Churton (Boston: Heath, 1900), p. 44; Kant, *Über Pädagogik*, ed. D. Friedrich Theodor Rink (Königsberg: Nicolovius, 1803), n.p. This is in the section on moral education; after this passage, Kant turns to the question of practical education.

21. See Friedrich Kluge, *Etymologisches Wörterbuch der Deutschen Sprache*, 18th ed., ed. Walter Mitzska (Berlin: Walter de Gruyter, 1960), s.v. "Froh," which also points to the Old High German *frao*, meaning "quick," or "hurried." Jakob and Wilhelm Grimm's classic *Deutsches Wörterbuch* evokes the Latin *laetus* I have used the 1877 edition, published by S. Hirzel in Leipzig.

22. Nietzsche, "Nietzsche contra Wagner," trans. Norman, pp. 281–82; *Nietzsche Werke*, pp. 436–37.

23. Friedrich Kluge's *Etymologisches Wörterbuch*, s.v. "Heiterkeit," which points to the Old High German term for "clear." The Grimm brothers mention the Latin synonyms *serenus, clarus,* and *resplendens,* as well as *hell* (bright) and *glanz* (shining).

24. "Dazu thut noth, tapfer bei der Oberfläche, der Falte, der Haut stehn zu bleiben, den Schein anzubeten, an Formen, an Töne, an Worte, an den ganzen *Olymp des Scheines* zu glauben." "Nietzsche contra Wagner," p. 437.

25. "Lapis Lazuli," in William Butler Yeats, *The Collected Poems of W. B. Yeats*, ed. Richard J. Finneran (New York: Collier, 1989), pp. 294–95. Since the poem is quite short, I omit line numbers. "Lapis Lazuli" is the second poem in Yeats's 1938 volume *New Poems*. It follows "The Gyres," which features the lines, "Hector is dead and there's a light in Troy; / We that look on but laugh in tragic joy." These lines provide the title for Thomas M. Greene's

influential account of Renaissance poetry, *The Light in Troy* (New Haven: Yale University Press, 1982), which offers an essentially melancholic vision of modern poetry as caught in a game of imitation with the ancients. "Lapis Lazuli," I will argue, offers a somewhat different vision of the relationship of poetry and history.

26. Yeats's interest in Nietzsche and gay song appears to have been serious and ongoing. He writes of Nietzsche in a letter to Lady Gregory as early as 1902 as "that strong enchanter." "I have read him so much," he goes on, "that I have made my eyes bad again.... Nietzsche completes Blake and has the same roots—I have not read anything with so much excitement since I got to love Morris's stories which have the same curious astringent joy." Letter of September 26, 1902, in *The Letters of W. B. Yeats*, ed. Allan Wade (London: Rupert Hart-Davis, 1954), p. 379.

27. In a letter to Dorothy Wellesley, Yeats stresses the heroic dimension of poetry at the current moment: "I think that the true poetic movement of our time is towards some heroic discipline. People much occupied with morality always lose heroic ecstasy." He cites a poem by Ernest Dowson that refers to the "bitter and gay" nature of the "heroic mood." And it is here that he mentions the lapis carving given to him: "A great piece carved by some Chinese sculptor." "Aesthetic, pupil, hard stone, eternal theme of the sensual east," he comments. "The heroic cry in the midst of despair. But no, I am wrong, the east has its solutions always and therefore knows nothing of tragedy. It is we, not the east, that must raise the heroic cry." Letter to Dorothy Wellesley of July 6, 1935, in *The Letters of W. B. Yeats*, pp. 836–37.

CHAPTER ELEVEN: IT IS AMAZING!

1. F. Scott Fitzgerald, *The Great Gatsby* (New York: Scribner, 2018), p. 9. The reference to spectroscopic gayety is on p. 44. It is how Fitzgerald describes the disapproval felt by the residents of old-moneyed East Egg who attend one of Gatsby's parties: "Instead of rambling this party had preserved a dignified homogeneity, and assumed to itself the function of representing carefully the staid nobility of the country-side—East Egg condescending to West Egg, and carefully on guard against its spectroscopic gayety." We might think of a party of Jane Austen's picnickers, lost in the frenzy of the twentieth century. The phrase from Nietzsche quoted earlier is from *The Gay Science*, trans. Josefine Nauckhoff (Cambridge: Cambridge University Press, 2001), p. 199. On the spectroscopic persistence of *Gatsby* through modern American culture, see Greil Marcus, *Under the Red White and Blue: Patriotism, Disenchantment, and the Stubborn Myth of the Great Gatsby* (New Haven: Yale University Press, 2020).

2. *The Boy Scouts Handbook* (New York: Boy Scouts of America, 1911), pp. 244–45.

3. Ibid., p. 7.

4. See Hochschild's classic study *The Managed Heart: Commercialization of Human Feeling* (Berkeley: University of California Press, 1983).

5. William James, *The Varieties of Religious Experience*, in *William James: Writings 1902–1910*, ed. Bruce Kuklick (New York: Library of America, 1987), pp. 87, 91, 93.

6. Orison Swett Marden, *Cheerfulness as a Life Power*, p. 8, accessed via Freeditorial.com at https://freeditorial.com/en/books/cheerfulness-as-a-life-power.

7. Ibid., p. 21.

8. Ibid., p. 52. We can contrast these patriotic discussions of cheer with the writing of the widely read French journalist Max O'Rell, who published several articles at the turn of the century on the overwhelming "cheerfulness" of the French, which he links to good food, wine, and an active sex life. See, for example, "Studies in Cheerfulness-I," *The North American Review* 167.505 (1898), pp. 690–97.

9. Norman Vincent Peale, *The Power of Positive Thinking* (New York: Simon and Schuster, 2015), p. 1.

10. In a later work, *Enthusiasm Makes the Difference* (New York: Fireside Books, 1967), written during the social upheavals of the 1960s, Peale recasts the patriotic theme in generational terms, opposing "the optimistic, the cheerful, the hopeful" (p. 3) against "the rebels who defy not only their parents and teachers but their barbers" (p. 4).

11. Peale, *The Power of Positive Thinking*, p. 163.

12. Ibid., p. 59.

13. Ibid., pp. 60 and 61.

14. Ibid., pp. 162 and 163. It is worth noting that Dale Carnegie's *How to Win Friends and Influence People*, the other Bible of American self-improvement, stresses cheerfulness in Scout-influenced language, focusing more on the body: "Whenever you go out-of-doors, draw the chin in, carry the crown of the head high, and fill the lungs to the utmost; drink in the sunshine; greet your friends with a smile, and put soul into every handclasp . . . . Preserve a right mental attitude — the attitude of courage, frankness, and good cheer. To think rightly is to create . . . . We become like that on which our hearts are fixed. Carry your chin in and the crown of your head high. We are gods in the chrysalis." Dale Carnegie, *How to Win Friends and Influence People* (New York: Gallery Books, 1981), p. 69.

15. For this history, see James Gray, *Business without Boundary: The Story of General Mills* (Minneapolis: University of Minnesota Press, 1954), pp. 214–17.

CHAPTER TWELVE: "TAKE IT, SATCH!"

1. Theodor W. Adorno, "Is Art Lighthearted," in *Notes to Literature, II*, trans. Shierry Weber Nicholsen (New York: Columbia University Press, 1992), p. 249. The German appears in *Noten zur Literatur*, ed. Rolf Tiedmann (Frankfurt am Main: Suhrkamp, 1981), p. 600. In *Jazz as Critique: Adorno and Black Expression Revisited* (Stanford: Stanford University Press, 2018), Fumi Okiji quotes another version of the Adorno argument, in his *Aesthetic Theory*, that "cheerful" art (by which he seems to mean entertainment) is necessarily irresponsible in the modern world, since it constitutes an injustice to "accumulated, speechless pain." Okiji goes on, via a reading of Frederick Douglass, to apply Adorno's judgment to modern misreadings of African American sorrow songs as "cheerful." As I will be suggesting here, it would interesting to think, as Adorno does not, about the capacity of adaptation, reworking, and revision of the type carried out by Louis Armstrong, as a tool for reanimating cheer against the gloominess that Adorno associates with all legitimate art (for him, Beckett) and that, he argues, can provide only "something like pleasure"—another qualified phrase. See Adorno, *Aesthetic Theory*, trans. Robert Hullot-Kentor (Minnesota: University of Minnesota Press, 1997), p. 40.

2. Saidiya Hartman, *Scenes of Subjection: Terror, Slavery, and Self-Making in Nineteenth-Century America* (Oxford: Oxford University Press, 1997), pp. 32–42. My thanks to James Porter for pointing me to this material. For a different reading of the same episode, which stresses Lincoln's deep emotional depression at the time of the meeting, see David Herbert Donald, *Lincoln* (New York: Simon and Schuster, 1995), p. 89. Donald goes on to note that Lincoln was haunted by the scene. He returned to it, fourteen years later, in an August 24, 1855, letter to Joshua Speed lamenting the Kansas-Nebraska Act, which opened the territories to slavery, where he declares, "That sight was a continued torment to me" and makes no reference to the cheerfulness discerned earlier. See Donald, *Lincoln*, p. 166, and the Lincoln letter at http://144.208.79.222/~abraha21/alo/lincoln/speeches/speed.htm.

3. W. E. B. Du Bois, *The Souls of Black Folk*, in *Writings*, ed. Nathan Huggins (New York: Library of America, 1986), pp. 545–46. On the problems inherent in Du Bois's transcription of the songs into conventional musical script see Eric J. Sundquist, *To Wake the Nations: Race in the Making of American Literature* (Cambridge, MA: Harvard University Press, 1993), chapter 5. "Let Us Cheer the Weary Traveler" was quickly set in a choral arrangement by the well-known composer and arranger R. Nathaniel Dett, musical director of the Hampton Institute. See his *Religious Folk-Songs of the Negro as Sung at Hampton Institute* (Hampton: Hampton Institute Press, 1927).

4. For information on the history and composition of the tune, see the Wikipedia page "Shine (1910 song)." Terry Teachout, in *Pops* (New York: Houghton Mifflin, 2009), p. 173, reports that Armstrong's bandmates counted as many as 250 high Cs in a row. Okiji cites Fred Moten's idea of the "blur" of African American performance as something that escapes easy description. See *Jazz as Critique*, pp. 82–83. For a discussion of how Armstrong performs "alterity" in scat, see Brent Hayes Edwards, *Epistrophies: Jazz and the Literary Imagination* (Cambridge, MA: Harvard University Press, 2017), chapter 1.

5. For the history of the song, see the entry at JazzStandards.com, http://www.jazzstandards.com/compositions-0/onthesunnysideofthestreet.htm. Many artists play "happy music" and many entertainers — including many jazz entertainers — are exuberant. My claim for Armstrong's exceptional status is built on his achievement in demonstrating unprecedented virtuosity while pushing at the limits of his own talent through his asides, vocal creativity, self-commentary, and so on. This point is made as well by Hayes Edwards, who notes Gary Giddens's insight that Armstrong's genius is linked not only to singing or playing, but to a verbal physicality — a self-presentation through grunts, wisecracks, asides, gestures, and more. Edwards, *Epistrophies*, p. 37.

6. See Teachout, *Pops*, pp. 310–12, on the history and circumstances of the recording. See as well Ricky Riccardi's authoritative account of all of Armstrong's versions of the tune in "60 Years of 'Mack The Knife,'" at *The Wonderful World of Louis Armstrong*, https://dippermouth.blogspot.com/2015/09/60-years-of-mack-knife.html.

7. Bertolt Brecht, "The Literarization of the Theater," in *Brecht on Theater: The Development of an Aesthetic*, ed. and trans. John Willett (New York: Hill and Wang, 1992), p. 45.

8. Teachout, *Pops*, p. 310, claims that Armstrong is responding to a "shout" from somewhere off mike. This seems to me to misdescribe what is in fact a murmured aside.

9. We might, in this regard, think of Armstrong's irony in contrast to the — superficially quite different — ethos of "cool" that emerges at the end of the 1950s. The "cool" artist, such as Miles Davis, derives his affect from a projection of the sense that he has better things to do and is always partly absent from the current moment. Armstrong is doubly present, watching his own persona as it performs. On the genesis of the "cool" ethos, see Joel Dinerstein, *The Origins of Cool in Postwar America* (Chicago: University of Chicago Press, 2017).

10. For Armstrong's remark, "All the white folks call me Louie," see Gary Giddens, *Satchmo* (New York: Doubleday, 1988), p. 120. On the Betty Boop cartoon, see p. 126. For a good account of the *Hello, Dolly!* performance and its aftermath, see Teachout, *Pops*, chapter 12.

CONCLUSION: CHEER IN PANDEMIC DAYS

1. Lauren Berlant, *Cruel Optimism* (Durham: Duke University Press, 2011). On affect as the space of struggle in late capitalism, see Antonio Negri and Michael Hardt, "Value and Affect," *boundary 2* 26.2 (Summer 1999), pp. 77–88. I say "since the Renaissance" following Darrin McMahon's implication that one of the characteristics of modernity is the growing assumption that we should be able to control and manage our emotional lives for the better. I extrapolate from the argument of his book, *Happiness: A History* (New York: Grove Press, 2006).

2. For an excellent account of this history and of the effect of the emoji, see Luke Stark and Kate Crawford, "The Conservatism of Emoji: Work, Affect, and Communication," *Social Media + Society* 1.2 (July–December 2015), pp. 1–11. I am grateful to my colleague Jacob Gaboury for bringing this essay to my attention.

3. See "Trump Says He's a Cheerleader for USA: We Need a Quarterback," CNN.com, April 1, 2020, https://www.cnn.com/2020/04/01/opinions/trump-coronavirus-hyper-partisan-opinion-avlon/index.html.

4. We might also mention, in this context, the concept of "lightness" celebrated by Italo Calvino as a tool of redemption in times of danger. See his discussion in the first chapter of *Six Memos for the Next Millennium*, trans. Patrick Creagh (London: Jonathan Cape, 1992).

Index

Zone Books series design by Bruce Mau

Typesetting by Meighan Gale

Printed and bound by Maple Press